Russian

МАРТИЗАНСКАЯ

Portezonskaya - Blue Line

5 stops

Arbatskaya

АРБАТСКАЯ

3 green line – T.

4 Blue line –

lonely planet

phrasebooks
and
James Jenkin & Grant Taylor

Russian phrasebook
4th edition – March 2006

Published by
Lonely Planet Publications Pty Ltd ABN 36 005 607 983
90 Maribyrnong St, Footscray, Victoria 3011, Australia

Lonely Planet Offices
Australia Locked Bag 1, Footscray, Victoria 3011
USA 150 Linden St, Oakland CA 94607
UK 72-82 Rosebery Ave, London, EC1R 4RW

Cover illustration
7.30am to St Petersburg by Daniel New

ISBN 1 74104 151 1

10 9 8 7 6 5 4 3 2

Printed through the Bookmaker International Ltd
Printed in China

acknowledgments

Editor Jodie Martire would like to acknowledge the following people for their contributions to this phrasebook:

James Jenkin and Grant Taylor for the comprehensive translations in this book and their countless enthusiastic suggestions.

James is an English teacher trainer and Russian linguistics expert – he's part-way through his PhD-quest to develop the perfect English-Russian dictionary. He previously worked as Lonely Planet's Language Publishing Manager, and now works with the Holmes Institute in Melbourne, Australia. He bought himself an old Ford Cortina because it looked like a Lada.

James says a big *spasiba* to Michelle for her wit and insight.

Grant is an English language academic manager and Russian linguist who has studied and worked in Melbourne, Moscow, Kiev, Sakhalin Island, Kazakhstan, Vietnam and Shanghai. He now works with RMIT English Worldwide in Melbourne, Australia. He once lived in Stalin's wedding-cake building, in an apartment with a trap door to the secret metro line direct to the Kremlin.

Grant would like to thank Sherry for her unending patience and bottomless bowls of filling Chinese broccoli.

James and Grant would like to thank Anton Borshch and Kesha Gelbak for their up-to-the-minute insights on Russian slang, skiing and romance – and the entire LP team, especially our inspiring and ever-helpful editor Jodie Martire. *Spasiba bal'shoye!*

Thanks also to Yukiyoshi Kamimura for the inside illustrations.

Lonely Planet Language Products

Publishing Managers: Chris Rennie & Karin Vidstrup Monk
Commissioning Editor: Ben Handicott
Editor: Jodie Martire
Assisting Editors: Branislava Vladisavljevic & Meladel Mistica
Managing Editor: Annelies Mertens

Layout Designer: David Kemp
Senior Layout Designer: Sally Darmody
Layout Manager: Adriana Mammarella
Series Designer: Yukiyoshi Kamimura
Cartographer: Wayne Murphy
Production Manager: Jo Vraca
Project Manager: Annelies Mertens

make the most of this phrasebook ...

Anyone can speak another language! It's all about confidence. Don't worry if you can't remember your school language lessons or if you've never learnt a language before. Even if you learn the very basics (on the inside covers of this book), your travel experience will be the better for it. You have nothing to lose and everything to gain when the locals hear you making an effort.

finding things in this book

For easy navigation, this book is in sections. The Tools chapters are the ones you'll thumb through time and again. The Practical section covers basic travel situations like catching transport and finding a bed. The Social section gives you conversational phrases, pick-up lines, the ability to express opinions – so you can get to know people. Food has a section all of its own: gourmets and vegetarians are covered and local dishes feature. Safe Travel equips you with health and police phrases, just in case. Remember the colours of each section and you'll find everything easily; or use the comprehensive Index. Otherwise, check the two-way traveller's Dictionary for the word you need.

being understood

Throughout this book you'll see coloured phrases on each page. They're phonetic guides to help you pronounce the language. You don't even need to look at the language itself, but you'll get used to the way we've represented particular sounds. The pronunciation chapter in Tools will explain more, but you can feel confident that if you read the coloured phrase slowly, you'll be understood.

communication tips

Body language, ways of doing things, sense of humour – all have a role to play in every culture. 'Local talk' boxes show you common ways of saying things, or everyday language to drop into conversation. 'Listen for ...' boxes supply the phrases you may hear. They start with the script (so a local can find the phrase they want and point it out to you) and then lead in to the phonetic guide and the English translation.

introduction 8

tools 11

practical 45

CONTENTS

social 111

russian

official language   widely understood

For more details, see the **introduction**.

Russian is the language which unites the largest nation in the world, the 'riddle wrapped in a mystery inside an enigma' which covers two continents and 11 time zones. Spoken by over 150 million speakers within the Russian Federation, Russian is also used as a second language in the former republics of the USSR and is widely spoken throughout the nations of Eastern Europe. With a total number of speakers of more than 270 million people, it's the fifth most spoken language in the world and one of the six official languages of the United Nations.

Russian belongs to the East Slavic group of Slavonic languages, as do Belarusian and Ukrainian. These languages were initially considered so similar that they were classified as one language – Old Russian. Once the Cyrillic alphabet was adopted in the 10th century, Russian was recognised as a distinct, modern language.

Russians adopted both their current alphabet and Orthodox Christianity by way of Old Church Slavic, a South Slavic language used principally in religious literature. Written secular texts were much closer to the spoken East Slavic language. For centuries these two forms of Old Russian coexisted, and it was a third, 'middle' style which emerged in the 18th century as the basis of modern Russian. Pushkin, the language's first great poet, was essentially writing in the Russian of today when he published *Eugene Onegin* in 1831. The alphabet was radically simplified at two major turning points in Russian history – as part of Peter the

at a glance ...

language name:
Russian

name in language:
русский язык *rus*·ki yi-*zihk*

language family:
Slavonic

key countries:
Russian Federation

approximate number of speakers: over 270 million

close relatives:
Belarusian, Ukrainian

donations to English:
apparatchik, sputnik, steppe, tsar, tundra, vodka

introduction

9

Great's reforms at the turn of the 17th century, and after the October Revolution in 1917.

For a language spoken across such a vast geographical area, Russian is surprisingly uniform, and the regional differences (mainly in pronunciation) don't get in the way of communication. The language was standardised by the centralised education system in the USSR, which spread literacy and enforced 'literary' Russian. In practical terms, Russian is divided into the northern and the southern dialect groups, while Moscow's dialect has some characteristics of both. From the 16th century onward Muscovite Russian was the standard tongue, even after Peter the Great's court had moved to St Petersburg.

Some admirers of Russian literature have claimed that the *славянская душа* (Slavic soul) of writers such as Dostoevsky, Chekhov or Tolstoy simply can't be understood, or at least fully appreciated, in translation. All exaggeration aside, the Russian language boasts a rich vocabulary and highly colourful expressions. This linguistic flamboyance has thankfully resisted the influence of dour communist style and the 'socrealist' (or 'socialist realist') literature of the 20th century.

This book gives you the practical phrases you need to get by in Russian, as well as all the fun, spontaneous phrases that can lead to a better understanding of Russian speakers and their culture. Once you've got the hang of how to pronounce Russian words, the rest is just a matter of confidence. Local knowledge, new relationships and a sense of satisfaction are on the tip of your tongue. So don't just stand there, say something!

abbreviations used in this book

a	adjective	m	masculine
acc	accusative	n	neuter
adv	adverb	nom	nominative
dat	dative	perf	perfective
f	feminine	pl	plural
gen	genitive	pol	polite
imp	imperfective	prep	prepositional
inf	informal	sg	singular
inst	instrumental	v	verb
lit	literal translation		

introduction

Many of the sounds in Russian are also found in English, and those that are unfamiliar aren't difficult to master. Use the coloured pronunciation guides to become familiar with them, and then read from the Cyrillic alphabet when you feel more confident.

Despite the Russian Federation's vast expanse and the age of the language itself, there are remarkably few variations in Russian pronunciation and vocabulary – for much of the last century only the teaching of the 'literary' language has been permitted. This phrasebook is written in standard Russian as it's spoken around Moscow, and you're sure to be understood by Russian speakers everywhere.

vowel sounds

Russian vowels are relatively simple to pronounce:

symbol	english equivalent	russian example	transliteration
a	path	да	da
ai	aisle	май	mai
e	ten	это	e·ta
ey	they	бассейн	bas·*yeyn*
i	ski	мир	mir
ih	any	мыло	*mih*·la
o	more	дом	dom
oy	boy	сырой	sih·*roy*
u	put	ужин	*u*·zhihn

consonant sounds

Most consonants are similar to English sounds, so they won't cause you too much difficulty. The apostrophe is used (like in *бедность byed·nast'*) to show that the consonant before it is pronounced with a soft y sound.

symbol	english equivalent	russian example	transliteration
b	bit	брат	brat
ch	chip	чай	chai
d	day	вода	va·da
f	fun	кофе	ko·fi
g	goat	город	go·rat
k	king	сок	sok
kh	Bach	смех	smyekh
l	lump	лифт	lift
m	my	место	mye·sta
n	not	нога	na·ga
p	put	письмо	pis·mo
r	rib (but rolled)	река	ri·ka
s	sit	снег	snyek
sh	shop	душа	du·sha
t	ton	так	tak
ts	hits	отец	at·yets
v	vet	врач	vrach
y	toy	мой	moy
z	zoo	звук	zvuk
zh	pleasure	жизнь	zhihzn'
'	like a soft y	власть	vlast'

word stress

Russian stress is free (it can fall on any syllable) and mobile (it can change in different forms of the same word). Each word has only one stressed syllable, which you'll need to learn as you go. In the meantime, follow our pronunciation guides which have the stressed syllable marked in italics.

intonation

You can change a statement into a question by simply changing your intonation, or the way you raise or lower your voice in a sentence.

In a statement (like the one on the left below), keep your voice level and drop it in the last word.

In a yes/no question (on the right below) keep your voice level, but then raise your tone in the last word and drop it again right at the end.

This is our hotel.
Это наша гостиница.

Is this our hotel?
Это наша гостиница?

e·ta *na*·sha gas·*ti*·nit·sa

e·ta *na*·sha gas·*ti*·nit·sa

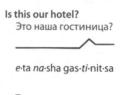

reading & writing

Russian uses a variant on the Cyrillic script, which was devised in the 9th century by the Greek missionary St Cyril. He used a modified Greek alphabet to translate the Bible into a language called Old Church Slavic.

The current Russian alphabet developed from this writing system. It consists of 31 letters and two signs – hard and soft. We've also included the letter Ё ё **yo** (which is used in dictionaries and grammars for non-natives) but in Russia it's usually written as Е е. For spelling purposes (like when you spell your name to book into a hotel), the pronunciation of each letter is provided on the next page. The order shown in the 'alphabet' box has been used in the **culinary reader** and **russian–english dictionary**.

alphabet

Аа	a	Кк	ka	Хх	kha
Бб	be	Лл	el	Цц	tse
Вв	ve	Мм	em	Чч	che
Гг	ge	Нн	en	Шш	sha
Дд	de	Оо	o	Щщ	shcha
Ее	ye	Пп	pe	Ъъ	*tvyor*·dih znak
Ёё	yo	Рр	er	Ыы	ih
Жж	zhe	Сс	es	Ьь	*myakh*·ki znak
Зз	ze	Тт	te	Ээ	e
Ии	i	Уу	u	Юю	yu
Йй	i·*krat*·ka·ye	Фф	ef	Яя	ya

The 'soft' sign ы and the 'hard' sign ъ don't have a sound of their own, but show in writing whether the consonant before them is pronounced 'soft' (with a slight y sound after it) or 'hard' (as it's written). The hard sign isn't included in our transliteration system as it's very rarely used.

Just like in the English alphabet, the pronunciation of some vowels and consonants in the Cyrillic alphabet can vary from the standard sound (shown below). Even so, if you read a Cyrillic word phonetically you should be understood, and as you listen to Russians speaking you'll pick up on the sound variations.

reading cyrillic

Just as letters in Latin script look different if they're in roman font (like 'a') or in italics (like '*a*'), so do Cyrillic letters. To eyes accustomed to English script, understanding that 'граница' and '*граница*' are different written forms of 'border' can be a challenge. Here's the Cyrillic alphabet in both roman and italic font to help you with menus, schedules and signs.

Аа	Бб	Вв	Гг	Дд	Ее	Ёё	Жж	Зз	Ии	Йй
Аа	*Бб*	*Вв*	*Гг*	*Дд*	*Ее*	*Ёё*	*Жж*	*Зз*	*Ии*	*Йй*

Кк	Лл	Мм	Нн	Оо	Пп	Рр	Сс	Тт	Уу	Фф
Кк	*Лл*	*Мм*	*Нн*	*Оо*	*Пп*	*Рр*	*Сс*	*Тт*	*Уу*	*Фф*

Хх	Цц	Чч	Шш	Щщ	Ъъ	Ыы	Ьь	Ээ	Юю	Яя
Хх	*Цц*	*Чч*	*Шш*	*Щщ*	*Ъъ*	*Ыы*	*Ьь*	*Ээ*	*Юю*	*Яя*

a–z phrasebuilder
фрэйзбилдэр

contents

The list below shows which grammatical structures you can use to say what you want. Look under each function – in alphabetical order – for information on how to build your own phrases. For example, to tell the taxi driver where your hotel is, look for **giving instructions** and you'll be directed to information on **case**, **demonstratives**, etc. A **glossary** of grammatical terms is included at the end of this chapter to help you. Abbreviations like nom and acc in the literal translations for each example refer to the case of the noun or pronoun – this is explained in the **glossary** and in **case**.

a–z phrasebuilder

15

adjectives & adverbs

Adjectives normally come before the noun, and they change their gender, number and case endings to agree with the nouns they describe. In our **dictionaries** and any others you may use, adjectives are given in the masculine form (generally ending in -ый *-ih*). This ending changes to -ая *-a·ya* to describe a feminine noun, -ое *-a·ye* for neuter nouns, and -ые *-ih·ye* for plural ones – we've used красивый kra·*si·*vih (beautiful) in the examples below. See also **case, gender** and **plurals.**

This is a beautiful city!
    Это красив**ый** город!   *e·*ta kra·*si·*vih *go·*rat
    (lit: this beautiful city-**m-nom**)

This is a beautiful river!
    Это красив**ая** река!   *e·*ta kra·*si·*va·ya ri·*ka*
    (lit: this beautiful river-**f-nom**)

Adverbs are formed by replacing the adjective endings with -о (-**o**, or -**a** if unstressed). They usually come before the verb.

He played beautifully!
    Он прекрасно играл!   on pri·*kras·*na i·*gral*
    (lit: he beautifully played)

You can use this -o form to make simple sentences.

It's cold!	Холодно!	*kho·*lad·na
(lit: cold-**o**)		
That's interesting!	Интересно!	in·tir·*yes·*na
(lit: interesting-**o**)		

articles

Russian doesn't have an equivalent for 'the' or 'a' – турист tu·*rist* means 'the tourist' or 'a tourist', depending on context.

be

doing things · negating

The Russian verb 'be' isn't used in the present tense (ie 'am', 'is' and 'are'). See also **verbs** for more information on past and future tenses.

I'm a tourist.
Я турист.   ya tu·*rist*
(lit: I-nom tourist-nom)

To make a sentence negative, just use the word не **nye** (not).

I'm not a tourist.
Я не турист.   ya nye tu·*rist*
(lit: I-nom not tourist-nom)

case

doing things · giving instructions · indicating location · naming people/things · possessing

Russian uses cases (shown by word endings) to indicate a noun or pronoun's role and its relationship to other words in a sentence. Russian has six cases, as shown opposite. The lists in this book and in the **dictionaries** and **culinary reader** provide words in the nominative case – this will always be understood, even when it isn't completely correct within a sentence.

Note that the genitive case is not only used to show possession, but also with amounts, prices and most quantifiers (like 'much' or 'many').

A hundred roubles.
Сто рублей.   sto rub·*lyey*
(lit: hundred roubles-gen)

I haven't got much money.
У меня мало денег.   u min·*ya ma*·la *dyen*·ik
(lit: at me-gen little money-gen)

nominative **nom** – shows the subject of a sentence

The guide has paid.
Гид уже заплатил.   git u·*zhe* za·pla·*til*
(lit: guide-**nom** already paid)

accusative **acc** – shows the direct object of a sentence

Did you see the play?
Вы посмотрели пьесу?   vih pas·mat·*rye*·li *pye*·su
(lit: you-**nom** saw play-**acc**)

genitive **gen** – shows possession 'of'

The price of the room is too high.
Цена номера слишком   tse·*na no*·mi·ra *slish*·kam
высокая.   vih·*so*·ka·ya
(lit: price-**nom** room-**gen** too high)

dative **dat** – shows the indirect object of a sentence

I gave my passport to the policeman.
Я дал паспорт   ya dal *pas*·part
милиционеру.   mi·lit·sih·an·*ye*·ru
(lit: I-**nom** gave passport-**acc** policeman-**dat**)

instrumental **inst** – shows how something is done

You need to write with a pen.
Нужно писать ручкой.   *nuzh*·na pi·*sat' ruch*·kay
(lit: must write pen-**inst**)

prepositional **prep** – is only used after the prepositions на na (on), в v (in) and о a (about)

The timetable is in the bag.
Расписание в сумке.   ras·pi·*sa*·ni·ye f *sum*·kye
(lit: timetable-**nom** in bag-**prep**)

Notice that all other prepositions aren't followed by the prepositional case. As in the next example, c s (with) is followed by the instrumental case. See also **prepositions**.

I'm here with my husband.
Я здесь с мужем.   ya zdyes' s *mu*·zhem
(lit: I-**nom** here with husband-**inst**)

Here are the most common case endings for nouns. For plural words, use the nominative plural ending (see **plurals**) and you'll be understood. You'll see that masculine and neuter nouns share most endings.

gender case	masculine (eg паспорт 'passport')	feminine (eg машина 'car')	neuter (eg блюдо 'dish')
nominative	consonant only паспорт *pas*·part	-a -a машина ma·*shih*·na	-o -o/a* блюдо *blyu*·da
accusative	consonant only паспорт *pas*·part	-у -u машину ma·*shih*·nu	-o -o/a* блюдо *blyu*·da
genitive	-a -a паспорта *pas*·par·ta	-ы -ih машины ma·*shih*·nih	-a -a блюда *blyu*·da
dative	-у -u паспорту *pas*·par·tu	-e -ye машине ma·*shihn*·ye	-у -u блюду *blyu*·du
instrumental	-ом -om/-am* паспортом *pas*·par·tam	-ой -oy/-ay* машиной ma·*shih*·nay	-ом -om/-am* блюдом *blyu*·dam
prepositional	-e -ye паспорте *pas*·part·ye	-e -ye машине ma·*shihn*·ye	-e -ye блюде *blyud*·ye

* Indicates alternative pronunciation of an ending (eg -o -o/-a) depending on the stress of the word it's attached to.

demonstratives

**giving instructions · indicating location ·
naming people/things · pointing things out**

The Russian word это *e*·ta means 'this/that is' and 'these/those are'. It never changes, and is followed by the nominative case. See also **case**.

This is my husband.

Это мой муж.   *e*·ta moy mush

(lit: this-is my husband-nom)

Those are your things.

Это ваши вещи.   *e*·ta *va*·shih *vye*·shi

(lit: those-are your things-nom)

gender

naming people/things

Russian nouns have gender – masculine m, feminine f or neuter n. You need to learn the grammatical gender for each noun as you go, but you can generally recognise it by the noun's ending – masculine nouns end in a consonant, feminine in -a -a, and neuter in -o -o. You need to know gender to mark case and form adjectives and past tense verbs. The nouns in this book's lists, **dictionaries** and **culinary reader** all have their gender marked.

паспорт m	*pas*·part	**passport**
виза f	*vi*·za	**visa**
консульство n	*kon*·sulst·va	**consulate**

See also **adjectives & adverbs**, **case** and **verbs**.

negatives

negating

Negative sentences are formed by adding the word не nye (not) before the verb:

I read Russian.

Я читаю порусски.   ya chi·*ta*·yu pa·*rus*·ki

(lit: I-nom read Russian)

I don't read Russian.

Я не читаю порусски.   ya nye chi·*ta*·yu pa·*rus*·ki

(lit: I-nom not read Russian)

nouns

naming people/things

Russian nouns have many forms – various endings are used to show their role in the sentence. See **case**, **gender** and **plurals**.

personal pronouns

doing things • giving instructions • naming people/things • possessing

Personal pronouns ('I', 'you', etc) change according to case to indicate the person's role in a sentence (eg whether the person is a subject or an object). In the table below, we've only laid out the nominative case of the pronouns. These forms won't always be correct in every sentence, but you'll be understood.

I want to eat.
Я хочу есть.   ya kha·*chu* yest'
(lit: I-**nom** want eat)

Give me a map.
Дайте мне карту.   *day*·tye mnye *kar*·tu
(lit: give me-**dat** map-**acc**)

I	я	ya	we	мы	mih
you sg inf	ты	tih	you pl inf&pol	вы	vih
you sg pol	вы	vih			
he	он	on			
she	она	a·*na*	they	они	a·*ni*
it	оно	a·*no*			

Note that Russian has a polite and an informal word for 'you' – see the box on page 106 for more information.

plurals

Russian generally uses the ending -ы ·ih to show plurals – it won't always be correct, but you should be understood fine. Just add -ы to a word ending in a consonant, and use it to replace the final -a ·a on feminine nouns. One exception: neuter nouns replace final -о ·o/-а with -a ·a. See also **gender**.

singular	plural
tourist турист m tu·*rist*	**We're tourists.** Мы туристы. mih tu·*ris*·tih (lit: we-**nom** tourists-**nom**)
apartment квартира f kvar·*ti*·ra	**Are those apartments?** Это квартиры? *e*·ta kvar·*ti*·rih (lit: those-are apartments-**nom**)
dish блюдо n *blyu*·da	**All the dishes are delicious.** Все блюда вкусные. fsye *blyu*·da *fkus*·nih·ye (lit: all dish-**nom** delicious)

possession

To say someone 'has' something, say у … есть … u … yest' … (lit: at someone-**gen** there-is something-**nom**).

Do you have a menu?
   У вас есть меню?   u vas yest' min·*yu*
   (lit: at you-**gen** menu-**nom**)

You can also use possessive terms (the equivalents of 'my', 'your', etc) to talk about ownership. The words его yi·*vo* (his), её yi·*yo* (her) and их ikh (their) don't change, but the translations of 'my' and 'your' take different endings to match the gender and case of the noun they describe. See also **case**, **gender** and **plurals**.

	masculine	feminine	neuter	plural
my	мой moy	моя ma·ya	моё ma·yo	мои ma·yi
your sg pol & pl inf&pol	ваш vash	ваша va·sha	ваше va·she	ваши va·shih

Here's my visa.
   Вот моя виза.   vot ma·ya vi·za
   (lit: here my visa-nom)

Is this your passport?
   Это ваш паспорт?   e·ta vash pas·part
   (lit: this your-pl passport-nom)

prepositions

indicating location • pointing things out

Russian uses prepositions – small words like в **v** (in/at) and на **na** (on) – to express where something is. After any preposition, add -e **-ye** to the noun:

bus   автобус   af·to·bus
   (lit: bus-nom)
in the bus   в автобусе   v af·to·bus·ye
   (lit: in bus-prep)

The following table shows some useful prepositions and the case of the noun they're attached to. See also **case**.

english	russian	translit	noun case
about	о	o	prepositional
in/at (place)	в	v	prepositional
near	рядом с	rya·dam s	instrumental
on/at (event)	на	na	prepositional
to	до	do	genitive
via	через	che·ris	accusative
with	с	s	instrumental

questions

You can change a statement into a yes/no question simply by making your voice rise and fall sharply towards the end of a sentence. To make it really clear that you're asking a question, you can also add the word да **da** (yes) at the end. See also the information on intonation in **pronunciation**, page 13.

This is my room.
Это мой номер.   *e·*ta moy *no·*mir
(lit: this my room-**nom**)

Is this my room?
Это мой номер?   *e·*ta moy *no·*mir
(lit: this my room-**nom**)

This is my room, isn't it?
Это мой номер, да?   *e·*ta moy *no·*mir da
(lit: this my room-**nom** yes)

To ask about specific information, just add one of the question words from the next table to the start of a sentence:

Where are you studying Russian?
Где вы изучаете   gdye vih i·zu·*cha·*i·tye
русский язык?   *rus·*ki yi·*zihk
(lit: where you-**pol-nom** study Russian language-**acc**)

How?	Как?	kak
How many/much?	Сколько?	*skol'·*ka
What?	Что?	shto
When?	Когда?	kag·*da*
Where?	Где?	gdye
Where to?	Куда?	ku·*da*
Who?	Кто?	kto
Why?	Почему?	pa·chi·*mu*

a–z phrasebuilder

25

Russian has only three tenses – past, present, and future. Tenses are formed by taking the infinitive (or 'dictionary form') of the verb, dropping the -ать -at' or -ить -it' endings, and adding the appropriate tense ending.

verb aspect

For an English verb, the dictionary usually gives two Russian infinitives – the entry for 'read' will give читать chi·tat' and прочитать pra·chi·tat'. The first form shows the 'imperfective aspect', and is used for habitual or continuing actions (ie when it's not important if the action is completed or not). It can be used both in the present and the past tense.

I often read in Russian.

Я часто читаю порусски.   ya *chas*·ta chi·*ta*·yu pa·*rus*·ki
(lit: I-nom often read-imp Russian)

Yesterday I did some reading.

Я вчера читала.   ya fchi·*ra* chi·*ta*·la
(lit: I-nom yesterday read-imp)

The second form shows the 'perfective aspect', and is used to emphasise the result of an action. This stresses that a single event is finished, and the main use is for completed past actions.

I finished reading the book yesterday.

Я вчера прочитала книгу.   ya fchi·*ra* pra·chi·*ta*·la *kni*·gu
(lit: I-nom read-perf book-acc yesterday)

present

The table overleaf shows the present tense endings for perfective and imperfective verbs ending in -ать -at' or -ить -it'. Both kinds of verb use the same set of endings.

	verb ending	eg читать 'read'	verb ending	eg говорить 'speak'
I	- ю -yu	читаю chi·ta·yu	- ю -yu	говорю ga·var·yu
you sg inf	- ешь -yish'	читаешь chi·ta·yish'	- ишь -ish'	говоришь ga·va·rish'
you sg pol	- ете -yit·ye	читаете chi·ta·yit·ye	- ите -it·ye	говорите ga·va·rit·ye
he/she	- ет -yit	читает chi·ta·yit	- ит -it	говорит ga·va·rit
we	- ем -yim	читаем chi·ta·yim	- им -im	говорим ga·va·rim
you pl inf&pol	- ете -yit·ye	читаете chi·ta·yit·ye	- ите -it·ye	говорите ga·va·rit·ye
they	- ют -yut	читают chi·ta·yut	- ят -yat	говорят ga·var·yat

Do you speak English?

Вы говорите по-английски?   vih ga·va·ri·tye pa·an·gli·ski
(lit: you-nom-sg-pol speak English)

past

Past tense endings depend on the gender and number of the subject doing the action. For most perfective and imperfective verbs, drop the final -ть -t' and add the endings in the table below. We've used the example купить ku·pit (buy).

singular subject			plural subject
masculine	**feminine**	**neuter**	**plural · 'you'** pol
-л -l	-ла -la	-ло -lo	-ли -li

He bought a ticket.

Он купил билет.   on ku·pil bil·yet
(lit: he-nom bought ticket-acc)

Did you buy a ticket?

Вы купили билет? pol   vih ku·pi·li bil·yet
(lit: you-nom-pol bought ticket-acc)

future

Grammatically, perfective and imperfective verbs take different forms in the future tense. An easy way to sidestep this is to say a sentence in the present tense, and add a 'future time marker' to it (just like in English). You can find these in the **dictionary**.

I'm working tomorrow.
> Я работаю завтра.   ya ra·*bo*·ta·yu *zaf*·tra
> (lit: I-nom work tomorrow)

word order

asking a question • doing things • giving instructions • making a statement • negating

Russian is often said to have free word order, as the case endings in words show who is doing what, but Russian word order is basically subject-verb-object like English. Pronoun objects like 'her' or 'it', however, come before verbs:

I love beer.
> Я люблю пиво.   ya lyub·*lyu pi*·va
> (lit: I-nom love beer-acc)

I love you.
> Я вас люблю.   ya vas lyub·*lyu*
> (lit: I-nom you love-pres)

Russians also start a sentence with background information, and build up to crucial new information – like a punchline in a joke.

There's no toilet on the bus!
> В автобусе нет туалета!   v af·*to*·bus·ye nyet tu·al·*ye*·ta
> (lit: in bus-prep no toilet-gen)

For more information on word order, see **adjectives & adverbs**, **negating** and **questions**.

glossary

accusative (case)	type of *case marking* used for the *object* of the sentence – 'the cosmonaut opened **the airlock**'
adjective	a word that describes something – 'she floated out into **deep** space'
adverb	a word saying how an action is done – 'she breathed **deeply** and started her spacewalk'
article	the words 'a', 'an' and 'the'
aspect	Russian verbs have two aspects – *perfective* and *imperfective*
case (marking)	word ending which tells us the role of a thing or person in the sentence
dative	type of *case marking* for the indirect *object* – 'she drifted towards **the Mir space station**'
gender	Russian nouns and pronouns are defined as masculine, feminine or neuter
genitive (case)	type of *case marking* showing possession – '**the space station's** door loomed before her'
imperfective	verb *aspect* showing an incomplete action – 'she **was waiting** for airlock clearance'
infinitive	the dictionary form of the verb – 'the door began **to open** …'
instrumental (case)	type of *case marking* which shows how something is done – 'and she pulled herself up **with the handrails**'
nominative (case)	type of *case marking* which shows the *subject* of the sentence – '**the crew** in the spaceship cheered wildly'

noun	a thing, person or idea – 'suddenly, **the spaceship** rocked'
number	whether a word is singular or plural – 'some small **meteorites** had hit the shuttle's tail'
object (direct)	the thing or person in the sentence that has the action directed to it – 'the science officer checked **the instrument panel**'
object (indirect)	the recipient of an action – 'the commander sent an order **to the people** in the tail'
perfective	verb *aspect* showing a complete action – 'they **fixed** the damage and **reported** back'
possessive pronoun	a word that means 'mine', 'yours', etc
preposition	a word like 'under' in '**under** the control panel'
prepositional (case)	type of *case marking* used after the prepositions на na (on), в v (in) and о a (about)
personal pronoun	a word that means 'I', 'you', etc
quantifiers	a word like 'some', 'all' or 'many'
subject	the thing or person in the sentence that does the action – '**the commander** transmitted a message to ground control'
tense	locates when an action happens – 'breathed' is past tense in 'the whole crew **breathed** a sigh of relief'
transliteration	pronunciation guide for words and phrases
verb	the word that tells you what action happened – 'the mission could safely **continue**'

language difficulties

Do you speak (English)?
Вы говорите
(по-английски)?

vih ga·va·*rit*·ye
(pa·an·*gli*·ski)

Does anyone speak (English)?
Кто-нибудь говорит
(по-английски)?

kto·ni·bud' ga·va·*rit*
(pa·an·*gli*·ski)

Do you understand?
Вы понимаете?

vih pa·ni·*ma*·it·ye

Yes, I understand.
Да, понимаю.

da pa·ni·*ma*·yu

No, I don't understand.
Нет, не понимаю.

nyet nye pa·ni·*ma*·yu

I (don't) understand.
Я (не) понимаю.

ya (nye) pa·ni·*ma*·yu

Pardon?
Простите?

pras·*tit*·ye

I speak (English).
Я говорю (по-английски).

ya ga·var·*yu* (pa·an·*gli*·ski)

I don't speak (Russian).
Я не говорю (по-русски).

ya nye ga·var·*yu* (pa·*ru*·ski)

I speak a little.
Я немного говорю.

ya nim·*no*·ga ga·var·*yu*

I would like to practise (Russian).
Я хочу говорить
(по-русски).

ya kha·*chu* ga·va·*rit'*
(pa·*ru*·ski)

Let's speak (Russian).
Давайте поговорим
(по-русски)!

da·*veyt*·ye pa·ga·va·*rim*
(pa·*ru*·ski)

What does 'пуп' mean?
Что обозначает
слово «пуп»?

shto a·baz·na·*cha*·it
slo·va pup

31

| **How do you say … in Russian?** | | |
| Как будет … по-русски? | | kak *bu*·dit … pa·*ru*·ski |

How do you …?	Как …?	kak …
pronounce this	это произносится	*e*·ta pra·iz·*no*·sit·sa
write 'Putin'	пишется «Путин»	*pi*·shiht·sa *pu*·tin

Could you please …?	…, пожалуйста.	… pa·*zhal*·sta
repeat that	Повторите	paf·ta·*rit*·ye
speak more slowly	Говорите помедленее	ga·va·*rit*·ye pa·mid·lin·*ye*·ye
write it down	Запишите	za·pi·*shiht*·ye

---

false friends

Beware *ложные друзья lozh*·nih·ye druz·*ya* (false friends) – words which sound like English words but have a different meaning altogether. Using them in the wrong context could confuse, or amuse, locals.

| интеллигентный m | in·ti·lig·*yent*·nih | cultured |
| **not** 'intelligent', which is *умный um*·nih | | |

| магазин m | ma·ga·*zin* | shop |
| **not** 'magazine', which is *журнал* zhur·*nal* | | |

| машина f | ma·*shih*·na | car |
| **not** 'machine', which is usually *станок* sta·*nok* | | |

| фамилия f | fa·*mi*·li·ya | surname |
| **not** 'family', which is *семья* sim·*ya* | | |

numbers & amounts

cardinal numbers

The numbers 'one' and 'two' are the only ones which take different forms for masculine, feminine and neuter words. Numbers also change form to reflect their case (see the **phrasebuilder**, page 18) but we've only included the nominative case here.

If you're counting in sequence (one, two, three ...) note that you use the word *раз* ras for 'one'.

1	один/одна/одно m/f/n	a-*din*/ad-*na*/ad-*no*
2	два/две m&n/f	dva/dvye
3	три	tri
4	четыре	chi-*tih*-ri
5	пять	pyat'
6	шесть	shest'
7	семь	syem'
8	восемь	*vo*-sim'
9	девять	*dye*-vit'
10	десять	*dye*-sit'
11	одиннадцать	a-*di*-nat-sat'
12	двенадцать	dvi-*nat*-sat'
13	тринадцать	tri-*nat*-sat'
14	четырнадцать	chi-*tihr*-nat-sat'
15	пятнадцать	pit-*nat*-sat'
16	шестнадцать	shihst-*nat*-sat'
17	семнадцать	sim-*nat*-sat'
18	восемнадцать	va-sim-*nat*-sat'
19	девятнадцать	di-vit-*nat*-sat'
20	двадцать	*dvat*-sat'
21	двадцать один	*dvat*-sat' a-*din*
22	двадцать два	*dvat*-sat' dva
30	тридцать	*trit*-sat'
40	сорок	*so*-rak
50	пятьдесят	pi-dis-*yat*
60	шестдесят	shihs-dis-*yat*

70	семьдесят	*syem'*·di·sit
80	восемьдесят	*vo*·sim'·di·sit
90	девяносто	di·vi·*no*·sta
100	сто	sto
132	сто тридцать два	sto *trit*·sat' dva
200	двести	*dvye*·sti
300	триста	*tri*·sta
400	четыреста	chi·*tih*·ri·sta
500	пятьсот	pit'·*sot*
600	шестьсот	shihst'·*sot*
700	семьсот	sim'·*sot*
800	восемьсот	va·sim'·*sot*
900	девятьсот	di·vit'·*sot*
1,000	тысяча	*tih*·si·cha
1,000,000	миллион	mi·li·*on*

making it count

If you're asking for a certain number of something in a shop, you need to use a word meaning 'thing' – *штука shtu*·ka – after the number. It changes form depending on the number before it, as shown below.

..., please!	..., пожалуйста!	... pa·*zhal*·sta
One	Одну штуку	ad·*nu shtu*·ku
Two/Three/Four	Две/Три/	dvye/tri/
	Четыре штуки	chi·*tih*·ri *shtu*·ki
Five	Пять штук	pyat' shtuk
Six (etc)	... штук	... shtuk

ordinal numbers

порядковые числительные

Ordinal numbers from 'first' to 'ninth' are irregular, so we've listed them on the next page. To form numbers above 'ninth', drop the ь (shown in the pronunciation guide by the apostrophe ') from the end of the cardinal number and add -ый -ih. For example, *двадцать dvat*·sat' (twenty) becomes *двадцатый dvat*·*sa*·tih (twentieth).

1st	первый	*pyer*·vih
2nd	второй	fta·*roy*
3rd	третий	*trye*·tih
4th	четвёртый	chit·*vyor*·tih
5th	пятый	*pya*·tih
6th	шестой	shih·*stoy*
7th	седьмой	sid'·*moy*
8th	восьмой	vas'·*moy*
9th	девятый	div·*ya*·tih
10th	десятый	dis·*ya*·tih

decimals & fractions

Russian decimals use a *запятая* za·pi·*ta*·ya (comma) instead of a dot – '2,5' means 'two and a half'. Saying decimals is quite complicated, and the easiest solution is to read out the numbers and the comma in the order you see them. In this example, *два запятая пять* dva za·pi·*ta*·ya pyat' (lit: two comma five) will get you by just fine.

a quarter	четверть	*chet*·virt'
a third	треть	tryet'
a half	половина	pa·la·*vi*·na
three-quarters	три четверти	tri *chet*·vir·ti
all	весь pl	vyes'
none	никаких pl	ni·ka·*kikh*

---

coinage of note

The currency of Russia is the *рубль* rubl' (rouble) which is divided into 100 *копейка* kap·*yey*·ka (kopecks). Abbreviations for the rouble are *py* or *p*. Coins come in denominations of one, five, 10 and 50 kopecks, and one, two and five roubles. Banknotes are available for 10, 50, 100, 500 and 1000 roubles.

The slang term for '50 roubles' is *полтинник* pal·*ti*·nik (lit: half) while *сотник* sot·nik (lit: hundred) means '100 roubles'.

useful amounts

How much/many?	Сколько?	skol'·ka
Please give me …	Дайте, пожалуйста …	deyt·ye pa·zhal·sta …
(50/100)	(пятьдесят/сто)	(pi·dis·yat/sto)
grams	грамм	gram
half a kilo	полкило	pol·ki·lo
a kilo	кило	ki·lo
a bottle	бутылку	bu·tihl·ku
a jar/tin	банку	ban·ku
a packet	пакет	pak·yet
a slice	кусок	ku·sok
a few	немного	nim·no·ga
less	меньше	myen'·she
(just) a little	(только)	(tol'·ka)
	немножко	nim·nosh·ka
a lot/many	много	mno·ga
more	больше	bol'·she
some	несколько	nye·skal'·ka

ancient history

It's useful to know how to read Cyrillic dates and abbreviations when you're checking out buildings, artworks and monuments. Centuries are written in Roman numerals.

год (г.)/лет	got/lyet	**year**
век (в.)	vyek	**century**
начало	na·cha·la	**beginning**
середина	si·ri·di·na	**middle**
конец	kan·yets	**end**
нашей эры (н.э.) (lit: of-our era)	na·shey e·rih	**AD**
до нашей эры (до н.э.) (lit: before our era)	da na·shey e·rih	**BC**

10th century AD

десятый век нашей эры	dis·ya·tih vyek na·shey e·rih

telling the time

The Russian word *час* chas (hour) also means 'o'clock'. It becomes *часа* chi·*sa* for two, three and four o'clock, and *часов* chi·*sof* for five o'clock and later hours.

What time is it?
    Который час?   ka·*to*·rih chas

It's one o'clock.
    Час.   chas

It's (two/three/four) o'clock.
    (Два/Три/Четыре) часа.   (dva/tri/chi·*tih*·ri) chi·*sa*

It's (ten) o'clock.
    (Десять) часов.   (*dye*·vit') chi·*sof*

Saying the minutes before or after the hour is a little more complicated. The easiest way is to give the hour plus the minutes, as in 'ten fifteen'. If the minutes are less than ten, say *ноль* nol' (zero) in the middle.

Five past (ten).
    (Десять) ноль пять.   (*dye*·sit') nol' pyat
    (lit: ten zero five)

Quarter past (ten).
    (Десять) пятнадцать.   (*dye*·sit') pit·*nat*·sat'
    (lit: ten fifteen)

Half past (ten).
    (Десять) тридцать.   (*dye*·sit') *trit*·sat'
    (lit: ten thirty)

Twenty to (eleven).
    (Десять) сорок.   (*dye*·sit') *so*·rak
    (lit: ten forty)

in the morning (5am-12pm)	утра	ut·*ra*
in the afternoon (12pm-5pm)	дня	dnya
in the evening (5pm-12am)	вечера	*vye*·chi·ra

At what time ...?
В котором часу ...?   f ka·*to*·ram chi·*su* ...

At (ten).
В (десять) часов.   v (*dye*·sit') chi·*sof*

At (7.57pm).
В (семь пятьдесят   f (syem' pi·dis·*yat*
семь вечера).   syem' *vye*·chi·ra)
(lit: at seven fifty seven in-the-evening)

the calendar

календарь

days

Monday	понедельник m	pa·ni·*dyel'*·nik
Tuesday	вторник m	*ftor*·nik
Wednesday	среда f	sri·*da*
Thursday	четверг m	chit·*vyerk*
Friday	пятница f	*pyat*·nit·sa
Saturday	суббота f	su·*bo*·ta
Sunday	воскресенье n	vas·kris·*yen'*·ye

months

January	январь m	yin·*var'*
February	февраль m	fiv·*ral'*
March	март m	mart
April	апрель m	ap·*ryel'*
May	май m	mey
June	июнь m	i·*yun'*
July	июль m	i·*yul'*
August	август m	*av*·gust
September	сентябрь m	sint·*yabr'*
October	октябрь m	akt·*yabr'*
November	ноябрь m	na·*yabr'*
December	декабрь m	di·*kabr'*

dates

What date is it today?
Какое сегодня число?   ka·*ko*·ye si·*vod*·nya chis·*lo*

It's 1 May.
Первое мая.   *pyer*·va·ye *ma*·ya

On what date?
Какого числа?   ka·*ko*·va chis·*la*

seasons

spring	весна f	vis·*na*
summer	лето n	*lye*·ta
autumn/fall	осень f	*o*·sin'
winter	зима f	zi·*ma*

time & dates

present

now	сейчас	si·*chas*
today	сегодня	si·*vod*·nya
tonight	сегодня вечером	si·*vod*·nya *vye*·chi·ram
this ...		
morning	сегодня утром	si·*vod*·nya ut·ram
afternoon	сегодня днём	si·*vod*·nya dnyom
week	на этой неделе	na *e*·tey nid·*yel*·ye
month	в этом месяце	v *e*·tam *mye*·sit·se
year	в этом году	v *e*·tam ga·*du*

past

day before yesterday	позавчера	pa·zaf·chi·*ra*
(three days) ago	(три дня) назад	(tri dnya) na·*zat*
since (May)	с (мая)	s (*ma*·ya)
yesterday ...	вчера ...	fchi·*ra* ...
morning	утром	ut·ram
afternoon	днём	dnyom
evening	вечером	*vye*·chi·ram
last ...		
night	вчера вечером	fchi·*ra vye*·chi·ram
week	на прошлой неделе	na *prosh*·ley nid·*yel*·ye
month	в прошлом месяце	f *prosh*·lam *mye*·sit·se
year	в прошлом году	f *prosh*·lam ga·*du*

whys and wherefores

Remember that the apostrophe ' in the pronunciation guide is said as a gentle 'y' sound after a consonant (as in nol') while the y is always pronounced like the 'y' in 'yes'.

future

day after tomorrow	послезавтра	pos·li·*zaf*·tra
in (six days)	через (шесть дней)	*che*·ris (shest' dnyey)
until (June)	до (июня)	da (i·*yun*·ya)
tomorrow ...	завтра ...	*zaf*·tra ...
morning	утром	*ut*·ram
afternoon	днём	dnyom
evening	вечером	*vye*·chi·ram
next ...		
week	на следующей неделе	na *slye*·du·yu·shi nid·*yel*·ye
month	в следующем месяце	f *slye*·du·yu·shim *mye*·sit·se
year	в следующем году	f *slye*·du·yu·shim ga·*du*

during the day

afternoon	после обеда	*pos*·lye ab·*ye*·da
dawn	рассвет m	ras·*vyet*
day	день m	dyen'
evening	вечер m	*vye*·chir
midday	полдень m	*pol*·din'
midnight	полночь f	*pol*·nach'
morning	утро n	*ut*·ra
night	ночь f	noch'
sunrise	восход солнца m	vas·*khot* sont·sa
sunset	заход солнца m	za·*khot* sont·sa

New Year (1 January)

Новый год   *no·vih got*

Russia's most important secular holiday – friends and family gather for a sumptuous feast on New Year's Eve, and turn on Radio Moscow to hear the Kremlin bells sound midnight. Everyone toasts with champagne, wishing each other *С Новым годом!* s *no·*vihm *go·*dam (Happy New Year!). A figure with red coat and white beard, *дед-мороз* dyet·ma·*ros* (Grandfather Frost), brings presents to all good children.

Defender of the Motherland Day (23 February)

День Защитника Родины   dyen' za·*shit·*ni·ka *ro·*di·nih

A day of great significance to Russian men, as most have served in the army. It's a de facto 'men's day' when women buy gifts like aftershave for the men in their lives.

Women's Day (8 March)

Восьмое марта   vas'·*mo·*ye *mar·*ta

Also called 'Mothers' Day', this celebration calls for men to give flowers to women, and boys to give a present to their female teachers. The men in a household may cook dinner to make up for the other 364 days of the year.

Orthodox Easter (March/April)

Пасха   *pas·*kha

Easter is of far greater significance than Christmas to Orthodox Christians, and families gather for lavish celebrations which begin on the Saturday evening. Just before midnight the priest opens the church doors and announces *Христос воскресе!* khris·*tos* vas·*kryes·*ye (Christ is risen!); the congregation responds *Воистину воскресе!* va·*yi·*sti·nu vas·*kryes·*ye (He is truly risen!). The priest then leads a procession around the church three times in a symbolic search for Christ's body.

Victory Day (9 May)

День Победы   dyen' pab·*ye·*dih

A day of military parades and veterans' gatherings which commemorates victory over the Nazis in WWII, remembered by Russians as the *Великая Отечественная война* vi·*li·*ka·ya at·ye·chist·vi·na·ya vey·*na* (Great Patriotic War). Over 20 million people in the former USSR were killed.

How much is it?
Сколько стоит? *skol'*·ka *sto*·it

It's free.
Это будет бесплатно. *e*·ta *bu*·dit bis·*plat*·na

It's (12) roubles.
Это будет (двенадцать) *e*·ta *bu*·dit (dvi·*nat*·sat')
рублей. rub·*lyey*

Can you write down the price?
Запишите, za·pi·*shiht*·ye
пожалуйста, цену. pa·*zhal*·sta *tse*·nu

Do I have to pay?
Нужно платить? *nuzh*·na pla·*tit'*

Do you accept …?	Вы принимаете оплату …?	vih pri·ni·*ma*·it·ye a·*pla*·tu …
credit cards	кредитной карточкой	kri·*dit*·ney *kar*·tach·key
debit cards	дебитной карточкой	*dye*·bit·ncy *kar*·tach·key
travellers cheques	дорожным чеком	da·*rozh*·nihm *che*·kam

I'd like …, please.	Будьте добры, я бы хотел/ хотела … m/f	*but*·ye da·*brih* ya bih khat·*yel*/ khat·*ye*·la …
my change	сдачу	*zda*·chu
some change	мелкими монетами	*myel*·ki·mi man·*ye*·ta·mi
smaller notes	мелкими купюрами	*myel*·ki·mi kup·*yu*·ra·mi
a receipt	квитанцию	kvi·*tant*·sih·yu
a refund	получить обратно деньги	pa·lu·*chit'* a·*brat*·na *dyen'*·gi
to return this	это вернуть	*e*·ta vir·*nut'*

Where's a/an …?	Где …?	gdye …
automated teller machine	банкомат	ban·ka·mat
foreign exchange office	обмен валюты	ab·myen val·yu·tih

I'd like to …	Я бы хотел … m	ya bih khat·yel …
	Я бы хотела … f	ya bih khat·ye·la …
cash a (travellers) cheque	разменять (дорожный) чек	raz·min·yat' (da·rozh·nih) chek
change money	поменять деньги	pa·min·yat' dyen'·gi
get a cash advance	снять деньги по кредитной карточке	snyat' dyen'·gi pa kri·dit·ney kar·tach·ki
withdraw money	снять деньги	snyat' dyen'·gi

What's the …?		
charge for that	Сколько нужно заплатить?	skol'·ka nuzh·na za·pla·tit'
exchange rate	Какой курс?	ka·koy kurs

How much is it per …?	Сколько стоит за …?	skol'·ka sto·it za …
caravan	автофургон	af·ta·fur·gon
day	день	dyen'
game	игру	i·gru
hour	час	chas
minute	минуту	mi·nu·tu
night	ночь	noch'
page	страницу	stra·nit·su
person	одного человека	ad·na·vo chi·lav·ye·ka
tent	палатку	pa·lat·ku
week	неделю	nid·yel·yu
vehicle	машину	ma·shih·nu
visit	один раз	a·din ras

For more money-related phrases, see **banking**, page 95.

getting around

средства передвижения

Which ... goes to (Minsk)?	Какой ... идёт в (Минск)?	ka·*koy* ... id·*yot* v (minsk)
Does this ... go to (Moscow)?	Этот ... идёт в (Москву)?	*e*·tat ... id·*yot* v (mask·*vu*)
boat	пароход	pa·ra·*khot*
bus	автобус	af·*to*·bus
plane	самолёт	sa·mal·*yot*
train	поезд	*po*·yist
trolleybus	троллейбус	tral·*yey*·bus
When's the ... (bus)?	Когда будет ... (автобус)?	kag·*da* bu·dit ... (af·*to*·bus)
first	первый	*pyer*·vih
last	последний	pas·*lyed*·ni
next	следующий	*slye*·du·yu·shi

What time does it leave?
Когда он отправляется?   kag·*da* on at·prav·*lya*·it·sa

How long does it take to get to (Volgograd)?
Сколько времени нужно ехать до (Волгограда)?   *skol'*·ka *vrye*·mi·ni *nuzh*·na *ye*·khat' da (*vol*·ga·gra·da)

How long will it be delayed?
На сколько он опаздывает?   na *skol'*·ka on a·*paz*·dih·*va*·yet

Is this seat available?
Это место занято?   *e*·ta *mye*·sta *za*·ni·ta

That's my seat.
Это моё место.   *e*·ta ma·*yo mye*·sta

Please tell me when we get to (Kursk).

Скажите, пожалуйста, когда мы подъедем к (Курску).

ska·*zhiht*·ye pa·*zhal*·sta kag·*da* mih pad·*ye*·dim k (*kurs*·ku)

Please stop here.

Остановитесь здесь, пожалуйста!

a·sta·na·*vi*·tis' zdyes' pa·*zhal*·sta

I'm going to throw up!

Меня тошнит!

min·*ya* tash·*nit*

---

tickety-boo

On crowded buses and trolleybuses, ask fellow passengers to validate your ticket for you:

Punch it, please!

Закомпостируйте, пожалуйста!

za·kam·pa·*sti*·ruy·tye pa·*zhal*·sta

---

tickets

Where do I buy a ticket?

Где можно купить билет?   gdye *mozh*·na ku·*pit'* bil·*yet*

A … ticket	Билет …	bil·*yet* …
(to Novgorod).	(на Новгород).	(na *nov*·ga·rat)
1st-class	в первом классе	f *pyer*·vam *klas*·ye
2nd-class	во втором классе	va fta·*rom klas*·ye
child's	для детей	dlya dit·*yey*
one-way	в один конец	v a·*din* kan·*yets*
return	в оба конца	v *o*·ba kant·*sa*
student	для студентов	dlya stud·*yen*·taf

How much is it?

Сколько стоит?   *skol'*·ka *sto*·it

(Ten) roubles' worth of tickets, please.

Билетов на (десять) рублей, пожалуйста!

bil·*ye*·taf na (*dye*·sit') rub·*lyey* pa·*zhal*·sta

How long does the trip take?

Сколько времени
уйдёт на эту поездку?

skol'·ka *vrye*·mi·ni
uyd·*yot* na *e*·tu pa·*yest*·ku

Is it a direct route?

Это прямой рейс?

e·ta pri·*moy* ryeys

What time is check in?

Во сколько начинается
регистрация?

va *skol'*·ka na·chi·*na*·yet·sa
ri·gi·*strat*·si·ya

I'd like	Я бы хотел … m	ya bih khat·*yel* …
a/an … seat.	Я бы хотела … f	ya bih khat·*ye*·la …
aisle	боковое место	ba·ka·*vo*·ye *mye*·sta
nonsmoking	место в отделении	*mye*·sta v a·dil·*ye*·ni·i
	для некурящих	dlya ni·kur·*ya*·shikh
smoking	место в отделении	*mye*·sta v a·dil·*ye*·ni·i
	для курящих	dlya kur·*ya*·shikh
window	место у окна	*myc*·sta u ak·*na*

listen for ...

Внимание!	vni·*ma*·ni·ye	**Attention!**
Билеты!	bil·*ye*·tih	**Tickets!**
Предъявите	prid·yi·*vit*·ye	**Passports, please!**
паспорт!	*pas*·part	
Все места	fsye mi·*sta*	**It's full.**
проданы.	*pro*·da·nih	
билетная касса f	bil·*yet*·na·ya *ka*·sa	**ticket office**
книжка талонов f	*knish*·ka ta·*lo*·naf	**book of tickets**
забастовка f	za·ba·*stof*·ka	**strike**
кассовый	*ka*·sa·vih	**ticket machine**
автомат m	af·ta·*mat*	
опаздывает	a·*paz*·dih·va·yet	**delayed**
отменили	at·mi·*ni*·li	**cancelled**
платформа f	plat·*for*·ma	**platform**
проводник m	pra·*vad*·nik	**carriage attendant/**
		conductor
расписание n	ras·pi·*sa*·ni·ye	**timetable**
то	to	**that one**
это	*e*·ta	**this one**

Is there (a) …?	Есть …?	yest' …
air conditioning	кондиционер	kan·dit·sih·an·yer
blanket	плед	plyet
heating	отопление	a·tap·lye·ni·ye
sick bag	гигиенический пакет	gi·gi·ye·ni·chi·ski pak·yet
toilet	туалет	tu·al·yet

I'd like to …	Я бы хотел/	ya bih khat·yel/
my ticket,	хотела … билет,	khat·ye·la … bil·yet
please.	пожалуйста. m/f	pa·zhal·sta
cancel	отменить	at·mi·nit'
change	поменять	pa·min·yat'
confirm	подтвердить	pat·vir·dit'

luggage

багаж

Where's a/the …?	Где …?	gdye …
baggage claim	выдача багажа	vih·da·cha ba·ga·zha
left-luggage office	багажное отделение	ba·gazh·na·ye o·dil·ye·ni·ye
luggage locker	камера-автомат	ka·mi·ra·af·ta·mat
trolley	тележка	til·yesh·ka

listen for …

жетон m	zhih·ton	token
доплатить	da·pla·tit'	pay extra v
перевес багажа m	pi·riv·yes ba·ga·zha	excess baggage
ручная кладь f	ruch·na·ya klat'	carry-on baggage

My luggage has been ...	Мой багаж ...	moy ba·*gash* ...
damaged	повредили	pa·vri·*di*·li
lost	пропал	pra·*pal*
stolen	украли	u·*kra*·li

That's (not) mine.

Это (не) моё.   *e*·ta (nye) ma·*yo*

Can I have some coins/tokens?

Дайте, пожалуйста,   *deyt*·ye pa·*zhal*·sta
монет/жетонов.   man·*yet*/zhih·*to*·naf

plane

Which gate for (Omsk)?

Какой выход на   ka·*koy vih*·khat na
посадку до (Омска)?   pa·*sat*·ku da (*om*·ska)

Where's (the) ...?	Где ...?	gdye ...
arrivals hall	зал прибытий	zal pri·*bih*·ti·ye
departures hall	зал отправлений	zal at·prav·*lye*·ni
duty-free	товары без	ta·*va*·rih byes
shops	пошлины	*posh*·li·nih
gate (number three)	выход на посадку (номер три)	*vih*·khat na pa·*sat*·ku (*no*·mir tri)

bus, trolleybus & coach

автобус и троллейбус

How often do buses come?
Как часто ходят автобусы?
kak *cha*·sta *kho*·dit af·*to*·bu·sih

Does it go to (Novgorod)?
Этот автобус
идёт в (Новгород)?
e·tat af·*to*·bus
id·*yot* v (*nov*·ga·rat)

What's the next stop?
Какая следующая
остановка?
ka·*ka*·ya *slye*·du·yu·sha·ya
a·sta·*nof*·ka

Please tell me when we get to (Magadan).
Объявите, пожалуйста,
когда мы подъедем
к (Магадану).
ab·yi·*vit*·ye pa·*zhal*·sta
kag·*da* mih pad·*ye*·dim
k (ma·ga·da·*nu*)

city a	городской m	ga·rat·*skoy*
intercity a	междугородный m	mizh·du·ga·*rod*·nih
local a	местный m	*myes*·nih
minibus (fixed-route taxi)	маршрутка f	marsh·*rut*·ka

For bus and trolleybus numbers, see **numbers & amounts**, page 33.

train & metro

Can I have a …?	…, пожалуйста.	… pa·*zhal*·sta
token	жетон	zhih·*ton*
monthly ticket	единый билет	yi·*di*·nih bil·*yet*

What station is this?
Какая эта станция? — ka·*ka*·ya e·ta *stant*·sih·ya

What's the next station?
Какая следующая
станция? — ka·*ka*·ya *slye*·du·yu·sha·ya *stant*·sih·ya

Which line goes to (Spartak)?
Какая линия идёт
в (Спартак)? — ka·*ka*·ya *li*·ni·ya id·*yot* f (spar·*tak*)

Does it stop at (Solntsevo)?
Поезд останавливается
в (Солнцево)? — *po*·yist a·sta·*nav*·li·va·yit·sa v (*sont*·si·va)

How long does the train take to (Domodedovo)?
Сколько времени идёт
электричка до
(Домодедово)? — *skol'*·ka·*vrye*·mi·ni id·*yot* el·ik·*trich*·ka da (da·mad·*ye*·da·va)

Do I need to change?
Мне нужно делать
пересадку? — mnye *nuzh*·na *dye*·lat' pi·ri·*sat*·ku

Which platform is for the Trans-Siberian Railway?
Транссибирский с
какой платформы? — trans·si·*bir*·ski s ka·*koy* plat·*for*·mih

---

a great train deal

As you travel on the Trans-Siberian Railway, the Russian passengers may introduce you to their favourite card game. Called *преферанс* pri·fi·*rans* (preference), it's derived from the French game Préférence. You play it with the full 52-card deck less the sixes, and involves taking tricks to win points. Some people call it 'bridge for children'.

How long do we stop here?

Сколько времени поезд
стоит на этой станции?

skol'·ka *vrye*·mi·ni *po*·ist
sta·*it* na *e*·tay *stant*·si

Can you please open/close the window?

Откройте/Закройте,
пожалуйста, окно.

at·*kroyt*·ye/za·*kroyt*·ye
pa·*zhal*·sta ak·*no*

The toilet is locked.

Туалет заперт.

tu·al·*yet za*·pirt

---

time-rich

The Russian Federation covers 11 time zones – when the
sun's setting in Kaliningrad, it's rising in Vladivostok – but
the entire country's rail and air networks run on Moscow
time. If you're not certain what time-zone you're running
on, ask for more information:

Is this Moscow time?

Это московское время?   *e*·ta ma·*skof*·ska·ye *vryem*·ya

Is this local time?

Это местное время?   *e*·ta *myes*·na·ye *vryem*·ya

Is it …?	Это …?	*e*·ta …
direct	прямой поезд	pri·*moy po*·yist
express	экспресс	iks·*pryes*
intercity	пассажирский	pa·sa·*zhihr*·ski
	поезд	*po*·yist
local (suburban)	электричка	e·lik·*trich*·ka

Where's the … carriage?	Где …?	gdye …
1st-class (sleeper)	спальный вагон	*spal'*·nih va·*gon*
2nd-class (sleeper)	купейный вагон	ku·*pey*·nih va·*gon*
3rd-class	плацкартный вагон	plats·*kart*·nih va·*gon*
4th-class	общий вагон	*op*·shi va·*gon*
dining	вагон-ресторан	va·*gon*·ri·sta·*ran*

boat

корабль

Is there a hydrofoil to (St Petersburg)?
Есть ракета до
(Санкт-Петербурга)?
yest' rak·*ye*·ta da
(sankt·pi·tir·*bur*·ga)

I want to book a cruise along the (Volga).
Я бы хотел/хотела
заказать круиз по (Волге). m/f
ya bih khat·*yel*/khat·*ye*·la
za·ka·*zat'* kru·is pa (*vol*·gye)

What's the water like today?
Какая сегодня вода?
ka·*ka*·ya si·*vod*·nya va·*da*

Are there life jackets?
Есть спасательные
жилеты?
yest' spa·*sa*·til'·nih·ye
zhihl·*ye*·tih

What island/beach is this?
Что это за остров/пляж?
shto *e*·ta za *o*·straf/plyash

I feel seasick.
Меня тошнит.
min·*ya* tash·*nit*

boat	пароход m	pa·ra·*khot*
cabin	каюта f	ka·*yu*·ta
captain	капитан m	ka·pi·*tan*
(car) deck	(автомобильная)	(af·ta·ma·*bil'*·na·ya)
	палуба f	*pa*·lu·ba
ferry	паром m	pa·*rom*
hydrofoil	ракета f	rak·*ye*·ta
lifeboat	спасательная лодка f	spa·*sa*·til'·na·ya *lot*·ka
life jacket	спасательный жилет m	spa·*sa*·til'·nih zhihl·*yet*
pirate	пират m	pi·*rat*
steamboat	пароход m	pa·ra·*khot*
terminal	речной вокзал m	rich·*noy* vag·*zal*
yacht	яхта f	*yakh*·ta

why, oh why

Remember that the apostrophe ' in the pronunciation
guide is said as a gentle 'y' sound after a consonant (like in
nol') while the y is always pronounced like the 'y' in 'yes'.

taxi

I'd like a taxi …	Мне нужно такси …	mnye *nuzh*·na tak·*si* …
at (9am)	в (девять	v (*dye*·vit'
	часов утра)	chi·*sof* u·*tra*)
now	сейчас	si·*chas*
tomorrow	завтра	*zaf*·tra

Where's the taxi rank?
Где стоянка такси?　　　　gdye sta·*yan*·ka tak·*si*

Is this taxi available?
Свободен?　　　　　　　　sva·*bo*·din

Please put the meter on.
Включите счётчик,　　　　fklyu·*chit*·ye *shot*·chik
пожалуйста!　　　　　　　pa·*zhal*·sta

How much is it to (Abramtsevo)?
Сколько стоит　　　　　　*skol'*·ka *sto*·it
доехать до (Абрамцево)?　da·*ye*·khat' da (ab·*ram*·tsih·va)

Please take me to (this address).
До (этого адреса)　　　　da (*e*·ta·va *a*·dri·sa)
не довезёте?　　　　　　　nye da·*viz*·yot·ye

How much is it?
Сколько с меня?　　　　　*skol'*·ka s min·*ya*

I'll give you (50) roubles.
Я вам дам (пятьдесят)　　ya vam dam (pi·dis·*yat*)
рублей.　　　　　　　　　rub·*lyey*

I want to get out!
Я хочу выйти!　　　　　　ya kha·*chu vih*·ti

---

alternative taxi

If you're about to travel with a *частник chas*·nik (private driver) instead of in an official taxi, sound confident and ask *Как мы будем ехать?* kak mih *bu*·dim *ye*·khat' (How are we getting there?). That way they may *think* you know where you're going, and feel less inclined to rip you off …

Please ...	..., пожалуйста!	... pa·*zhal*·sta
slow down	Не так быстро	ni tak *bih*·stra
step on it	Газуйте	ga·*zuyt*·ye
stop here	Остановитесь	a·sta·na·*vit*·yes'
	здесь	zdyes'
wait here	Подождите	pa·dazh·*dit*·ye
	здесь	zdyes'

For other useful phrases, see **directions**, page 65.

know your gender

Masculine and feminine markers (m and f) in our phrases always show the subject of a sentence – in the phrase *Я бы хотел/хотела* ... m/f ya bih khat·*yel*/khat·*ye*·la (I'd like ...), the m/f refers to the gender of the speaker.

car & motorbike

автомобиль и мотцикл

car & motorbike hire

I'd like to hire	Я бы хотел/	ya bih khat·*yel*/
a car (that's ...).	хотела взять	khat·*ye*·la vzyat'
	машину (...на	ma·*shih*·nu (... na
	прокат). m/f	pra·*kat*)
4WD	с полным	s *pol*·nihm
	приводом	pri·*vo*·dam
automatic	с автоматической	s af·ta·ma·*ti*·chi·skey
	трансмиссией	trans·*mi*·si·yey
manual	с ручным	s ruch·*nihm*
	переключением	pi·ri·klyu·*che*·ni·yem
	передач	pi·ri·*dach*
with ...	с ...	s ...
air	кондиционером	kan·dit·sih·an·*ye*·ram
conditioning		
a driver	шофёром	shaf·*yo*·ram

transport

55

I'd like to hire a motorbike.
> Я бы хотел/хотела   ya bih khat·*yel*/khat·*ye*·la
> взять мотоцикл в прокат. **m/f**   vzyat' ma·tat·*sihkl* f pra·*kat*

How much for daily/weekly hire?
> Сколько стоит однодневный/   *skol*'·ka *sto*·it ad·nad·*nyev*·nih/
> недельный прокат?   nid·*yel*'·nih pra·*kat*

Does that include insurance?
> Сюда входит страховка?   syu·*da* fkho·dit stra·*khof*·ka

Do you have a guide to the road rules (in English)?
> Есть правила уличного   yest' *pra*·vi·la *u*·lich·na·va
> движения (на английском)?   dvi·*zhe*·ni·ya (na an·*gli*·skam)

Do you have a road map?
> У вас есть карта дорог?   u vas yest' *kar*·ta da·*rok*

on the road

What's the speed limit?
> Какое ограничение   ka·*ko*·ye a·gra·ni·*che*·ni·ye
> скорости?   *sko*·ra·sti

Is this the road to (Kursk)?
> Эта дорога   *e*·ta da·*ro*·ga
> ведёт в (Курск)?   vid·*yot* f (kursk)

Where's a petrol station?
> Где заправка?   gdye za·*praf*·ka

Is it self-service?

Здесь самообслуживание?   zdyes' sa·ma·aps·*lu*·zhih·van·i·ye

Please fill it up.

Заполните бак,   za·*pol*·nit·ye bak
пожалуйста.   pa·*zhal*·sta

I'd like (15) litres.

(Пятнадцать) литров,   (pit·*nat*·sat') *li*·traf
пожалуйста.   pa·*zhal*·sta

diesel	дизельное	*di*·zil'·na·ye
	топливо n	*to*·pli·va
LPG	СУГ m	es·u·*ge*
octane level	октановое число n	ak·*ta*·na·va·ye chis·*lo*
premium	бензин	bin·*zin* no·mir
	номер 98 m	di·vi·*no*·sta *vo*·sim'
regular	бензин	bin·*zin* no·mir
	номер 93 m	di·vi·*no*·sta tri
unleaded	очищенный бензин m	a·*chi*·shi·nih bin·*zin*

Can you check	Проверьте,	prav·*yert*·ye
the ...?	пожалуйста, ...	pa·*zhal*·sta ...
oil	масло	*mas*·la
tyre pressure	давление колёс	dav·*lye*·ni·ye kal·*yos*
water	воду	*vo*·du

(How long) Can I park here?

(Сколько) Здесь   (*skol'*·ka) zdyes'
можно стоять?   *mozh*·na sta·*yat'*

Do I have to pay?

Нужно платить?   *nuzh*·na pla·*tit'*

---

listen for ...

бесплатно	bis·*plat*·na	**free** a
водительские	va·*di*·til'·ski·ye	**drivers licence**
права n pl	pra·*va*	
километров m pl	ki·lam·*ye*·traf	**kilometres**
стояночный	sta·*ya*·nach·nih	**parking meter**
счётчик m	*shot*·chik	

These signs are provided in upper-case letters. If you have trouble reading a sign, it might be in lower-case or italics (see the box on page 14 for details).

БЕРЕГИСЬ (ТРАМВАЯ)!	bi·ri·*gis'* (tram·*va*·ya)	**Look Out For (Trams)**
ВНИМАНИЕ	vni·*ma*·ni·ye	**Caution**
ВПЕРЕДИ ВЕДУТСЯ РАБОТЫ	fpi·ri·*di* vi·*dut*·sa ra·*bo*·tih	**Roadworks In Progress**
ВЪЕЗД	vyest	**Entrance**
ВЫЕЗД	*vih*·yest	**Exit**
ГАИ	ge·a·*el*	**Police**
ОБЪЕЗД	ab·*yest*	**Detour**
ОДНОСТОРОННЕЕ ДВИЖЕНИЕ	ad·na·sta·*ro*·ni·ye dvi·*zhe*·ni·ye	**One-Way**
ОПАСНО	a·*pas*·na	**Danger**
ПРОЕЗД ЗАПРЕЩЕН	pra·*yest* za·pri·*shon*	**No Entry**
СТОП	stop	**Stop**
СТОЯНКА ЗАПРЕЩЕНА	sta·*yan*·ka za·pri·shi·*na*	**No Parking**
УСТУПИ ДОРОГУ	u·stu·*pi do*·ra·gu	**Give Way**

problems

I need a mechanic.

Мне нужен автомеханик. mnye *nu*·zhihn af·ta·mi·*kha*·nik

I've had an accident.

Я потерпел аварию. m ya pa·tir·*pyel* a·*va*·ri·yu

Я потерпела аварию. f ya pa·tir·*pye*·la a·*va*·ri·yu

The car has broken down (at Kursk).

Машина сломалась ma·*shih*·na sla·*ma*·las'

в (Курске). v (*kur*·skye)

The motorbike has broken down (five kilometres) from here.

Мотоцикл сломался ma·tat·*sihkl* sla·*mal*·sa

(пять километров) отсюда. (pyat' ki·lam·*ye*·traf) at·*syu*·da

I have a flat tyre.

У меня лопнула шина. u min·*ya* lop·*nu*·la *shih*·na

The car/motorbike won't start.
Машина/мотоцикл
не заводится.

ma·*shih*·na/ma·tat·*sihkl*
nye za·*vo*·dit·sa

I've lost my car keys.
Я потерял/потеряла
ключи от машины. m/f

ya pa·tir·*yal*/pa·tir·*ya*·la
klyu·*chi* at ma·*shih*·nih

I've locked the keys inside.
Я закрыл/закрыла
ключи в машине. m/f

ya za·*krihl*/za·*krih*·la
klyu·*chi* v ma·*shihn*·ye

I've run out of petrol.
У меня кончился бензин.

u min·*ya kon*·chil·sa bin·*zin*

Can you fix it (today)?
Вы это можете
сделать (сегодня)?

vih e·ta *mo*·zhiht·ye
zdye·lat' (si·*vod*·nya)

When will the car be ready?
Когда машина
будет готова?

kag·*da* ma·*shih*·na
bu·dit ga·*to*·va

When will the motorbike be ready?
Когда мотоцикл
будет готов?

kag·*da* ma·tat·*sihkl*
bu·dit ga·*tof*

petrol/gas
бензин m
bin·*zin*

windscreen
лобовое стекло n
la·ba·*vo*·ye sti·*klo*

battery
батерея f
ba·tar·*ye*·ya

engine
двигатель m
dvi·*ga*·til'

tyre
шина f
shih·na

headlights
фары f pl
fa·rih

bicycle

I'd like to ...	Я бы хотел ... m	ya bih khat·*yel* ...
a bicycle.	Я бы хотела ... f	ya bih khat·ye·la ...
buy	купить	ku·*pit'*
	велосипед	vi·la·sip·*yet*
hire	взять велосипед	vzyat' vi·la·sip·*yet*
	на прокат	na pra·*kat*
I'd like a ... bike.	Я бы хотел/	ya bih khat·*yel*/
	хотела ...	khat·*ye*·la ...
	велосипед. m/f	vi·la·*sip*·yet
mountain	горный	*gor*·nih
racing	спортивный	spar·*tiv*·nih
second-hand	подержанный	pad·*yer*·zha·nih
How much is it	Сколько стоит	*skol'*·ka *sto*·it
per ...?	прокат в ...?	pra·*kat* f ...
day	сутки	*sut*·ki
hour	час	chas

Do I need a helmet?
Нужно носить шлем?   *nuzh*·na na·*sit'* shlyem

Are there bicycle paths?
Велодорожки есть?   vi·la·da·*rosh*·ki yest'

Is there a bicycle-path map?
Есть карта велодорожек?   yest' *kar*·ta vi·la·da·ro·zhek

I have a puncture.
У меня лопнула шина.   u min·*ya lop*·nu·la *shih*·na

Where can I get my bicycle repaired?
Где можно починить   gdye *mozh*·na pa·chi·*nit'*
велосипед?   vi·la·sip·*yet*

border crossing

I'm here ...	Я здесь ...	ya zdyes' ...
for study	учусь	u·*chus'*
on business	по бизнесу	pa *biz*·ni·su
on holiday	в отпуске	v *ot*·pus·kye

I'm here for ...	Я здесь ...	ya zdyes' ...
(10) days	(десять) дней	(*dye*·sit') dnyey
(three) weeks	(три) недели	(tri) nid·*ye*·li
(two) months	(два) месяца	(dva) *mye*·sit·sa

I'm going to (Lithuania) through (Belarus).
Я еду в (Литву)   ya *ye*·du v (lit·*vu*)
через (Беларусь).   che·riz (bi·la·*rus'*)

I'm going to (Akademgorodok).
Я еду в (Академгородок).   ya *ye*·du v (a·ka·dim·ga·ra·*dok*)

a clean sweep

Russia is a country with more bureaucracy than you may
be used to. You'll come across people who Russians would
scornfully condemn as a *совок* sa·*vok* (dustpan) – someone
who demonstrates an old-school Soviet mind-set and is
generally unhelpful and interfering.

If you're in an official situation and you've had enough of
so much dust-panning, don't lose your cool – talk about the
weather, and imagine your joy if you could say *Ой, какая
волокита!* oy ka·*ka*·ya va·la·*ki*·ta (God, what red tape!).

I'm staying at (the Kosmos).
Я останавливаюсь
в (Космосе).
ya as·ta·*nav*·li·va·yus'
v (*kos*·mas·ye)

The children are on this passport.
Дети вписаны в паспорт.
dye·ti *fpi*·sa·nih f *pas*·part

I'm a citizen of (Australia).
Я гражданин (Австралии). m
ya grazh·da·*nin* (af·*stra*·li·i)
Я гражданка (Австралии). f
ya grazh·*dan*·ka (af·*stra*·li·i)

Do you have this form in (English)?
У вас есть этот бланк
на (английском) языке?
u vas yest' *e*·tat blank
na (an·*gli*·skam) yi·zihk·*ye*

Do I need a visa?
Нужна ли виза?
nuzh·*na* li *vi*·za

Where can I have my visa registered?
Где регистрировать визу?
gdye re·gist·*ri*·ra·vat' *vi*·zu

signs

These signs are provided in upper-case letters. If you have
trouble reading a sign, it might be in lower-case or italics
(see the box on page 14 for details).

ИММИГРАЦИЯ	i·mi·*grat*·si·ya	**Immigration**
КАРАНТИН	ka·ran·*tin*	**Quarantine**
ПАСПОРТНЫЙ КОНТРОЛЬ	*pas*·part·nih kan·*trol'*	**Passport Control**
ТАМОЖЕННЫЙ КОНТРОЛЬ	ta·*mo*·zhih·nih kan·*trol'*	**Customs**
ТОВАРЫ БЕЗ ПОШЛИНЫ	ta·*va*·rih bis *posh*·li·nih	**Duty-Free**

at customs

I have nothing to declare.
Мне нечего
декларировать.

mnye *nye*·chi·va
di·kla·*ri*·ra·vat'

I have something to declare.
Мне нужно что-то
задекларировать.

mnye *nuzh*·na *shto*·ta
za·di·kla·*ri*·ra·vat'

Do I have to declare this?
Это нужно
декларировать?

e·ta *nuzh*·na
di·kla·*ri*·ra·vat'

Everything is for personal use.
У меня только вещи
личного пользования.

u min·*ya tol'*·ka *vye*·shi
lish·na·va *pol'*·za·va·ni·ya

That's (not) mine.

Это (не) моё. e·ta (nye) ma·*yo*

I didn't know I had to declare it.

Я не знал/знала, ya ni znal/*zna*·la
что это нужно shta e·ta *nuzh*·na
декларировать. m/f di·kla·*ri*·ra·vat'

For phrases on payments and receipts, see **money**, page 43.

For phrases on payments and receipts, see **money**, page 43.

listen for ...		
билет m	bil·*yet*	ticket
группа f	*gru*·pa	group
иммиграционная карточка f	i·mi·grat·sih·o·na·ya *kar*·tach·ka	immigration card
один m	a·*din*	alone
одна f	ad·*na*	alone
паспорт m	*pas*·part	passport
регистрация виз f	ri·gist·*rat*·si·ya vis	visa registration
семья f	sim·*ya*	family
таможенная декларация f	ta·*mo*·zhih·na·ya di·kla·*rat*·si·ya	customs declaration form

Откуда вы прилетели? **Where have you flown from?**
at·*ku*·da vih pri·lit·ye·li

На сколько вы приехали? **How long are you here for?**
na *skol'*·ka vih pri·*ye*·kha·li

Наличные есть? **Are you carrying cash?**
na·*lich*·nih·ye yest'

Ждите здесь! **Wait here!**
zhdih·tye zdyes'

Ввоз в Российскую **The importation of Justin**
Федерацию компакт-дисков **Timberlake CDs into the**
Джастина Тимберлейка **Russian Federation is**
строго воспрещается. **strictly prohibited.**
vos v ra·*si*·sku·yu
fi·di·*rat*·sih·yu *kom*·pakt·*dis*·kav
dzha·sti·na *tim*·bir·ley·ka
stro·ga vas·pri·*sha*·yit·sa

Where's a/the ... (around here)?	Где (здесь) ...?	gdye (zdyes') ...
bank	банк	bank
market	рынок	*rih*·nak
tourist office	туристическое бюро	tu·ri·*sti*·chi·ska·ye byu·*ro*

How do I get there?
Как туда попасть? — kak tu·*da* pa·*past'*

Do you know the way?
Вы знаете дорогу? — vih *zna*·yi·tye da·*ro*·gu

Is it nearby/far away?
Близко/Далеко? — *blis*·ka/da·li·*ko*

What's the address?
Какой адрес? — ka·*koy a*·dris

Can you show me (on the map)?
Покажите мне, пожалуйста (на карте). — pa·ka·*zhih*·tye mnye pa·*zhal*·sta (na *kart*·ye)

---

name the place

Here are placenames and their written abbreviations.

бульвар (бул.) m	bul'·*var*	boulevard
город (г.) m	*go*·rat	city
дом (д.) m	dom	housing complex
дорога (дор.) f	da·*ro*·ga	road
деревня (дер.) f	dir·*yev*·nya	village
квартира (кв.) f	kvar·*ti*·ra	apartment
корпус (корп.) m	*kor*·pus	building (in a complex)
переулок (пер.) m	pi·ri·*u*·lak	lane
площадь (пл.) f	*plo*·shit'	square
проспект (пр.) m	prasp·*yekt*	avenue
район (р./р-н) m	ra·*yon*	suburb
улица (ул.) f	*u*·lit·sa	street

north	север	*sye*·vir
south	юг	yuk
east	восток	va·*stok*
west	запад	*za*·pat

It's ...

close	Близко.	*blis*·ka
far	Далеко.	da·li·*ko*
here	Здесь.	zdyes'
on the corner	На углу.	na u·*glu*
straight ahead	Прямо.	*prya*·ma
that side	С той стороны.	s toy sta·ra·*nih*
this side	С этой стороны.	s e·toy sta·ra·*nih*
there	Там.	tam

It's ...

behind ...	За ...	za ...
in front of ...	Перед ...	*pye*·rit ...
near ...	Около ...	*o*·ka·la ...
next to ...	Рядом с ...	*rya*·dam s ...
opposite ...	Напротив ...	na·*pro*·tif ...

Turn (at the) ...	Поверните ...	pa·vir·*nit*·ye ...
corner	за угол	*za*·u·gal
left	налево	nal·*ye*·va
right	направо	na·*pra*·va
traffic lights	на светофоре	na svi·ta·*for*·ye

listen for ...		
километров	ki·lam·*ye*·traf	**kilometres**
метров	*mye*·traf	**metres**
минут	mi·*nut*	**minutes**

PRACTICAL

Russians typically write addresses in the reverse order to English speakers – they start with the country, then the city, suburb, street, and finally the person's name. As in the example below, the abbreviation *г.* for *город gó·rat* (city) appears before the name of the city, and likewise for the abbreviations for streets, buildings, etc.

Россия	**Russia**
г. Москва 117334	**Moscow City, Postcode 117334**
ул. Некрасова	**Nekrasov Street**
д. 33, корп. 2, кв. 15	**Complex 33, Building 2, Apartment 15**
ПАВЛОВУ М.И.	**M.I. Pavlov**

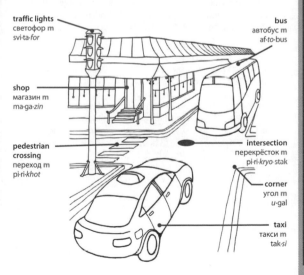

traffic lights
светофор m
svi·ta·*for*

bus
автобус m
af·to·bus

shop
магазин m
ma·ga·*zin*

pedestrian crossing
переход m
pi·ri·*khot*

intersection
перекрёсток m
pi·ri·*kryo*·stak

corner
угол m
u·gal

taxi
такси m
tak·*si*

directions

67

by ...		
bus	автобусом	af·*to*·bu·sam
foot	пешком	pish·*kom*
taxi	на такси	na tak·*si*
train	электричкой	e·lik·*trich*·key

What ... is this?	Что это за ...?	shto *e*·ta za ...
street	улица	*u*·lit·sa
suburb	район	ra·*yon*
village	деревня	dir·*yev*·nya

accommodation

finding accommodation

в поисках жилья

Where's a …?	Где …?	gdye …
boarding house	пансионат	pan·si·a·*nat*
camping ground	кемпинг	*kyem*·ping
hotel	гостиница	ga·*sti*·nit·sa
hut	сторожка	sta·*rosh*·ka
motel	мотель	mat·*yel'*
room (for rent)	комната (для съёма)	*kom*·na·ta (dlya *syo*·ma)
tourbase	турбаза	tur·*ba*·za
youth hostel	общежитие	ap·shi·*zhih*·ti·ye

Can you recommend somewhere …?	Вы можете порекомендовать что-нибудь …?	vih *mo*·zhiht·ye pa·ri·ka·min·da·*vat'* *shto*·ni·bud' …
cheap	дешёвое	di·*sho*·va·ye
luxurious	роскошное	ras·*kosh*·na·ye
nearby	близко отсюда	*blis*·ka at·*syu*·da
romantic	романтичное	ra·man·*tich*·na·ye

Where can I find a room in a private flat?

Где можно снять комнату в частной квартире? — gdye *mozh*·na snyat' *kom*·na·tu f *chas*·nay kvar·*tir*·ye

What's the address?

Какой адрес? — ka·*koy a*·dris

For phrases on how to get there, see **directions**, page 65.

listen for …		
всё занято	fsyo *zan*·yi·ta	**full**
паспорт m	*pas*·part	**passport**
сколько суток?	*skol'*·ka *su*·tak	**How many nights?**
сколько человек?	*skol'*·ka chi·lav·*yek*	**How many people?**

booking ahead & checking in

I'd like to book a room, please.

Я бы хотел/хотела
забронировать номер. m/f

ya bih khat·*yel*/khat·*ye*·la
za·bra·*ni*·ra·vat' *no*·mir

I have a reservation.

Я заказал номер. m
Я заказала номер. f

ya za·ka·*zal no*·mir
ya za·ka·*za*·la *no*·mir

My surname is …

Моя фамилия …

ma·*ya* fa·*mi*·li·ya …

Overnight only.

Только сутки.

tol'·ka *sut*·ki

For (three) nights.

(Трое) суток.

(*tro*·ye) *su*·tak

From (5 July) to (8 July).

С (пятого июля)
по (восьмое июля).

s (*pya*·ta·va i·*yul*·ya)
pa (vas'·*mo*·ye i·*yul*·ya)

Do you have a … room?	У вас есть …?	u vas yest' …
single	одноместный номер	ad·nam·*yes*·nih *no*·mir
double	номер с двуспальней кроватью	*no*·mir z dvu·*spaln*·yey kra·*vat*·yu
twin	двухместный номер	dvukh·*myes*·nih *no*·mir

local talk

charming	прелестно	pril·*yes*·na
comfortable	удобно	u·*dob*·na
rat-infested	наводнено крысами	na·vad·ni·*no krih*·sa·mi
a dive	дыра f	dih·*ra*
a real find	настоящая находка f	na·sta·*ya*·shi·ya na·*khot*·ka

How much is it per/for …?	Сколько стоит за …?	*skol'*·ka *sto*·it za …
night	ночь	noch'
two people	двоих	dva·*ikh*
week	неделю	nid·*yel*·yu

The price is very high.
Цена очень высокая. — tsih·*na* o·chin' vih·*so*·ka·ya

Can I see it?
Можно посмотреть? — *mozh*·na pas·mat·*ryet'*

Are there other rooms?
У вас есть другие номера? — u vas yest' dru·*gi*·ye na·mi·*ra*

I'll take it.
Я беру. — ya bi·*ru*

Do I need to pay a deposit/upfront?
Нужно платить аванс/вперёд? — *nuzh*·na pla·*tit'* a·*vans*/fpir·*yot*

Can I pay by …?	Можно расплатиться …?	*mozh*·na ras·pla·*tit'*·sa …
credit card	кредитной карточкой	kri·*dit*·nay *kar*·tach·kay
debit card	дебитной карточкой	di·*bit*·nay *kar*·tach·kay
travellers cheque	дорожным чеком	da·*rozh*·nihm *che*·kam

For other methods of payment, see **banking**, page 95, and **money**, page 43.

When/Where is breakfast served?
Когда/Где завтрак? kag·*da*/gdye *zaf*·trak

Please wake me at (seven).
Позвоните мне, paz·va·*nit*·ye mnye
пожалуйста, в (семь) часов. pa·*zhal*·sta v (syem') chi·*sof*

Is hot water available all day?
Горячая вода бывает gar·*ya*·chi·ya va·*da* bih·*va*·yit
целый день? *tse*·lih dyen'

Can I use the ...?	Можно восполь-зоваться ...?	*mozh*·na vas·*pol*'·za·vat'·sa ...
kitchen	кухней	*kukh*·nyey
laundry	прачечной	*pra*·chich·nay
telephone	телефоном	ti·li·*fo*·nam

Do you have a/an ...?	У вас есть ...?	u vas yest' ...
lift/elevator	лифт	lift
laundry service	прачечная	*pra*·chich·na·ya
message board	доска объявлений	da·*ska* ob·yiv·*lye*·ni
safe	сейф	syeyf
satellite TV	спутниковое телевидение	*sput*·ni·ka·va·ye ti·li·*vi*·di·ni·ye
swimming pool	бассейн	bas·*yeyn*

Can I ... here?	Здесь можно ...?	zdyes' *mozh*·na ...
change money	поменять деньги	pa·min·*yat'* dyen'·gi
join a tour	присоединиться к экскурсии	pri·sa·yi·di·*nit*'·sa k iks·*kur*·si

listen for ...		
ключ	klyuch	**key**
регистрация	ri·gi·*strat*·sih·ya	**reception**

Could I have (a/an) …, please?	Дайте, пожалуйста …	*dayt*·ye pa·*zhal*·sta …
(extra) blanket	(ещё) одеяло	(yi·*sho*) a·di·*ya*·la
bulb	лампочку	*lam*·pach·ku
receipt	квитанцию	kvi·*tant*·sih·yu
my key	ключ от моего номера	klyuch at ma·yi·*vo no*·mi·ra

on the floor

Each floor of a Russian hotel is supervised by a *дежурная* di·*zhur*·na·ya (floor lady). You can rely on her for help with:

горячая вода	gar·*ya*·cha·ya va·*da*	**hot water**
стирка	*stir*·ka	**laundry**
подсматривание	pat·sma·tri·*va*·ni·ye	**spying**

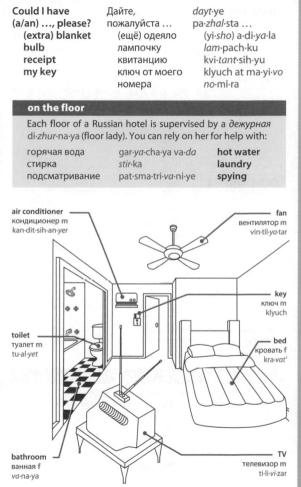

air conditioner
кондиционер m
kan·dit·sih·an·*yer*

fan
вентилятор m
vin·til·*ya*·tar

key
ключ m
klyuch

bed
кровать f
kra·*vat'*

toilet
туалет m
tu·al·*yet*

bathroom
ванная f
va·na·ya

TV
телевизор m
ti·li·*vi*·zar

accommodation

73

Is there a message for me?

Мне передавали? mnye pi·ri·da·*va*·li

Can I leave a message for someone?

Вы можете передать vih *mo*·zhiht·ye pi·ri·*dat'*
кому-то? ka·*mu*·ta

I'm locked out of my room.

Я забыл ключ в номере. m ya za·*bihl* klyuch v *no*·mir·ye
Я забыла ключ в номере. f ya za·*bih*·la klyuch v *no*·mir·ye

complaints

жалобы

It's too ...	В комнате очень ...	f *kom*·nat·ye *o*·chin' ...
bright	ярко	*yar*·ka
cold	холодно	*kho*·lad·na
dark	темно	tim·*no*
noisy	шумно	*shum*·na
small	тесно	*tyes*·na

The ... doesn't work.	... не работает.	... nye ra·*bo*·ta·yit
air conditioner	Кондиционер	kan·dit·sih·an·*yer*
heater	Отопление	a·tap·*lye*·ni·ye
toilet	Туалет	tu·al·*yet*

a knock at the door ...

Who is it?	Кто там?	kto tam
Just a moment.	Одну минуту!	ad·*nu* mi·*nu*·tu
Come in.	Заходите!	za·kha·*dit*·ye
Come back later, please.	Приходите попозже, пожалуйста.	pri·kha·*dit*·ye pa·*po*·zhe pa·*zhal*·sta
I'm not decent!	Я переодеваюсь!	ya pi·ri·a·di·*va*·yus'

This (pillow) isn't clean.
Эта (подушка) грязная.   e·ta (pa·*dush*·ka) *gryaz*·na·ya

There's no (hot water).
Нет (горячей воды).   nyet (gar·*ya*·chey va·*dih*)

I/We can't sleep because of (the renovations).
(Ремонт) мешает   (ri·*mont*) mi·*sha*·yet
мне/нам спать.   mnye/nam spat'

checking out

What time is checkout?
Когда нужно   kag·*da nuzh*·na
освободить номер?   as·va·ba·*dit'* no·mir

Can you call a taxi for me (for 11 o'clock)?
Мне нужно такси   mnye *nuzh*·na tak·*si*
(на одиннадцать часов).   (na a·*di*·nat·sat' chi·*sof*)

I'm leaving now.
Я сейчас уезжаю.   ya si·*chas* u·yi·*zha*·yu

We're leaving now.
Мы сейчас уезжаем.   mih si·*chas* u·yi·*zha*·im

Can I have the bill, please?
Приготовьте счёт,   pri·ga·*toft*·ye shot
пожалуйста.   pa·*zhal*·sta

There's a mistake in the bill.
Меня обсчитали.   min·*ya* ap·shi·*ta*·li

Can I leave my bags here?
Здесь можно   zdyes' *mozh*·na
оставлять багаж?   a·stav·*lyat'* ba·*gash*

Could I have my ..., please?	Дайте, пожалуйста ...	*dayt*·ye pa·*zhal*·sta ...
deposit	мой аванс	moy a·*vans*
passport	мой паспорт	moy *pas*·part
valuables	мои ценности	ma·*i tse*·nas·ti

I'll be back …
Я вернусь … ya vir·*nus'* …

    in (three) days
    через (три) дня *che*·ris (tri) dnya

    on (Monday)
    в (понедельник) f (pa·nid·*yel'*·nik)

I had a great stay, thank you.
Спасибо, я отлично spa·*si*·ba ya at·*lich*·na
провёл/провела время. m/f prav·*yol*/pra·vi·*la vryem*·ya

camping

Who's in charge here?
Кто здесь заведующий? kto zdyes' zav·*ye*·du·yu·shi

Can I camp here?
Можно устроить *mozh*·na u·*stro*·it'
стоянку здесь? sta·*yan*·ku zdyes'

Can I park next to my tent?
Можно поставить машину *mozh*·na pa·*sta*·vit' ma·*shih*·nu
рядом с палаткой? *rya*·dam s pa·*lat*·kay

Is the water drinkable?
Эту воду можно пить? *e*·tu *vo*·du *mozh*·na pit'

---

signs

These signs are provided in upper-case letters. If you have trouble reading a sign, it might be in lower-case or italics (see the box on page 14 for details).

НЕ ДЛЯ ПИТЬЯ	nye dlya pi·*tya*	**Not For Drinking**
ПИТЬЕВАЯ ВОДА	pi·ti·*va*·ya va·*da*	**Drinking Water**
ПРАВИЛА	*pra*·vi·la	**Site Regulations**
ВНУТРЕННЕГО	vnu·tri·ni·va	
РАСПОРЯДКА	ras·par·*yat*·ka	
РАЗЖИГАТЬ КОСТРЫ	ra·zhih·*gat'* kast·*rih*	**No Campfires**
ЗАПРЕЩАЕТСЯ	za·pri·*sha*·it·sa	
СТОЯНКА ТУРИСТОВ	sta·*yan*·ka tu·*ri*·staf	**No Camping**
ЗАПРЕЩЕНА	za·pri·shi·*na*	

How much is it per ...?	Сколько стоит за ...?	skol'·ka sto·it za ...
caravan	автофургон	af·ta·fur·gon
person	одного	ad·na·vo
	человека	chi·lav·ye·ka
tent	палатку	pa·lat·ku
vehicle	машину	ma·shi·nu

Do you have (a) ...?	Здесь есть ...?	zdyes' yest' ...
electricity	электричество	e·lik·tri·chist·va
laundry	прачечная	pra·chich·na·ya
shower facilities	душ	dush
site	место	mye·sta
tents for hire	палатки	pa·lat·ki
	напрокат	na·pra·kat

Is it coin-operated?
Это монетно? — e·ta man·yet·na

Could I borrow ...?
Можно взять взаймы ...? — mozh·na vzyat' vzay·mih ...

renting

снятие квартиры

Do you have a/an ... for rent?	У вас сдаётся ...?	u vas zda·yot·sa ...
apartment	квартира	kvar·ti·ra
holiday house	дача	da·cha
house	дом	dom
room	комната	kom·na·ta
traditional country house	изба	iz·ba

car space	место для	mye·sta dlya
	машины n	ma·shih·nih
furniture	мебель f	mye·bil'
security door	бронированные	bra·ni·ro·va·nih·ye
	двери f pl	dvye·ri

staying with locals

Can I stay at your place?
Можно пожить у вас?   *mozh·na pa·zhiht' u vas*

I have my own ...   У меня есть ...   *u min·ya yest' ...*
    mattress   матрац   *ma·trats*
    sleeping bag   спальный мешок   *spal'·nih mi·shok*

Is there anything I can do to help?
Разрешите вам помочь!   *raz·ri·shiht·ye vam pa·moch'*

Let me ...   Разрешите мне ...   *raz·ri·shiht·ye mnye ...*
    buy the   сделать   *zdye·lat'*
      groceries   покупки   *pa·kup·ki*
    clear the table   убрать со стола   *u·brat' sa sta·la*
    do the dishes   помыть посуду   *pa·miht' pa·su·du*
    set the table   накрыть на стол   *na·kriht' na·stal*
    take out   вынести мусор   *vih·ni·sti mu·sar*
      the rubbish

Many thanks for your hospitality.
Огромное спасибо за   *a·grom·na·ye spa·si·ba za*
ваше гостеприимство.   *va·shih ga·sti·pri·imst·va*

To compliment your hosts' cooking, see **eating out**, page 170.

visiting etiquette

When visiting Russians at home it's customary to take a small gift. There are no strict rules – a bottle of wine or vodka, a box of chocolates or flowers are fine. If it's winter, a gift of fruit shows that you've made an effort. Children will appreciate small gifts such as chocolate bars.

PRACTICAL

looking for ...

Where's a (supermarket)?
Где (универсам)?   gdye (u·ni·vir·*sam*)

Where can I buy (a padlock)?
Где можно купить   gdye *mozh*·na ku·*pit'*
(нависной замок)?   (na·vis·*noy* za·*mok*)

Where's the bus to (IKEA)?
Откуда идёт   at·*ku*·da id·*yot*
автобус до (ИКЕА)?   af·*to*·bus da (ik·*ye*·a)

For more items and shopping locations, see the **dictionary**.

listen for ...		
Вам помочь?	vam pa·*moch'*	**Can I help you?**
Что ещё?	shto yi·*sho*	**Anything else?**
У нас нету.	u nas *nye*·tu	**No, we don't have any.**
Редко поступает к нам.	*ryet*·ka pa·stu·*pa*·it k nam	**It's in short supply.**
Платите в кассу.	pla·*tit*·ye f *ka*·su	**Pay at the cashier.**

making a purchase

Be prepared for the 'three queue system' in older shops. When you choose an item, ask the shop assistant for a docket: *Выпишите, пожалуйста* vih·pi·shiht·ye pa·*zhal*·sta (Please write it out). Take this docket to a *касса ka*·sa (cashier), where you pay and have your docket stamped. Finally, proceed to the counter with your docket and collect your purchase.

Could you help me?
Будьте добры!   *but*·ye da·*brih*

I'd like to buy (an adaptor plug).
Я бы хотел купить   ya bih khat·*yel'* ku·*pit'*
(адаптер). **m**   (a·*dap*·tir)

I'd like to buy (a pocket knife).
Я бы хотела купить   ya bih khat·*ye*·la ku·*pit'*
(карманный ножик). **f**   (kar·*ma*·nih *no*·zhik)

I'm just looking.
Я просто смотрю.   ya *pros*·ta smat·*ryu*

How much is it?
Сколько стоит?   *skol'*·ka *sto*·it

Can you write down the price?
Запишите, пожалуйста, цену.   za·pi·*shiht*·ye pa·*zhal*·sta *tse*·nu

Do you have any others?
У вас есть другие?   u vas yest' dru·*gi*·ye

Can I look at it?
Покажите, пожалуйста.   pa·ka·*zhiht*·ye pa·*zhal*·sta

That's just what I want.
Это как раз.   *e*·ta kak ras

I'll take it.
Возьму.   vaz'·*mu*

Do I pay here?
Вам платить?   vam pla·*tit'*

Please write me out a docket.
Выпишите, пожалуйста.   *vih*·pi·shiht·ye pa·*zhal*·sta

Who's the last in the queue?
Кто последний?   kto pas·*lyed*·ni

are you being served?

Russians will often attract the attention of shop assistants
with the words *Девушка!* *dye*·vush·ka (girl) and *Бабушка!*
ba·bush·ka (grandmother). A more respectful version is *Вы
обслуживаете?* vih aps·*lu*·zhih·va·it·ye (Are you serving?).
If you want to get served, then politeness (and flattery)
always go a long way.

Do you accept ...?	Вы принимаете оплату ...?	vih pri·ni·*ma*·it·ye a·*pla*·tu ...
credit cards	кредитной карточкой	kri·*dit*·ney *kar*·tach·key
debit cards	дебитной карточкой	*dye*·bit·ney *kar*·tach·key
travellers cheques	дорожным чеком	da·*rozh*·nihm *che*·kam

Could I have (a) ..., please?	Дайте ..., пожалуйста.	*deyt*·ye ... pa·*zhal*·sta
bag	пакет	pak·*yet*
receipt	квитанцию	kvi·*tant*·sih·yu
some change	мелкими монетами	*myel*·ki·mi man·*ye*·ta·mi
smaller notes	мелкими купюрами	*myel*·ki·mi kup·*yu*·ra·mi

I don't need a bag, thanks.
Пакет не нужен. pak·*yet* nye *nu*·zhihn

Could I have it wrapped?
Заверните, пожалуйста. za·vir·*nit*·ye pa·*zhal*·sta

Does it have a guarantee?
Есть гарантия? yest' ga·*ran*·ti·ya

Can I have it sent abroad?
Вы можете переслать это за границу? vih *mo*·zhiht·ye pi·ris·*lat'* e·ta za gra·*nit*·su

Can you order it for me?
Я хочу это заказать. ya kha·*chu* e·ta za·ka·*zat'*

Can I pick it up later?
Я заберу это позже. ya za·bi·*ru* e·ta *po*·zhe

It's faulty.
Это браковано. e·ta z bra·*ko*·va·na

Can you repair this?
Вы можете это починить? vih *mo*·zhiht·ye e·ta pa·chi·*nit'*

When will it be ready?
Когда будет готово? kag·*da bu*·dit ga·*to*·va

I'd like …	Будьте добры, я бы хотел/ хотела … m/f	*but*·ye da·*br'* ya bih khat·*yel*/ khat·*ye*·la …
a refund	получить обратно деньги	pa·lu·*chit'* ab·*rat*·na *dyen'*·gi
my change	сдачу	*zda*·chu
to return this	это возвратить	*e*·ta vaz·vra·*tit'*

bargaining

поторгуемся

That's too expensive.
Это очень дорого.   *e*·ta *o*·chin' *do*·ra·ga

Can you lower the price?
Вы можете снизить цену?   vih *mo*·zhiht·ye *sni*·zit' *tse*·nu

Do you have something cheaper?
Есть подешевле?   yest' pa·di·*shev*·li

I'll give you (100) roubles.
Я вам дам (сто) рублей.   ya vam dam (sto) rub·*lyey*

books & reading

Do you have …?	У вас есть …?	u vas yest' …
a novel by	роман	ra·*man*
(Pasternak)	(Пастернака)	(pas·tir·na·*ka*)
an entertainment	список местных-	*spi*·sak *myes*·nihkh
guide	развлечений	raz·vli·*che*·ni

Is there an	Есть …	yest' …
(English-)	(английской)	(an·*gli*·skey)
language …?	книги?	*kni*·gi
bookshop	магазин	ma·ga·*zin*
section	секция	*syekt*·sih·ya

I'd like a …	Я бы хотел … m	ya bih khat·*yel* …
	Я бы хотела … f	ya bih khat·*ye*·la …
dictionary	словарь	sla·*var'*
newspaper	газету	gaz·*ye*·tu
(in English)	(на английском)	(na an·*gli*·skam)
notepad	блокнот	blak·*not*

Can you recommend a book for me?

Вы можете	vih *mo*·zhiht·ye
порекомендовать	pa·ri·ka·min·da·*vat'*
мне книгу?	mnye *kni*·gu

clothes

My size is (40).
Мой размер (сорок).   moy raz·*myer* (*so*·rak)

Can I try it on?
Можно это примерить?   *mozh*·na *e*·ta prim·*ye*·rit'

It doesn't fit.
Это не подходит.   *e*·ta nye pat·*kho*·dit

How do I look in this?
Как выгляжу в этом?   kak *vih*·gli·zhu v *e*·tam

Fabulous!
Классно!   *klas*·na

For different types of clothing, see the **dictionary**, and for sizes, see **numbers & amounts**, page 33.

electronic goods

Where can I buy duty-free electronic goods?
Где можно купить   gdye *mozh*·na ku·*pit'*
беспошлинную   bes·*posh*·li·nu·yu
электронику?   e·lik·*tro*·ni·ku

Is this the latest model?
Это последняя модель?   *e*·ta pas·*lyed*·nya·ya mad·*yel'*

Is this (240) volts?
Это на (двести сорок) вольт?   *e*·ta na (*dvye*·sti *so*·rak) volt

hairdressing

I'd like (a) ...	..., пожалуйста.	... pa·*zhal*·sta
blow wave	Сделайте	*zdye*·leyt·ye
	укладку феном	u·*klat*·ku *fye*·nam
colour	Сделайте	*zdye*·leyt·ye
	окраску	a·*kras*·ku
haircut/trim	Постригите	pas·tri·*git*·ye
my beard	Подстригите	pat·stri·*git*·ye
trimmed	бороду	*bo*·ra·du
shave	Побрейте	pab·*ryeyt*·ye

Don't cut it too short.
    Не слишком коротко.   nye *slish*·kam *ko*·rat·ka

That's plenty.
    Так достаточно.   tak das·*ta*·tach·na

You're a genius.
    У вас блестящие   u vas blist·*ya*·shi·ye
    способности.   spa·*sob*·na·sti

What have you done to me?!
    Что это вы тут натворили!   shto *e*·ta vih tut nat·va·*ri*·li

---

curds & whey

The ey in the pronunciation guide is always pronounced
the same as in 'they' or 'way'.

---

music & DVD

музыка и DVD

I'd like a …	Я бы хотел … m	ya bih khat·*yel* …
	Я бы хотела … f	ya bih khat·*ye*·la …
blank tape	чистую кассету	*chis*·tu·yu kas·*ye*·tu
CD	компакт-диск	kam·*pakt*·disk
DVD	DVD	di·vi·*di*
video	видеокассету	vi·di·o·kas·*ye*·tu

I'm looking for something by (Pavel Kashin).
    Я ищу что-нибудь   ya ish·*yu* shto·ni·bud'
    (Павла Кашина).   (*pav*·la *ka*·shih·na)

What's his/her best recording?
    Какая его/её самая   ka·*ka*·ya yi·*vo*/yi·*yo* sa·ma·ya
    лучшая запись?   *luch*·sha·ya za·pis'

Can I listen to this?
    Можно послушать?   *mozh*·na pas·*lu*·shat'

Will this work on any DVD player?
    Это сработает на   *e*·ta sra·*bo*·ta·yit na
    любом DVD-плейере?   lyu·*bom* di·vi·*di*·plyey·ir·ye

video & photography

I need ... film for this camera.	Мне нужна ... плёнка на эту камеру.	mnye nuzh·na ... plyon·ka na e·tu kam·ye·ru
APS	APS	a·pe·es
B&W	чёрно-белая	chor·nab·ye·la·ya
colour	цветная	tsvet·na·ya
slide	слайд-овая	slaid·a·va·ya
(high) speed	(высоко-) чувствительная	(vih·sa·ko·) chus·vi·til'·na·ya

Can you ...?	Вы можете ...?	vih mo·zhiht·ye ...
develop digital photos	проявить цифровые снимки	pra·yi·vit' tsihf·ra·vih·ye snim·ki
develop/load this film	проявить/ вложить эту плёнку	pra·yi·vit'/ vla·zhiht' e·tu plyon·ku
recharge the battery for my digital camera	перезарядить батарейку на мою цифровую камеру	pi·ri·za·ri·dit' ba·tar·yey·ku na ma·yu tsihf·ra·vu·yu kam·ye·ru
transfer photos from my camera to CD	перебросить снимки с камеры на компакт-диск	pi·ri·bro·sit' snim·ki s kam·ye·rih na kam·pakt·disk

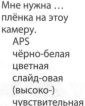

Do you have ... for this camera?	У вас есть ... на этоу видеокамеру?	u vas yest' ... na e·tu vi·di·o·kam·ye·ru
batteries	батарейки	ba·tar·yey·ki
memory cards	карты памяти	kar·tih pam·ya·ti

I need a cable to connect my camera to a computer.

Мне нужен кэйбл, чтобы соединить камеру с компьютером.

mnye *nu*·zhihn keybl *shto*·bih sa·yi·di·*nit'* *kam*·ye·ru s kamp·*yu*·ti·ram

I need a cable to recharge this battery.

Мне нужен кэйбл, чтобы перезарядить батарейку.

mnye *nu*·zhihn keybl *shto*·bih pi·ri·za·ri·*dit'* ba·tar·*yey*·ku

I need a video cassette for this camera.

Мне нужна видеокассета на этоу камеру.

mnye nuzh·*na* vi·di·o·kas·ye·ta na *e*·tu *kam*·ye·ru

Is this for a (PAL/NTSC) system?

Это на систему (PAL/NTSC)?

e·ta na sist·*ye*·mu (pel/en·ti·es·*si*)

I need a passport photo taken.

Мне нужно фотографироваться на визу.

mnye *nuzh*·na fa·ta·gra·*fi*·ra·vat'·sa na *vi*·zu

When will it be ready?

Когда она будет готова?

kag·*da* a·*na* bu·dit ga·*to*·va

How much is it?

Сколько стоит?

skol'·ka *sto*·it

I'm not happy with these photos.

Эти снимки меня не устраивают.

e·ti *snim*·ki min·*ya* nye ust·*ra*·i·va·yut

I don't want to pay the full price.

Я не буду платить полную цену.

ya nye *bu*·du pla·*tit'* *pol*·nu·yu *tse*·nu

abacus	счёты m pl	*sho*·tih
amber	янтарь m	yin·*tar'*
antique	антиквар m	an·tik·*var*
badge	значок m	zna·*chok*
balalaika	балалайка f	ba·la·*ley*·ka
chess set	шахматы f pl	*shakh*·mat·ih
fur hat	меховая	mi·kha·*va*·ya
	шапка f	*shap*·ka
handicrafts	изделия ручной	iz·*dye*·li·ya ruch·*noy*
	работы n pl	ra·*bot*·ih
icon	икона f	i·*ko*·na
jewellery	ювелирные	yu·vi·*lirn*·ih·ye
	изделия n pl	iz·*dye*·li·ya
lace	кружево n	*kru*·zhih·va
peasant doll	матрёшка f	mat·*ryosh*·ka
piece of crap	пустяк m	pust·*yak*
pottery	керамика f	ki·*ra*·mi·ka
rug	коврик m	*kov*·rik
Russian cigarettes	папиросы f pl	pa·pi·*ro*·sih
samovar	самовар m	sa·ma·*var*
Soviet posters	советские	sav·*yet*·ski·ye
	плакаты m pl	pla·*ka*·tih
stamps	марки f pl	*mar*·ki
toy	игрушка f	i·*grush*·ka
wooden carving	резьба по	riz'·*ba* pa
	дереву f	*dye*·ri·vu
woollen scarf	шерстяной	shir·stih·*noy*
	шарф m	sharf

communications

the internet

интернет

Where's the local Internet café?
Где здесь интернет-кафе?   gdye zdyes' in·ter·*net*·ka·*fe*

I'd like to …	Я бы хотел … m	ya bih khat·*yel* …
	Я бы хотела … f	ya bih khat·*ye*·la …
check my	проверить	prav·*ye*·rit'
email	свой и-мэйл	svoy i·*meyl*
get Internet	подключиться	pat·klyu·*chit'*·sa
access	к интернету	k in·ter·*ne*·tu
use a printer	воспользоваться	vas·*pol'*·za·vat'·sa
	принтером	in·ter·*ne*·tam
use a scanner	воспользоваться	vas·*pol'*·za·vat'·sa
	сканером	*skan*·ye·ram

Do you have …?	Есть …?	yest' …
Macs	компьютеры	kam·*pyu*·ti·rih
	Макинтош	ma·kin·*tosh*
PCs	ПК	pe·*ka*
a Zip drive	зип-драйв	*zip*·dreyf
How much per …?	Сколько стоит …?	*skol'*·ka *sto*·it …
minute	минута	mi·*nu*·ta
half-hour	полчаса	pol·chi·*sa*
hour	час	chas
page	страница	stra·*nit*·sa

How do I log on?

Как подключиться?　　　　　　kak pat·klyu·*chit'*·sa

Please change it to the (English)-language setting.

Включите, пожалуйста,　　　　fklyu·*chit*·ye pa·*zhal*·sta
(английский) алфавит.　　　　　(an·*gli*·ski) al·*fa*·vit

Do you have (English) keyboards?

Есть (английская)　　　　　　 yest' (an·*gli*·ska·ya)
клавиатура?　　　　　　　　　kla·vi·a·*tu*·ra

It's crashed.

Сломался.　　　　　　　　　　sla·*mal*·sa

I've finished.

Я закончил/закончила. m/f　　 ya za·*kon*·chil/za·*kon*·chi·la

> **'allo 'allo**
>
> When you answer the phone, say *Алло!* al·*yo* instead of *Здравствуйте!* zdrast·vuyt·ye for 'hello'.

mobile/cell phone

мобильный телефон

I'd like a …	Я бы хотел … m	ya bih khat·*yel* …
	Я бы хотела … f	ya bih khat·*ye*·la …
charger for	зарядное	zar·*yad*·na·ye
my phone	устройство на	ust·*royst*·va
	телефон	ti·li·*fon*
mobile/cell	взять	vzyat'
phone for hire	мобильный	ma·*bil'*·nih
	телефон напрокат	ti·li·*fon* nap·ra·*kat*
prepaid mobile/	предоплаченный	pri·da·*pla*·chi·nih
cell phone	телефон	ti·li·*fon*
SIM card	СИМ-карту	*sim*·kar·tu

What are the rates?

Какие тарифы?　　　　　　　ka·*ki*·ye ta·*ri*·fih

(Five) roubles per (30) seconds.

(пять) рублей за　　　　　　　(pyat') *rub*·lyey za
(тридцать) секунд.　　　　　　(*trit*·sat') si·*kunt*

phone

What's your phone number?

| Можно ваш номер | *mozh*·na vash *no*·mir |
| телефона? | ti·li·*fo*·na |

Where's the nearest pay phone?

| Где ближайший | gdye bli·*zhey*·shi |
| телефон-автомат? | ti·li·*fon*·af·ta·*mat* |

I'd like to …	Я бы хотел … m	ya bih khat·*yel* …
	Я бы хотела … f	ya bih khat·*ye*·la …
buy a	купить	ku·*pit'*
phonecard	телефонную	ti·li·*fo*·nu·yu
	карточку	*kar*·tach·ku
buy a token	купить жетон	ku·*pit'* zhih·*ton*
call (Singapore)	позвонить	paz·va·*nit'*
	(в Сингапур)	(v sin·ga·*por*)
make an inter-	позвонить	paz·va·*nit'*
national call	за границу	za gra·*nit*·su
reverse	позвонить	paz·va·*nit'*
the charges	с оплатой	s a·*pla*·tey
	вызываемого	vih·zih·*va*·yi·ma·va
speak for	поговорить	pa·ga·va·*rit'*
(three) minutes	(три) минуты	(tri) mi·*nu*·tih

listen for …

Вы не туда попали.	vih ni tu·*da* pa·*pa*·li	**Wrong number.**
Слушаю.	*slu*·sha·yu	**Speaking.**
Представьтесь, пожалуйста.	prit·*staft*·yes' pa·*zhal*·sta	**Who's calling?**
С кем вы хотите говорить?	s kyem vih kha·*tit*·ye ga·va·*rit'*	**Who do you want to speak to?**
Минутку.	mi·*nut*·ku	**One moment.**
Его нету.	yi·*vo nye*·tu	**He isn't here.**
Её нету.	yi·*yo nye*·tu	**She isn't here.**

communications

91

How much does each minute cost?
Сколько стоит минута?   *skol'·ka sto·it mi·nu·ta*

The number is …
Телефон …   *ti·li·fon …*

What's the code for (New Zealand)?
Какой код (Новой Зеландии)?   *ka·koy kot (no·vey zi·lan·di)*

It's engaged.
Занято.   *zan·ya·ta*

I've been cut off.
Меня превали.   *min·ya pri·va·li*

The connection's bad.
Плохо слышно.   *plo·kha slihsh·na*

Hello.
Алло!   *al·yo*

Can I speak to …?
Позовите, пожалуйста, …   *pa·za·vit·ye pa·zhal·sta …*

It's …
Это …   *e·ta …*

Please tell him/her that … called.
Передайте, пожалуйста,   *pi·ri·deyt·ye pa·zhal·sta*
что позвонил/позвонила …   *shto paz·va·nil/paz·va·ni·la …*

Can I leave a message for him/her?
Вы можете передать   *vih mo·zhiht·ye pi·ri·dat'*
ему/ей?   *yi·mu/yey*

My number is …
Мой телефон …   *moy ti·li·fon …*

I don't have a contact number.
У меня нет телефона.   *u min·ya nyet ti·li·fo·na*

I'll call back later.
Я перезвоню попозже.   *ya pi·riz·van·yu pa·po·zhe*

Bye!
Пока!   *pa·ka*

Speak to you soon!
Созвонимся!   *saz·va·nim·sa*

For telephone numbers, see **numbers & amounts**, page 33.

post office

Where's the post office?
Где здесь почта?   gdye zdyes' *poch*·ta

I want to send a ...	Я хочу послать ...	ya kha·*chu* pas·*lat'* ...
fax	факс	faks
letter	письмо	pis'·*mo*
parcel (small)	бандероль	ban·di·*rol'*
parcel (large)	посылку	pa·*sihl*·ku
postcard	открытку	at·*kriht*·ku

I want to buy ...	Я хочу купить ...	yak ha·*chu* ku·*pit'* ...
an envelope	конверт	kan·*vyert*
a (10 rouble)	марку	*mar*·ku
stamp	(за десять рублей)	(za *dye*·sit' rub·*lyey*)
a (100 unit)	телефонную	te·le·*fo*·nu·yu
phonecard	карточку	*kar*·tach·ku
	(на сто единиц)	(na sto i·*di*·nits)

customs declaration	таможенная декларация f	ta·*mo*·zhih·na·ya di·kla·*rat*·sih·ya
domestic mail	внутренняя почта f	vnu·tri·ni·ya *poch*·ta
fragile a	хрупкий m	*khrup*·ki
international mail	международная почта f	mizh·du·na·*rod*·na·ya *poch*·ta
mail	почта f	*poch*·ta
mailbox	почтовый ящик m	pach·*to*·vih *ya*·shik
PO box	абонементный ящик m	a·ba·nam·*yent*·nih *ya*·shik
postcode	почтовый индекс m	pach·*to*·vih *in*·diks

snail mail

by ... mail	... почтой	... *poch*·tay
air	авиа	*a*·vi·a
express	экспресс	iks·*pres*
registered	заказной	za·kaz·*noy*
regular	обычной	a·*bihch*·nay

Please send it by regular mail to (Australia).

Пошлите, пожалуйста,
обычной почтой
в (Австралию).

pash·*lit*·ye pa·*zhal*·sta
a·*bihch*·ney *poch*·tey
v (af·*stra*·li·yu)

It contains (souvenirs).

Там (сувениры).

tam (su·vi·*ni*·rih)

Where's the poste restante section?

Где окно до
востребования?

gdye ak·*no* da
vas·tri·ba·*va*·ni·ya

Is there any mail for me?

Есть почта для меня?

yest' *poch*·ta dlya min·*ya*

What time does the bank open?

Когда открывается/
закрывается банк?

kag·*da* at·krih·*va*·yit·sa/
za·krih·va·yit·sa bank

Where can I ...?	Где можно ...?	gdye *mozh*·na ...
I'd like to ...	Я бы хотел ... m	ya bih khat·*yel* ...
	Я бы хотела ... f	ya bih khat·*ye*·la ...
cash a (travellers) cheque	обменять (дорожный) чек	ab·min·*yat'* (da·*rozh*·nih) chek
change money	поменять деньги	pa·min·*yat'* *dyen'*·gi
get a cash advance	снять деньги по кредитной карточке	snyat' *dyen'*·gi pa kri·*dit*·ney *kar*·tach·kye
withdraw money	снять деньги	snyat' *dyen'*·gi
Where's a/an ...?	Где ...?	gdye ...
automated teller machine	банкомат	ban·ka·*mat*
foreign exchange office	обмен валюты	ab·*myen* val·*yu*·tih
What's the ...?		
exchange rate	Какой курс?	ka·*koy* kurs
charge for that	Сколько нужно заплатить?	*skol'*·ka *nuzh*·na za·pla·*tit'*

---

listen for ...

невозможно	ni·vaz·*mozh*·na	**impossible**
недостаточно	ni·da·*sta*·tach·na	**insufficient funds**
паспорт m	*pas*·part	**passport**
проблема f	prab·*lye*·ma	**problem**
распишитесь	ras·pi·*shiht*·yes'	**sign v**
удостоверение личности n	u·da·sta·vir·*ye*·ni·ye *lich*·na·sti	**identification**

How much can I take out in one day?

Сколько можно взять в один день?

skol'·ka mozh·na vzyat' v a·din dyen'

Has my money arrived yet?

Мои деньги уже пришли?

moy dyen'·gi u·zhe prish·li

How long will it take to arrive?

Как быстро деньги придут?

kak bihst·ra dyen'·gi pri·dut

The automated teller machine took my card.

Банкомат съел мою карточку.

ban·ka·mat syel ma·yu kar·tach·ku

I've forgotten my PIN.

Я забыл свой номер. m

ya za·bihl svoy no·mir

Я забыла свой номер. f

ya za·bih·la svoy no·mir

sightseeing

осмотр достопримечательностей

I'd like a …	Я бы хотел … m	ya bih khat·*yel* …
	Я бы хотела … f	ya bih khat·*ye*·la …
catalogue	каталог	ka·ta·*lok*
guide	гида	*gi*·da
guidebook	путеводитель	pu·ti·va·*dit*·yel'
(in English)	(на английском)	(na an·*gli*·skam)
	языке	yi·zihk·*ye*
(city) map	карту (города)	*kar*·tu (*go*·ra·da)
Do you have information on … sights?	У вас есть информация о … достопримеча- тельностях?	u vas yest' in·far·*mat*·sih·ya a … da·sta·pri·mi·*cha*· til'·nast·yakh
cultural	культурных	kul'·*tur*·nihkh
historical	исторических	i·sta·*ri*·chi·skikh
religious	религиозных	ri·li·gi·*oz*·nihkh
Soviet era	советских	sav·*yet*·skikh

I'd like to see …		
Я бы хотел посетить … m	ya bih khat·*yel* pa·si·*tit'* …
Я бы хотела посетить … f	ya bih khat·*ye*·la pa·si·*tit'* …

What's that?
Что это?   shto *e*·ta

Who made it?
Кто это делал?   kto *e*·ta *dye*·lal

How old is it?
Когда это построили?   kag·*da* e·ta past·*tro*·i·li

sightseeing

Could you take a photo of me?

Сфотографируйте
меня, пожалуйста.

sfa·ta·gra·*fi*·ruy·tye
min·*ya* pa·*zhal*·sta

Can I take a photo (of you)?

Можно
сфотографировать (вас)?

mozh·na
sfa·ta·gra·*fi*·ra·vat' (vas)

I'll send you the photo.

Я вышлю вам фотографию.

ya *vihsh*·lyu vam fa·ta·*gra*·fi·yu

getting in

What time does it open/close?

Когда открывается/
закрывается?

kag·*da* at·krih·*va*·yit·sa/
za·krih·*va*·yit·sa

What's the admission charge?

Сколько стоит
входной билет?

skol'·ka *sto*·it
fkhad·*noy* bil·*yet*

Is there a discount for …?	Есть скидка для …?	yest' *skit*·ka dlya …
children	детей	dit·*yey*
families	семей	sim·*yey*
groups	групп	grup
older people	пожилых людей	pa·zhih·*lihkh* lyud·*yey*
pensioners	пенсионеров	pin·si·an·*ye*·raf
students	студентов	stud·*yen*·taf

blowing it

If you whistle indoors or in an enclosed space like a car, it's believed that *денег не будет dye*·nik ni *bu*·dit' (you won't have money).

PRACTICAL

98

tours

Can you recommend a tour?
Вы можете
порекомендовать
экскурсию?

vih *mo*·zhiht·ye
pa·ri·ka·min·da·*vat'*
eks·*kur*·si·yu

When's the next tour?
Когда следующая
экскурсия?

kag·*da slye*·du·yu·sha·ya
eks·*kur*·si·ya

Is ... included? Цена
включает ...?

tse·*na*
fklyu·*cha*·yit ...

   accommodation помещение pa·mi·*she*·ni·ye
   food обед ab·*yet*
   transport транспорт *tran*·spart

The guide will pay.

Гид будет платить.   gid *bud*·it pla·*tit'*

The guide has paid.

Гид уже заплатил.   git u·*zhe* za·pla·*til*

How long is the tour?

Как долго продолжается	kag *dol*·ga pra·dal·*zha*·yit·sa
экскурсия?	eks·*kur*·si·ya

What time should we be back?

Когда мы возвращаемся?   kag·*da* mih vaz·vra·*sha*·yim·sa

I'm with them.

Я с ними.   ya s *ni*·mi

I've lost my group.

Я потерял свою группу. m	ya pa·tir·*yal* sva·*yu gru*·pu
Я потеряла свою группу. f	ya pa·tir·*ya*·la sva·*yu gru*·pu

We've seen enough (churches)!

Мы насмотрелись	mih nas·mat·*rye*·lis'
(церквей)!	(tsihrk·*vyey*)

doing business

по бизнесу

I'm attending a ...	Я на ...	ya na ...
conference	конференции	kan·fir·*yent*·sih
meeting	собрании	sa·*bra*·ni
trade fair	торговой ярмарке	tar·*go*·vey *yar*·mark·ye
Where's the ...?	Где находится ...?	gdye na·*kho*·dit·sa ...
business centre	бизнес-центр	*biz*·nes·tsentr
conference	конференция	kan·fir·*yent*·sih·ya
meeting	собрание	sa·*bra*·ni·ye
I need (a/an) ...	Я бы хотел ... m	ya bih khat·*yel* ...
	Я бы хотела ... f	ya bih khat·*ye*·la ...
computer	компьютер	kam·*pyu*·tir
Internet connection	подключение к интернету	pat·klyu·*che*·ni·ye k in·ter·*ne*·tu
interpreter	переводчика	pi·ri·*vot*·chi·ka
business cards	визитные карточки	vi·*zit*·nih·ye *kar*·tach·ki
to send a fax	послать факс	pas·*lat'* faks
Here's my ...	Вот ...	vot ...
address	мой адрес	moy *a*·dris
business card	моя визитная карточка	ma·*ya* vi·*zit*·na·ya *kar*·tach·ka
email address	мой и-мейл	moy i·*meyl*
fax number	номер моего факса	*no*·mir ma·yi·*vo* *fak*·sa
mobile/cell number	мой мобильный номер	moy ma·*bil'*·nih *no*·mir
pager number	номер моего пэйджера	*no*·mir ma·yi·*vo* *peyd*·zhe·ra
phone number	мой номер	moy *no*·mir

Can I have yours?
    Можно ваш?   *mozh*·na vash

That went very well.
    Всё прошло очень   fsyo prash·*lo* o·chin'
    успешно.   usp·*yesh*·na

A pleasure to do business.
    Приятно иметь   pri·*yat*·na im·*yet'*
    дело с вами!   *dye*·la s *va*·mi

Thank you for your time.
    Спасибо за ваше время!   spa·*si*·ba za *va*·she *vryem*·ya

Shall we go for a drink/meal?
    Хотите пойти в ресторан? kha·*tit*·ye pey·*ti* v ri·sta·*ran*

It's on me.
    Сегодня я угощаю.   si·*vod*·nya ya u·ga·*sha*·yu

---

paying attention

If you're working in Russia, be prepared for the zealous attentions of the *налоговая инспекция* na·*lo*·ga·va·ya in·*spyekt*·sih·ya (tax inspection service) and *пожарники* pa·*zhar*·ni·ki (fire safety officers). They often prefer bribes to smooth their business and property inspections.

looking for a job

в поисках работы

Where are jobs advertised?
    Где рекламируется   gdye ri·kla·*mi*·ru·yit·sa
    работа?   ra·*bo*·ta

I'm enquiring about the position advertised.
    Я хочу справиться   ya kha·*chu* spra·vit'·sa
    относительно   at·na·*si*·til'·na
    объявления о работе.   ab·yiv·*lye*·ni·ya o ra·*bot*·ye

I've had experience.
    У меня есть рабочий стаж. u min·*ya* yest' ra·*bo*·chi stash

What are the chances for work here?
Как здесь насчёт работы?   kag zdyes' na·*shot* ra·bo·tih

What's the wage?
Какая будет зарплата?   ka·*ka*·ya *bu*·dit zar·*pla*·ta

I'm looking for	Я ищу работу …	ya i·*shu* ra·bo·tu …
work as a/an …		
editor	редактором	ri·*dak*·ta·ram
(English)	учителем/	u·*chi*·ti·lim/
teacher	учительницей	u·*chi*·til'·nit·sey
	(английского	(an·*gli*·ska·va
	языка) m/f	yi·zih·*ka*)
journalist	журналистом m	zhur·na·*lis*·tam
	журналисткой f	zhur·na·*list*·key
labourer	рабочим m	ra·bo·chim
	рабочей f	ra·bo·chey
radio announcer	диктором	*dik*·ta·ram
translator	переводчиком m	pi·ri·*vot*·chi·kam
	переводчицей f	pi·ri·*vot*·chit·sey
waiter	официантом	a·fit·sih·*an*·tam
waitress	официанткой	a·fit·sih·*ant*·key

I'm looking for	Я ищу …	ya i·*shu* …
… work.		
casual	временную	*vrye*·mi·nu·yu
	работу	ra·bo·tu
full-time	работу на	ra·bo·tu na
	полную ставку	*pol*·nu·yu *staf*·ku
part-time	работу на	ra·bo·tu na
	пол-ставки	pol·*staf*·ki

Do I need (a) …?	Нужно иметь …?	*nuzh*·na im·*yet'* …
car	машину	ma·*shih*·nu
contract	контракт	kan·*trakt*
experience	рабочий стаж	ra·bo·chi stash
insurance	страхование	stra·kha·*va*·ni·ye
paperwork	документы	da·kum·*yen*·tih
uniform	форму	*for*·mu
work permit	разрешение	raz·ri·*she*·ni·ye
	на работу	na ra·bo·tu

business

103

What time do I ...?	Во сколько ...?	va skol'·ka ...
start	начинается	na·chi·na·yit·sa
	рабочий день	ra·bo·chi dyen'
have a break	перерыв	pi·ri·rihf
finish	кончается	kan·cha·yit·sa
	рабочий день	ra·bo·chi dyen'

I can start ...	Я могу выйти ...	ya ma·gu vih·ti ...
Can you start ...?	Вы можете	vih mo·zhiht·ye
	выйти ...?	vih·ti ...
at (eight) o'clock	в (восемь) часов	v (vo·sim') chi·sof
today	сегодня	si·vod·nya
tomorrow	завтра	zaf·tra
next week	на следующей	na slye·du·yu·shey
	неделе	nid·yel·ye

Here is/are my ...	Вот ...	vot ...
bank account details	подробности	pa·drob·na·sti
	моего счёта	ma·yi·vo sho·ta
CV/résumé	моё резюме	ma·yo riz·yu·mey
visa	моя виза	ma·ya vi·za
work permit	моё разрешение	ma·yo raz·ri·she·ni·ye
	на работу	na ra·bo·tu

advertisement	объявление n	ab·yiv·lye·ni·ye
contract	контракт m	kan·trakt
employee	служащий m	slu·zha·shi
	служащая f	slu·zha·sha·ya
employer	работодатель m	ra·bo·ta·dat·yil'
job	работа f	ra·bo·ta
work experience	производственная	pra·iz·votst·vi·na·ya
	практика f	prak·ti·ka

keeping the situation in hand

It's polite to take your gloves off before you shake hands, but don't shake hands or pass anything через порог che·ris pa·rok (over a threshold) as it's believed to lead to arguments.

senior & disabled travellers

особые нужды

I have a disability.
Я инвалид.
ya in·va·*lit*

I need assistance.
Мне нужна помощь.
mnye nuzh·*na* po·mash

What services do you have for people with a disability?
Какие виды услуг вы
оказываете инвалидам?
ka·*ki*·ye *vi*·dih us·*luk* vih
a·*ka*·zih·va·yit·ye in·va·*li*·dam

Are there disabled toilets?
Есть туалет для инвалидов?
yest' tu·al·*yet* dlya in·va·*li*·daf

Is there wheelchair access?
Есть доступ для
инвалидной коляски?
yest' *do*·stup dlya
in·va·*lid*·ney kal·*ya*·ski

How wide is the entrance?
Какова ширина входа?
ka·ka·*va* shih·ri·*na* fkho·da

I'm deaf.
Я глухой/глухая. m/f
ya glu·*khoy*/glu·*kha*·ya

I have a hearing aid.
У меня слуховой аппарат.
u min·*ya* slu·kha·*voy* a·pa·*rat*

My companion's blind.
Мой приятель слепой. m
moy pri·*ya*·til' sli·*poy*
Моя приятельница слепая. f
ma·*ya* pri·*ya*·til'·nit·sa sli·*pa*·ya

Are guide dogs permitted?
Можно войти с
собакой-поводырём?
mozh·na vey·*ti* s
sa·*ba*·key·pa·va·dihr·*yom*

How many steps are there?
Сколько здесь ступенек?
skol'·ka zdyes' stup·*yen*·yek

Is there a lift/elevator?
Есть лифт?
yest' lift

Are there rails in the bathroom?
В ванной есть перила?
v *va*·ney yest' pi·*ri*·la

Could you help me cross the street safely?

Помогите мне, пожалуйста, перейти через дорогу!   pa·ma·*git*·ye mnye pa·*zhal*·sta pi·*rey*·ti che·riz da·*ro*·gu

Is there somewhere I can sit down?

Можно посидеть где-нибудь?   *mozh*·na pa·sid·*yet*' *gdye*·ni·but'

person with a disability	инвалид m	in·va·*lit*
guide dog	собака-поводырь f	sa·*ba*·ka·pa·va·*dihr*'
older person	пожилой человек m	pa·zhih·*loy* chi·lav·*yek*
ramp	уклон m	u·*klon*
walking frame	ходильная рама f	kha·*dil*'·na·ya *ra*·ma
walking stick	трость m	trost'
wheelchair	кресло для инвалидов n	*kryes*·la dlya in·va·*li*·daf

it's all about you

When speaking in Russian you need either polite (**pol**) or informal (**inf**) language. The informal *ты* tih form (meaning 'you' **sg inf**) can be used with individual friends or relatives, while the *вы* vih form (you **sg pol & pl inf/pol**) must be used for strangers, important people, or more than one friend or relative. As a traveller, it's best to use the *вы* form with new people you meet. Nouns, verbs and personal pronouns ('you', 'she', 'we' and so on) will change depending on whether you're being polite or informal. For more information, see the **phrasebuilder**.

In this book we've chosen the appropriate form for the situation that the phrase is used in – this is normally the polite form unless we've marked it otherwise. For phrases where either form might be suitable, we've given both.

travelling with children

Is there a …?	Есть …?	yest' …
baby change room	комната, оборудованная для ухода за младенцами	*kom*·na·ta a·ba·*ru*·da·va·na·ya dlya u·*kho*·da za mlad·*yent*·sa·mi
child-minding service	служба по присмотру за детьми	*sluzh*·ba pa pris·*mo*·tru za dit'·*mi*
child's portion	детская порция	*dyet*·ska·ya *port*·sih·ya
children's menu	детское меню	*dyet*·ska·ye min·*yu*
crèche	детские ясли	*dyet*·ski·ye *yas*·li
discount for children	скидка для детей	*skit*·ka dlya dit·*yey*
family ticket	семейный билет	sim·*yey*·nih bil·*yet*
I need a/an …	Я хочу …	ya kha·*chu* …
baby seat	детское сиденье	*dyet*·ska·ye sid·*yen*·ye
(English-speaking) babysitter	няню, говорящую (по-английски)	*nyan*·yu ga·var·*ya*·shu·yu (pa·an·*gli*·ski)
cot	детскую кроватку	*dyet*·sku·yu kra·*vat*·ku
highchair	детский стульчик	*dyet*·ski *stul'*·chik
plastic bag	пластиковый пакет	*pla*·sti·ka·vih pak·*yet*
plastic sheet	пластиковый лист	*pla*·sti·ka·vih list
potty	горшок	gar·*shok*
pram/stroller	детскую коляску	*dyet*·sku·yu kal·*yas*·ku
sick bag	гигиенический пакет	gi·gi·i·*ni*·chi·ski pak·*yet*

Do you sell …? — Здесь продаются …? — zdyes' pra·da·*yut*·sa …

baby wipes	подгузники	pad·*guz*·ni·ki
disposable nappies/diapers	одноразовые пелёнки	ad·na·*ra*·zav·nih·ye pil·*yon*·ki
painkillers for infants	болеутоляющие для младенцев	bo·li·u·tol·*ya*·yu·shi·ye dlya mlad·*yent*·sef
tissues	бумажные салфетки	bu·*mazh*·nih·ye salf·*yet*·ki

Where's the nearest …? — Где здесь …? — gdye zdyes' …

drinking fountain	фонтанчик для питья	fan·*tan*·chik dlya pit·*ya*
park	парк	park
playground	площадка для игр	pla·*shat*·ka dlya igr
swimming pool	бассейн	bas·*yeyn*
tap	кран	kran
theme park	парк культуры	park kul'·*tu*·rih
toyshop	игрушечный магазин	i·*gru*·shihch·nih ma·ga·*zin*

Are children allowed?
Детям вход разрешён? — *dyet*·yam fkhot raz·ri·*shon*

Do you mind if I breast-feed here?
Можно здесь покормить ребёнка грудью? — *mozh*·na zdes' pa·kar·*mit'* rib·*yon*·ka *grud*·yu

Where can I change a nappy/diaper?
Где можно перепеленать ребёнка? — gdye *mozh*·na pi·rip·ye·li·nat' rib·*yon*·ka

Is there space for a pram/pushchair?
Для детской коляски хватает места? — dlya *dyet*·skey kal·*yas*·ki khva·*ta*·yit *mye*·sta

Are there any good places to take children around here?
Поблизости есть развлечения для детей? — pa·*bli*·za·sti yest' raz·vli·*che*·ni·ya dlya dit·*yey*

Is this suitable for (seven)-year-old children?
Это подходит (семи)летнему ребёнку? — *e*·ta pat·*kho*·dit (si·mi·)*lyet*·ni·mu rib·*yon*·ku

Could I have some paper and pencils, please?

Дайте, пожалуйста, бумаги
и цветные карандаши.

deyt·ye pa·*zhal*·sta bu·*ma*·gi
i tsvit·*nih*·ye ka·ran·da·*shih*

Do you know a doctor who is good with children?

Вы не знаете
врача, который хорошо
обращается с детьми?

vih nye *zna*·yit·ye
vra·*cha* ka·*to*·rih kha·ra·*sho*
ab·ra·*sha*·yit·sa z dit'·*mi*

Do you know a dentist who is good with children?

Вы не знаете зубного
врача, который хорошо
обращается с детьми?

vih nye *zna*·yit·ye *zub*·no·va
vra·*cha* ka·*to*·rih kha·ra·*sho*
ab·ra·*sha*·yit·sa z dit'·*mi*

If your child is sick, see **health**, page 197.

talking with children

In this section, phrases are in the informal *мы* tih (you) form only.
If you're not sure what this means, see the box on page 106.

What's your name?

Как тебя зовут?

kak tib·*ya* za·*vut*

How old are you?

Сколько тебе лет?

skol'·ka tib·*ye* lyet

When's your birthday?

Когда твой день рождения?

kag·*da* tvoy dyen' razhd·*ye*·ni·ya

Do you go to school/kindergarten?

Ты ходишь в
школу/детский сад?

tih *kho*·dish f
shko·lu/*dyet*·ski sat

What grade are you in?

Ты в каком классе?

tih f ka·*kom* klas·ye

Do you like ...?	Тебе нравится ...?	tib·*ye* nra·*vit*·sa ...
school	школа	*shko*·la
sport	спорт	sport
your teacher	твоя	tva·*ya*
	учительница f	u·*chi*·til'·nit·sa

What do you do after school?

Чем ты занимаешься
после школы?

chem tih za·ni·*ma*·yish·sa
pos·lye *shko*·lih

Do you learn (English)?

Ты учишь
(английский) язык?

tih *u*·chish'
(an·*gli*·ski) ya·*zihk*

talking about children

How many children do you have?

Сколько у вас детей?

skol'·ka u vas dit·*yey*

What a beautiful child!

Какой красивый ребёнок!

ka·*koy* kra·*si*·vih rib·*yo*·nak

How old is he/she?

Сколько ему/ей лет?

skol'·ka yi·*mu*/yey lyet

Does he/she go to school?

Он/Она учится?

on/a·*na* u·chit·sa

What's his/her name?

Как его/её зовут?

kak yi·*vo*/yi·*yo* za·*vut*

---

that'll learn ya

Education is highly valued in Russia, so parents compete
to send their kids to good schools and often have them
study in big cities or abroad over the summer break.
Classic questions for parents are:

What type of school do your children go to?

В какую школу ходят
ваши дети?

f ka·*ku*·yu *shko*·lu *kho*·dit
va·shih *dye*·ti

Where do you send your children in summer?

Куда вы летом
отправляете своих
детей?

ku·*da* vih *lye*·tam
at·prav·*lya*·yit·ye sva·*ikh*
dit·*yey*

---

basic language

простые фразы

Yes.	Да.	da
No.	Нет.	nyet
Please.	Пожалуйста.	pa·*zhal*·sta
Thank you	Спасибо	spa·*si*·ba
(very much).	(большое).	(bal'·*sho*·ye)
You're welcome.	Пожалуйста.	pa·*zhal*·sta
Excuse me.	Извините,	iz·vi·*nit*·ye
(attention/apology)	пожалуйста.	pa·*zhal*·sta
Excuse me.	Разрешите,	raz·ri·*shiht*·ye
(to get past)	пожалуйста.	pa·*zhal*·sta

greetings & goodbyes

приветствия

Russian society is generally quite affectionate – both men and women hug, hold hands and walk around arm-in-arm. Young women kiss and hug to greet each other, while older women kiss each other on the cheek a couple of times. Shaking hands is a given between men, but a man generally doesn't extend his hand to a woman – in a business meeting, he may offer a soft handshake, but otherwise it's up to the woman to offer first. In other circumstances, men just nod hello.

Hello.	Здравствуйте!	*zdrast*·vuyt·ye
Hi.	Привет!	priv·*yet*
Good …		
afternoon/day	Добрый день!	*do*·brih dyen'
evening	Добрый вечер!	*do*·brih *vye*·chir
morning	Доброе утро!	*do*·bra·ye *u*·tra

How are you?
Как дела? kag dyi·*la*

Fine.
Спасибо, хорошо. spa·*si*·ba kha·ra·*sho*

And you?
А у вас? a u vas

What's your name?
Как вас зовут? kak vaz za·*vut*

My name is (Jane).
Меня зовут (Джейн). min·*ya* za·*vut* (dzheyn)

My name is (Jane Brown).
Меня зовут (Джейн), min·*ya* za·*vut* (dzheyn)
а фамилия (Браун). a fa·*mi*·li·ya (braun)
(lit: my name Jane with surname Brown)

I'd like to introduce Познакомьтесь, paz·na·*komt*·yes'
you to … это … e·ta …
This is my … Это … e·ta …

child	мой ребёнок	moy rib·*yo*·nak
colleague	мой коллега m	moy kal·*ye*·ga
	моя коллега f	ma·*ya* kal·*ye*·ga
friend	мой друг m	moy druk
	моя подруга f	ma·ya pa·*dru*·ga
husband	мой муж	moy mush
partner	мой парень m	moy *pa*·rin
(intimate)	моя девушка f	ma·*ya* dye·vush·ka
wife	моя жена	ma·*ya* zhih·*na*

For more kinship terms, see **family**, page 119.

I'm pleased Очень приятно. o·chin' pri·*yat*·na
to meet you.
See you again До скорой da *sko*·rey
soon. встречи! fstrye·chi
Goodbye. До свидания! da svi·*dan*·ya
Bye. Пока! pa·*ka*
Good night. Спокойной ночи! spa·*koy*·ney *no*·chi
Bon voyage! Счастливого пути! shis·*li*·va·va pu·*ti*
All the best! Всего хорошего! fsi·*vo* kha·*ro*·shih·va

russian good humour		
What's new?	Что нового?	shto *no*·va·va
Nothing new.	Ничего нового нету!	ni·chi·*vo no*·va·va *nye*·tu
How's life?	Как жизнь?	kag zhihzn'
Great!	Отлично!	at·*lich*·na
Fine!	Нормально!	nar·*mal'*·na
Not good, not bad.	Не хорошо, не плохо!	nye kha·ra·*sho* nye *plo*·kha
Can't complain.	Не жалуюсь!	nye *zha*·lu·yus'
I can barely keep going!	Еле на ногах держусь!	*yel*·ye na na·*gakh* dyir·*zhus'*
Is this really life?	Разве это жизнь?	*raz*·vye e·ta zhihzn'
This isn't life, this is torment!	Не жизнь, а мученье!	nye zhihzn' a mu·*chen*·ye

titles & addressing people

как обращаться к людям

When you're addressing someone politely, use their first name and patronymic (not their family name). A 'patronymic' is a middle name derived from the person's father's name, and means 'son/daughter of' – Ivan's son Sergey would be called *Сергей Иванович* sir·*gey* i·*va*·nich (Sergey Ivanovich). There are words for 'Mr' and 'Ms/Miss/Mrs' – *господин* ga·spa·*din* (lit: citizen) and *госпожа* ga·spa·*zha* (lit: citizeness) – but these are only used in official contexts. In informal situations, you can use your first name as in English.

Mr	господин	ga·spa·*din*
Sir	сэр	ser
Ms/Mrs/Miss	госпожа	ga·spa·*zha*
Madam	мадам	ma·*dam*

meeting people

113

There are very few taboo topics of conversation in today's Russia. Politics is the most popular topic of all, and even on a first meeting, it's quite acceptable to ask someone in detail about their work, salary and personal life. Although Russia is a multiethnic society with citizens from many cultural backgrounds, you may come across controversial attitudes to nationality and religion.

making conversation

ведение разговоров

What a beautiful day!
Какой прекрасный день!
ka·*koy* pri·*kras*·nih dyen'

Nice/Awful weather, isn't it?
Какая хорошая/
плохая погода!
ka·*ka*·ya kha·*ro*·sha·ya/
pla·*kha*·ya pa·*go*·da

Do you live here?
Вы здесь живёте?
vih zdyes' zhihv·*yot*·ye

Where are you going?
Далеко собираетесь?
da·li·*ko* sa·bi·*ra*·yit·yes'

What are you doing?
Чем вы занимаетесь?
chem vih za·ni·*ma*·yit·yes'

Have you been waiting long? (in a queue)
Вы давно стоите?
vih dav·*no* sta·*it*·ye

What's your star sign?
Какой ваш знак?
ka·*koy* vash znak

Do you like it here?
Вам здесь нравится?
vam zdyes' *nra*·vit·sa

I love it here.
Мне здесь очень нравится!
mnye zdyes' *o*·chin' *nra*·vit·sa

What's this called?
Как это называется?   kak *e*·ta na·zih·*va*·yit·sa

That's (beautiful), isn't it!
Как (красиво)!   kak (kra·*si*·va)

How long are you here for?
Как долго вы здесь будете?   kag *dol*·ga vih zdyes' *bu*·dit·ye

I'm here for (five) weeks/days.
Я буду здесь (пять) недель/дней.   ya *bu*·du zdyes' (pyat') nid·*yel'*/dnyey

Are you here on holiday?
Вы здесь в отпуске?   vih zdyes' v *ot*·pusk·ye

I'm here …	Я здесь …	ya zdyes' …
for a holiday	в отпуске	v *ot*·pusk·ye
on business	по бизнесу	pa *biz*·ni·su
for study	учусь	u·*chus'*

---

the luck of the devil

Russian has three ways of wishing someone good luck – *С богом!* z bo·gam (With God!), *Ни пуха ни пера!* ni *pu*·kha ni *pi*·ra (Neither down nor feathers!) or *Желаю успеха!* zhih·*la*·yu usp·*ye*·kha (I wish you luck!). The correct response to all three is always *К чёрту!* k *chor*·tu (To the devil!).

---

nationalities

Where are you from?
Вы откуда?   vih at·*ku*·da

I'm from …	Я из …	ya iz …
Australia	Австралии	af·*stra*·li·i
Canada	Канады	ka·*na*·dih
China	Китая	ki·*ta*·ya

local talk

Hey!	Эй!	ey
Hey guys!	Здорово, мужики!	zda·*ro*·va mu·zhih·*ki*
Great!	Здорово!	*zdo*·ra·va
Sure.	Конечно!	kan·*yesh*·na
Maybe.	Может быть.	*mo*·zhiht biht'
No way!	Вы шутите!	vih *shu*·tit·ye
Oh!	Ой!	oy
Just a minute.	Минутку!	mi·*nut*·ku
Just joking.	Я шучу!	ya shu·*chu*
It's OK.	Хорошо!	kha·ra·*sho*
No problem.	Ничего!	ni·chi·*vo*
Don't ask!	Не спрашивайте!	nye *spra*·shih·veyt·ye
Look!	Посмотрите!	pas·ma·*trit*·ye
Listen!	Послушайте!	pas·*lu*·sheyt·ye
Shame!	Ай-ай-ай!	ey·ey·*ey*
It's (im)possible.	Это (не)возможно.	*e*·ta (nye·)vaz·*mozh*·na

age

возраст

How old …?	Сколько … лет?	*skol'*·ka … lyet
are you	вам	vam
is your daughter	вашей дочке	*va*·shey *doch*·kye
is your son	вашему сыну	*va*·shih·mu *sih*·nu

I'm … years old.
Мне … лет. mnye … lyet

He/She is … years old.
Ему/Ей … лет. ye·*mu*/yey … lyet

I'm younger than I look.
Я выгляжу моложе своих лет. ya *vih*·gli·zhu ma·*lo*·zhe sva·*ikh* lyet

For your age, see **numbers & amounts**, page 33.

SOCIAL

116

occupations & studies

What's your occupation?
Кем вы работаете? kyem vih ra·bo·ta·yit·ye

I'm a/an …	Я …	ya …
accountant	бухгалтер	bu·*gal*·tir
businessperson	бизнесмен	biz·nis·*myen*
chef	шеф-повар	shef·*po*·var
doctor	врач	vrach
engineer	инженер	in·zhihn·*yer*
journalist	журналист m	zhur·na·*list*
	журналистка f	zhur·na·*list*·ka
mechanic	механик	mi·*kha*·nik
nurse	медсестра	mid·sist·*ra*
priest	священник	svi·*she*·nik
student	студент m	stud·*yent*
	студентка f	stud·*yent*·ka
teacher	учитель m	u·*chi*·til'
	учительница f	u·*chi*·til'·nit·sa

body language

Russians nod their heads for 'yes', shake their heads for 'no', point and beckon in the same ways that English speakers do. There are, however, some distinctively Russian gestures you should know:

- a movement like cutting your throat with your hand means 'I'm full!'

- flicking your throat with your index finger indicates drinking – usually 'Let's drink!' or 'He/She is drunk'.

- nodding your head in one direction means 'Let's go!' – for a serious talk, a fight, or possibly a sexual proposition

- a hand placed on one hip means 'So what?'

- tapping your forehead with your finger means someone is stupid

I work in ...	Я работаю ...	ya ra·*bo*·ta·yu ...
government	на	na
	государственной	ga·su·*darst*·vi·ney
	службе	*sluzh*·bye
health	в	v
	здравоохранении	zdra·va·a·khran·*ye*·ni·ye
marketing	в маркетинге	v mark·*ye*·ting·ye

I'm ...	Я ...	ya ...
retired	на пенсии	na *pyen*·si·i
self-	имею свой	im·*ye*·yu svoy
employed	собственный	*sopst*·vi·nih
	бизнес	*biz*·nis
unemployed	безработный m	byiz·ra·*bot*·nih
	безработная f	biz·ra·*bot*·na·ya

What are you studying?
Что вы изучаете? shto vih i·zu·*cha*·yit·ye

I'm studying ...	Я изучаю ...	ya i·zu·*cha*·yu ...
humanities	гуманитарные	gu·ma·ni·*tar*·nih·ye
	науки	na·*u*·ki
Russian	русский язык	*rus*·ki yi·*zihk*
science	естественные	yist·*yest*·vi·nih·ye
	науки	na·*u*·ki

SOCIAL

118

family

Do you have a ...?	У вас есть ...?	u vas yest' ...
I have a ...	У меня есть ...	u min·ya yest' ...
brother	брат	brat
daughter	дочка	*doch*·ka
family	семья	sim·ya
granddaughter	внучка	*vnuch*·ka
grandfather	дедушка	*dye*·dush·ka
grandmother	бабушка	*ba*·bush·ka
grandson	внук	vnuk
husband	муж	mush
partner	парень m	*pa*·rin'
(intimate)	девушка f	*dye*·vush·ka
sister	сестра	sist·*ra*
son	сын	sihn
wife	жена	zhih·*na*

in-laws

Compared to Russian, English is so simplistic when it comes to naming the in-laws ...

brother-in-law

деверь	*dye*·vir'	husband's brother
зять	zyat'	sister's husband
шурин	*shu*·rin	wife's brother

sister-in-law

заловка	za·*lof*·ka	husband's sister
невестка	ni·*vyest*·ka	brother's wife
свояченица	sva·*ya*·chi·nit·sa	wife's sister

father-in-law

свёкор	*svyo*·kar	husband's father
тесть	tyest'	wife's father

mother-in-law

свекровь	svi·*krof*'	husband's mother
тёща	*tyo*·sha	wife's mother

Are you married?
Вы женаты? (to a man)   vih zhih·*na*·tih
Вы замужем? (to a woman)   vih *za*·mu·zhihm

I live with someone.
Я живу с кем-то.   ya zhih·*vu* s *kyem*·ta

I'm ...	Я ...	ya ...
married	женат m	zhih·*nat*
	замужем f	*za*·mu·zhihm
separated	не живу с	nye zhih·*vu* s
	женой/мужем m/f	zhih·*noy/mu*·zhihm
single	холост/холоста m/f	*kho*·last/kha·la·*sta*

well-wishing		
Congratulations!	Поздравляю!	paz·drav·*lya*·yu
Happy Birthday!	С днём	z dnyom
	рождения!	razh·*dye*·ni·ya
Merry Christmas!	С Рождеством	s razh·dist·*vom*
	Христовым!	khri·*sto*·vihm

farewells

прощание

(Tomorrow) is my last day here.
(Завтра) мой   (*zaf*·tra) moy
последний день.   pas·*lyed*·ni dyen'

It's been great meeting you.
Было очень приятно   *bih*·la o·chin' pri·*yat*·na
познакомиться!   paz·na·*ko*·mit'·sa

Keep in touch!
Не забывайте!   nye za·bih·*veyt*·ye

Here's my ...	Вот мой ...	vot moy ...
What's your ...?	Можно ваш ...?	*mozh*·na vash ...
address	адрес	*a*·dris
email address	и-мейл	i·*meyl*
phone number	номер телефона	*no*·mir ti·li·*fo*·na

---

interests

интересы

common interests

общие интересы

What do you do in your spare time?
Чем вы занимаетесь
в свободное время?
chem vih za·ni·*ma*·yit·yes'
f sva·*bod*·na·ye *vryem*·ya

Do you like ...?	Вам нравится ...?	vam *nra*·vit·sa ...
I (don't) like ...	Мне (не) нравится ...	mnye (nye) *nra*·vit·sa ...
computer games	играть в компьютерные игры	i·*grat'* f kamp·*yu*·tir·nih·ye *i*·grih
cooking	готовить	ga·*to*·vit'
dancing	танцевать	tant·sih·*vat'*
dominoes	домино	da·mi·*no*
drawing	рисовать	ri·sa·*vat'*
films	кино	ki·*no*
gardening	садоводство	sa·da·*vots*·tva
hiking	пешеходный туризм	pi·shih·*khod*·nih tu·*rizm*
music	музыка	*mu*·zih·ka
painting	живопись	*zhih*·va·pis'
photography	фотографировать	fa·ta·gra·*fi*·ra·vat'
reading	читать	chi·*tat'*
shopping	ходить по магазинам	kha·*dit'* pa ma·ga·*zi*·nam
socialising	встречаться с друзьями	fstri·*chat'*·sa z druz·*ya*·mi
sport	спорт	sport
surfing the Internet	интернет	in·ter·*net*
travelling	путешествовать	pu·ti·*shest*·va·vat'
watching TV	смотреть телевизор	smat·*ryet'* ti·li·*vi*·zar

For types of sports, see **sport**, page 153, and the **dictionary**.

interests

121

astrology	астрология f	ast·ra·*lo*·gi·ya
ballet	балет m	bal·*yet*
bathhouse	баня f	*ban*·ya
chess	шахматы m pl	*shakh*·ma·tih
ice skating	катание на	ka·*ta*·ni·ye na
	коньках n	kan'·*kakh*
mushrooming	собирание	sa·bi·*ra*·ni·ye
	грибов n	gri·*bof*
playing cards	карты m pl	*kar*·tih
sauna	сауна f	*sa*·u·na
theatre	театр m	ti·*atr*

music

музыка

Do you …?	Вы …?	vih …
dance	танцуете	tant·*su*·it·ye
go to concerts	ходите на	*kho*·dit·ye na
	концерты	kant·*ser*·tih
listen to music	слушаете	*slu*·sha·yit·ye
	музыку	*mu*·zih·ku
play an	играете на	i·*gra*·yit·ye na
instrument	каком-нибудь	ka·*kom*·ni·bud'
	инструменте	ins·trum·*yent*·ye
sing	поёте	pa·*yot*·ye
Which … do you like?	… вы любите?	… vih *lyu*·bit·ye
bands	Какие группы	ka·*ki*·ye *gru*·pih
music	Какую музыку	ka·*ku*·yu *mu*·zih·ku
singers	Каких певцов	ka·*kikh* pift·*sof*

blues	блюз m	blyus
classical music	классическая музыка f	kla·si·chi·ska·ya mu·zih·ka
electronic music	электронная музыка f	e·lik·tro·na·ya mu·zlh·ka
folk songs	народные песни f pl	na·rod·nih·ye pyes·ni
jazz	джаз m	dzhas
pop	поп m	pop
rock	рок m	rok
traditional music	традиционная музыка f	tra·dit·sih·o·na·ya mu·zih·ka
world music	мировая музыка f	mi·ra·va·ya mu·zih·ka

Planning to go to a concert? See **tickets**, page 46, and **going out**, page 135.

cinema & theatre

I feel like going to a …
  Мне хочется пойти на …   mnye kho·chit·sa pey·ti na …
Do you have tickets for the …?
  Есть билеты на …?   yest' bil·ye·tih na …
How did you like the …?
  Как вам понравился …?   kak vam pan·ra·vil·sa …

ballet	балет m	bal·yet
concert	концерт m	kant·sert
film	фильм m	film
opera	опера f	o·pi·ra
play	пьеса f	pye·sa

new arrivals

When you enter a restaurant or the theatre, leave your coat, hat and boots at the *гардероб* gar·di·rop (cloakroom). On arriving at a friend's home, remove your shoes and you'll be offered *тапочки* ta·pach·ki (slippers).

interests

123

Are there any extra tickets?
Есть лишние билеты?   yest' *lish*·ni·ye bil·*ye*·tih

I'd like to get (cheap/the best) tickets.
Я бы хотел/хотела   ya bih khat·*yel*/khat·*ye*·la
билеты (подешевле/   bil·*ye*·tih (pa·di·*shev*·lye/
получше). m/f   pa·*luch*·she)

What's showing at the cinema/theatre tonight?
Что идёт в кино/театре?   shto id·*yot* f ki·*no*/ti·*at*·rye

Is there a matinée show?
Есть дневной спектакль?   yest' dniv·*noy* spik·*takl'*

Is it in (English)?
Это на (английском)?   *e*·ta na (an·*gli*·skam)

Does it have (English) subtitles?
Этот фильм с субтитрами   *e*·tat film s sub·*ti*·tra·mi
на (английском)?   na (an·*gli*·skam)

Is this seat taken?
Это место занято?   *e*·ta *mye*·sta *zan*·ya·ta

Have you seen (October)?
Вы смотрели (Октябрь)?   vih smat·*rye*·li (akt·*yabr'*)

Who's in it?
Кто играет в этом фильме?   kto i·*gra*·yit v *e*·tam *film*·ye

It stars (Matveev).
Главную роль   *glav*·nu·yu rol'
играет (Матвеев).   i·*gra*·yet (mat·*vyey*·if)

---

know your gender

Masculine and feminine markers (m and f) in our phrases always show the subject of a sentence – in the phrase Я бы хотел/хотела ... m/f ya bih khat·*yel*/khat·*ye*·la (I'd like ...), the m/f refers to the gender of the speaker.

theatre-going

balcony	балкон m	bal·*kon*
box (theatre)	ложа f	*lo*·zha
cloakroom	гардероб m	gar·di·*rop*
concert hall	концертный зал m	kant·*sert*·nih zal
drama theatre	драматический театр m	dra·ma·*ti*·chi·ski ti·*atr*
dress circle	бельэтаж m	byel'·i·*tash*
inconvenient place	неудобное место n	nyi·u·*dob*·na·ye *mye*·sta
orchestra	оркестр m	ark·*yestr*
row	ряд m	ryat
seat	место n	*mye*·sta
stalls	партер m	par·*ter*
(1st/2nd/ 3rd) tier	(первый/второй/ третий) ярус m	(*pyer*·vih/fta·*roy*/ *trye*·ti) *ya*·rus

What's he/she saying?
Что он/она говорит? shto on/a·*na* ga·va·*rit*

Shhh!
Т-с-с-с! t·s·s·s

I (don't) like ...	Я (не) люблю ...	ya (nye) lyub·*lyu* ...
action movies	боевики	ba·i·vi·*ki*
animated films	мультфильмы	mult·*fil'*·mih
comedies	комедии	kam·*ye*·di
documentaries	документальные фильмы	da·ku·min·*tal'*·nih·ye *fil'*·mih
drama	драму	*dra*·mu
horror movies	фильмы ужасов	*fil'*·mih u·zha·saf
(Russian) cinema	(русское) кино	(*rus*·ka·ye) ki·*no*
sci-fi	научную фантастику	na·*uch*·nu·yu fan·*tas*·ti·ku
short films	коротко- метражные фильмы	ka·rat·ka· mi·*trazh*·nih·ye *fil'*·mih
thrillers	сенсационные фильмы	sin·sat·sih·*o*·nih·ye *fil'*·mih
war movies	фильмы о войне	*fil'*·mih a veyn·*ye*

interests

125

I thought it was ...	По-моему, было ...	pa·*mo*·i·mu *bih*·la ...
excellent	отлично	at·*lich*·na
long	слишком долго	*slish*·kam *dol*·ga
OK	нормально	nar·*mal*'·na
pretentious	претенциозно	pri·tint·sih·*oz*·na

written in the stars

A favourite topic of conversation in Russia is *астрология* ast·ra·*lo*·gi·ya (astrology) and the *зодиак* zo·di·*ak* (zodiac). Even business meetings can begin with a run down of everyone's *знак* znak (star sign) and a summary of planetary positions to help with strategic planning.

What's your star sign?

Какой ваш знак? **pol**		ka·*koy* vash znak
Какой твой знак? **inf**		ka·*koy* tvoy znak

My star sign is ...	Мой знак ...	moy znak ...
Aries	Овен	av·*yen*
Taurus	Телец	til·*yets*
Gemini	Близнецы	bliz·nit·*sih*
Cancer	Рак	rak
Leo	Лев	lyef
Virgo	Дева	*dye*·va
Libra	Весы	vi·*sih*
Scorpio	Скорпион	skar·pi·*on*
Sagittarius	Стрелец	stril·*yets*
Capricorn	Козерог	ka·zi·*rok*
Aquarius	Водолей	va·dal·*yey*
Pisces	Рыбы	*rih*·bih

I'm on the cusp.

Я на стыке знаков.	ya na *stih*·kye *zna*·kaf

We're compatible!

Мы идеально	mih i·di·*al*'·na
подходим друг другу!	pat·*kho*·dim drug *dru*·gu

feelings & opinions
чувства и мнения

feelings

чувства

I'm (not) …	Я (не) …	ya (nye) …
afraid	боюсь	ba·*yus'*
annoyed	злюсь	zlyus'
cold	замёрз m	zam·*yors*
	замёрзла f	zam·*yorz*·la
disappointed	разочарован m	ra·za·chi·*ro*·van
	разочарована f	ra·za·chi·*ro*·va·na
embarrassed	смущён m	smu·*shon*
	смущена f	smu·shi·*na*
grateful	благодарен m	bla·ga·*da*·rin
	благодарна f	bla·ga·*dar*·na
happy	счастлив m	shas·*lif*
	счастлива f	shas·*li*·va
hot	умираю от жары	u·mi·*ra*·yu ad zha·*rih*
hungry	голоден m	*go*·la·din
	голодна f	ga·lad·*na*
in a hurry	спешу	spi·*shu*
sad	грущу	gru·*shu*
shy	стесняюсь	stis·*nya*·yus'
sorry (condolence)	скорблю	skarb·*lyu*
sorry (regret)	сожалею	sa·zhal·*ye*·yu
surprised	удивляюсь	u·div·*lya*·yus'
thirsty	хочу пить	kha·*chu* pit'
tired	устал m	u·*stal*
	устала f	u·*sta*·la
well	чувствую себя	*chust*·vu·yu sib·*ya*
	хорошо	kha·ra·*sho*
worried	беспокоюсь	bis·pa·*ko*·yus'
What about you?	А вы?	a vih

If you're not feeling well, see **health**, page 197.

a little	немного	nim·*no*·ga
I'm a little tired.	Я немного устал. m	ya nim·*no*·ga u·*stal*
	Я немного устала. f	ya nim·*no*·ga u·*sta*·la
very	очень	*o*·chin'
I'm very happy.	Я очень счастлив. m	ya *o*·chin' shas·*lif*
	Я очень счастлива. f	ya *o*·chin' shas·*li*·va

opinions

мнения

Did you like it?

Вам это понравилось? vam *e*·ta pan·*ra*·vi·las'

How do you like it?

Как вы думаете об этом? kak vih *du*·ma·yit·ye ab *e*·tam

I thought it was …	По-моему, было …	pa·*mo*·i·mu *bih*·la …
It's …	Это …	*e*·ta …
awful	ужасно	u·*zhas*·na
beautiful	красиво	kra·*si*·va
boring	скучно	*skush*·na
great	здорово	*zdo*·ra·va
interesting	интересно	in·tir·*yes*·na
OK	нормально	nar·*mal'*·na
strange	странно	*stra*·na
too expensive	слишком дорого	*slish*·kam *do*·ra·ga

politics & social issues

Who do you vote for?
За кого вы голосуете?   za ka·*vo* vih ga·la·*su*·yit·ye

Do you support (Putin)?
Вы поддерживаете   vih pad·*yer*·zhih·va·yit·ye
(Путина)?   (*pu*·ti·na)

I support the (communists).
Я поддерживаю   ya pad·*yer*·zhih·va·yu
(коммунистов).   (ka·mu·*ni*·staf)

I'm a member   Я член ... партии.   ya chlyen ... *par*·ti
of the ... party.

communist	коммунисти-ческой	ka·mu·ni·*sti*·chi·skey
conservative	консервативной	kan·sir·va·*tiv*·ney
democratic	демократической	di·ma·kra·*ti*·chi·skey
green	зелёной	zil·*yo*·ney
liberal	либеральной	li·bi·*ral*'·ney
social	социал-	sat·sih·*al*·
democratic	демократической	di·ma·kra·*ti*·chi·skey
socialist	социалисти-ческой	sat·sih·a·li·*sti*·chi·skey

---

you could hear ...

Most Russians, particularly the older ones, are very open in expressing their frustration at their social and economic circumstances – even in the post-Soviet era. Here are some phrases that are in surprisingly common usage:

В нормальной стране ...   **In a normal country ...**
  v nar·*mal*'·ney stran·ye ...   **(ie not Russia)**

Раньше ...   **Earlier ...**
  ran'·she ...   **(ie before 1991)**

Я боюсь за свою родину.   **I'm concerned for my country.**
  ya ba·*yus*' za sva·*yu* ro·di·nu

Кошмар!   **It's a nightmare!**
  kash·*mar*

feelings & opinions

life of the party

Some of Russia's most prominent political parties are listed below. They're ordered according to their standard English translations.

Edinaya Rossiya (United Russia)
Единая Россия — yi·*di*·na·ya ra·*si*·ya

Kompartiya (Communists)
Компартия — kam·*par*·ti·ya

LDP (Liberal Democrats)
Либерально- — li·bi·*ral'*·na·
демократическая — di·ma·kra·*ti*·chi·ska·ya
партия (ЛДП) — *par*·ti·ya (el·de·*pe*)

Soyuz Pravykh Sil (Union of Right Forces)
Союз правых сил — sa·*yus pra*·vihkh sil

Yabloko (Liberals)
Яблоко — *ya*·bla·ka

Did you hear about …?
Вы слышали про …? — vih *slih*·sha·li pra …

Do you agree with it?
Вы согласны? — vih sa·*glas*·nih

I (don't) agree with …
Я (не) согласен/с … m — ya (nye) sa·*gla*·sin s …
Я (не) согласна с … f — ya (nye) sa·*glas*·na s …

How do people feel about …?
Как думают про …? — kak *du*·ma·yut pra …

How can we protest against …?
Как мы можем — kak mih *mo*·zhihm
протестовать против …? — pra·ti·sta·*vat' pro*·tif …

How can we support …?
Как мы можем — kak mih *mo*·zhim
поддерживать …? — pad·*yer*·zhih·vat' …

SOCIAL

130

abortion	аборт m	a·*bort*
animal rights	права животных n pl	pra·*va* zhih·*vot*·nihkh
atheism	атеизм m	a·ti·*izm*
anti-Semitism	антисемитизм m	an·ti·si·mi·*tizm*
black market	чёрный рынок m	*chor*·nih *rih*·nak
bureaucracy	бюрократия f	byu·ra·*kra*·ti·ya
centralisation	централизация f	tsihn·tra·li·*zat*·sih·ya
communism	коммунизм m	ka·mu·*nizm*
crime	преступность f	pri·*stup*·nast'
discrimination	дискриминация f	dis·kri·mi·*nat*·sih·ya
drugs	наркотики f pl	nar·*ko*·ti·ki
the economy	экономика f	e·ka·*no*·mi·ka
education	образование n	a·bra·za·*va*·ni·ye
the environment	окружающая	a·kru·*zha*·yu·sha·ya
	среда f	sri·*da*
ethnic minorities	национальности f pl	nat·sih·a·*nal*'·na·sti
equal opportunity	равные	*rav*·nih·ye
	возможности n pl	vaz·*mozh*·na·sti
euthanasia	эйтаназия f	ey·ta·*na*·zi·ya
glasnost	гласность f	*glas*·nast'
globalisation	глобализация f	gla·ba·li·*zat*·sih·ya
Gulags	ГУЛАГ m	gu·*lak*
human rights	права человека n pl	pra·*va* chi·lav·*ye*·ka
immigration	иммиграция f	i·mi·*grat*·sih·ya
inequality	неравенство n	ni·*ra*·vinst·va
inflation	инфляция f	inf·*lyat*·sih·ya
Leninism	Ленинизм m	li·ni·*nizm*
mafia	мафия f	*ma*·fi·ya
market economy	рыночная	*rih*·nach·na·ya
	экономика f	e·ka·*no*·mi·ka
Marxism	марксизм m	mark·*sizm*
nationalism	национализм m	nat·sih·a·na·*lizm*
'new Russians'	новые русские m pl	*no*·vih·ye *ru*·ski·ye
(nouveaux riches)		
perestroika	перестройка f	pi·ri·*stroy*·ka
party politics	политика f	pa·*li*·ti·ka
poverty	нищета f	ni·shi·*ta*
privatisation	приватизация f	pri·va·ti·*zat*·sih·ya
racism	расизм m	ra·*sizm*
reforms	реформы f pl	ri·*for*·mih

sexism	сексизм m	sik·*sizm*
shortages	недостатки m pl	ni·da·*stat*·ki
Soviet era	советский	sav·*yet*·ski
	период m	pi·ri·*ot*
Stalinism	сталинизм m	sta·li·*nizm*
terrorism	терроризм m	ti·ra·*rizm*
tycoons	олигархи m pl	a·li·*gar*·khi
tsarist era	царский период m	*tsar*·ski pi·ri·*ot*
social welfare	социальное	sat·sih·*al'*·na·ye
	обеспечение n	a·bis·pye·*chi*·ni·ye
unemployment	безработица f	bis·ra·*bo*·tit·sa
the war in	война в	vey·*na* f
(Chechnya)	(Чечне) f	(chich·*nye*)
westernisation	вестернизация f	vi·stir·ni·*zat*·sih·ya

the environment

окружающая среда

Is this a	Это	*e*·ta
protected …?	заповедный …?	za·pav·*yed*·nih …
forest	лес	lyes
park	парк	park
species	вид	vit

Is there a … problem here?
Здесь есть проблема …?   zdyes' yest' prab·*lye*·ma …

What should be done about …?
Как быть с …?   kag biht' s …

acid rain	кислый дождь m	*kis*·lih dosht'
conservation	консервация f	kan·sir·*vat*·sih·ya
Chornobyl disaster	чернобыльская катастрофа f	chir·*no*·bihl·ska·ya ka·tas·*tro*·fa
deforestation	обезлесение n	a·biz·*lye*·si·ni·ye
drought	засуха f	*za*·su·kha
ecosystem	экосистема f	e·ko·sist·*ye*·ma
endangered species	вымирающие виды m pl	vih·mi·*ra*·yu·shi·ye *vi*·dih
erosion	эрозия f	e·*ro*·zi·ya
fertilisers	удобрения n pl	u·dab·*rye*·ni·ya
gas pipelines	газопроводы m pl	ga·za·*pro*·va·dih
genetically modified food	генетически модифициро- ванная еда f	gi·ni·*ti*·chi·ski ma·di·fit·sih·*ro*· va·na·ya yi·*da*
hunting	охота f	a·*kho*·ta
hydroelectricity	гидроэлек- тричество n	gi·dra·e·lik· *tri*·chist·va
industrial waste	промышленные стоки m pl	pra·*mihsh*·li·nih·ye *sto*·ki
irrigation	ирригация f	i·ri·*gat*·sih·ya
nuclear energy	ядерная энергия f	*ya*·dir·na·ya in·*yer*·gi·ya
nuclear power stations	атомные электростанции f pl	*a*·tam·nih·ye e·lik·tra·*stant*·sih
nuclear testing	испытания ядерного оружия n pl	is·pih·*ta*·ni·ya *ya*·dir·na·va a·*ru*·zhih·ya
oil spills	утечки нефти f pl	ut·*yech*·ki *nyef*·ti
ozone layer	озонный слой m	a·*zo*·nih sloy
pesticides	пестициды f pl	pi·stit·*sih*·dih
pollution	загрязнение n	za·griz·*nye*·ni·ye
radiation	радиация f	ra·di·*at*·sih·ya
recycling programme	рециклирование n	rit·sih·kli·ra·*va*·ni·ye
salination	засоление n	za·sal·*ye*·ni·ye
toxic waste	токсичные стоки m pl	tak·*sich*·nih·ye *sto*·ki
water supply	водоснабжение n	va·da·snab·*zhe*·ni·ye

To find out how Russian speakers really feel about life, you should get familiar with some of their idioms …

You've got no hope in hell!
Руки коротки. *ru*·ki *ko*·rat·ki
(lit: your hands are too short)

Don't mess with them!
Пальца в рот не клади! *palt*·sa v rot nye kla·*di*
(lit: don't put your finger in their mouth)

They don't know if they're Arthur or Martha.
Семь пятниц на неделе. syem' *pyat*·nits na ni·*dyel*·ye
(lit: seven Fridays in their week)

Like getting blood from a stone.
Как от козла молока. kak at kaz·*la* ma·la·*ka*
(lit: like milk from a he-goat)

This is the root of the problem.
Вот где собака зарыта. vot gdye sa·*ba*·ka za·*rih*·ta
(lit: here's where the dog's buried)

They've disappeared into thin air.
Как корова языком kak ka·*ro*·va yi·zih·*kom*
слизала. sli·*za*·la
(lit: like a cow licked them away)

Completely packed.
Как сельдей в бочке. kak sil'·*dyey* v *boch*·kye
(lit: like herrings in a barrel)

Living in the lap of luxury.
Полная чаша. *pol*·na·ya *cha*·sha
(lit: full cup)

This is impossible to pronounce!
Язык сломаешь. yi·*zihk* sla·*ma*·yish'
(lit: you'll break your tongue)

Unexpected problems.
Подводные камни. pad·*vod*·nih·ye *kam*·ni
(lit: underwater rocks)

going out

выход в свет

where to go

What's there to do in the evenings?
Что можно делать
по вечерам?

shto *mozh*·na *dye*·lat'
pa vi·chi·*ram*

I feel like	Мне хочется	mnye *kho*·chit·sa
going to a …	пойти …	pey·*ti* …
ballet	на балет	na bal·*yet*
bathhouse	в баню	v *ban*·yu
bar	в бар	v bar
café	в кафе	f ka·*fe*
circus	на цирк	na tsihrk
concert	на концерт	na kant·*sert*
film	в кино	v ki·*no*
football/soccer match	на футбольный матч	na fud·*bol*'·nih mach
hockey match	на хоккейный матч	na khak·*yey*·nih mach
nightclub	в ночной клуб	v nach·*noy* klup
opera	на оперу	na *o*·pi·ru
party	на тусовку	na tu·*sof*·ku
performance	на представление	na prit·stav·*lye*·ni·ye
play	в пьесу	f *pye*·su
pub	в пивную	f piv·*nu*·yu
restaurant	в ресторан	v ri·sta·*ran*
theatre	в театр	f ti·*atr*

For other forms of entertainment, see **interests**, page 121, and **sport**, page 153.

What's on …?	Что идёт …?	shto id·yot …
locally	в этом районе	v e·tam ra·yon·ye
today	сегодня	si·vod·nya
tonight	сегодня	si·vod·nya
	вечером	vye·chi·ram
this weekend	на этих	na e·tikh
	выходных	vih·khad·nihkh

Where can I find …?	Где находятся …?	gdye na·kho·dit·sa …
clubs	клубы	klu·bih
gay venues	гей-клубы	gyey·klu·bih
places to eat	рестораны	ri·sta·ra·nih
pubs	пивные	piv·nih·ye

For more on bars, drinks and partying, see **romance**, page 141, and **eating out**, page 163.

invitations

Are you free …?	Вы свободны …?	vih sva·bod·nih …
now	сейчас	si·chas
tonight	сегодня	si·vod·nya
	вечером	vye·chi·ram
this weekend	в субботу	f su·bo·tu

Would you like to go (for a) …?	Вы не хотите пойти …?	vih nye kha·tit·ye pey·ti …
coffee	в кафе	f ka·fe
dancing	потанцевать	pa·tan·sih·vat'
drink	в бар	v bar
meal	в ресторан	v ri·sta·ran
out somewhere	куда-нибудь	ku·da·ni·bud'
walk	погулять	pa·gul·yat'

Do you know a good restaurant?
Вы знаете, где
хороший ресторан?

vih *zna*·it·ye gdye
kha·*ro*·shih ri·sta·*ran*

Do you want to go to a (disco) with me?
Вы не хотите пойти
со мной в (дискотеку)?

vih nye kha·*tit*·ye pey·*ti*
sa mnoy v (di·skat·*ye*·ku)

Come to our place for a party.
Поедем к нам на тусовку.

pa·*yed*·yem k nam na tu·*sof*·ku

You should come.
Приезжайте!

pri·i·*zheyt*·ye

Drop in sometime!
Заходите как-нибудь!

za·kha·*dit*·ye *kak*·ni·bud'

For other invitations, see **romance**, page 141.

responding to invitations

Sure!
Обязательно!

ab·ya·*za*·til'·na

Yes, I'd love to.
Я с удовольствием.

ya s u·da·*volst*·vi·yem

That's very kind of you.
Благодарю вас.

bla·ga·dar·*yu* vas

Where shall we go?
Куда?

ku·*da*

It's a date.
Договорились!

da·ga·va·*ri*·lis'

No, I'm afraid I can't.
Спасибо, но я не могу.

spa·*si*·ba no ya nye ma·*gu*

Sorry, I can't sing/dance.
К сожалению, я не
умею петь/танцевать.

k sa·zhal·*ye*·ni·yu ya nye
um·*ye*·yu pyet'/tant·sih·*vat'*

What about (tomorrow)?
Как насчёт (завтра)?

kak na·*shot* (*zaf*·tra)

Going to the *баня* ban·ya (communal bathhouse) is a ritual enjoyed by all vodka-blooded Russians, a place for physical and moral purification. Russians go to the same bathhouse at the same time each week to meet up with friends. Unlike their Turkish or Finnish counterparts, Russian *баня* participants thrash themselves or their friends with a *веник* vye·nik – a bunch of oak or birch twigs – which detoxifies the body while releasing delightful forest aromas. The sexes are segregated, either by coming to the *баня* on alternate days or bathing on different floors of the same building.

When you go to a *баня*, take a *полотенце* pa·lat·yent·se (towel), *шампунь* sham·pun' (shampoo), *туфли* tuf·li (plastic shoes) and *чай* chey (tea) or *пиво* pi·va (beer). You strip in the change room, buy your twigs and move to the *парилка* pa·ril·ka (steam room). Sit on a wooden bench and dip your twig-bundle into a bucket of hot water to soften it before the thrashing begins. After five minutes or so, you can escape and immerse yourself in the *бассейн* bas·yeyn (cold pool). Then you can drink your tea or beer and have a chat before starting all over again. Russians wish each other good health after the bathhouse experience with the expression *С лёгким паром!* s lyokh·kim pa·ram (With light steam!)

Apparently rival mafia leaders in Chicago used to hold meetings in the city's Russian baths, as it was difficult to conceal weapons on their naked bodies …

arranging to meet

What time will we meet?
Во сколько встретимся?   va skol'·ka fstrye·tim·sa

Where will we meet?
Где встретимся?   gdye fstrye·tim·sa

Where will you be?
Где вы будете ждать?   gdye vih bu·dit·ye zhdat'

Let's meet at … Встретимся … *fstrye·tim·sa …*
   (seven) o'clock в (семь) часов f (syem') chi·*sof*
   the (entrance) перед (входом) *pye·*rit (*fkho·*dam)

I'll pick you up.
   Я зайду за вами. ya zey·*du* za *va·*mi

Are you ready?
   Вы готовы? vih ga·*to·*vih

I'm ready.
   Я готов/готова. m/f ya ga·*tof*/ga·*to·*va

See you later/tomorrow.
   До встречи/завтра! da *fstrye·*chi/*zaf·*tra

Sorry I'm late.
   Извините, что я опоздал. m iz·vi·*nit·*ye shto ya a·paz·*dal*
   Извините, что я опоздала. f iz·vi·*nit·*ye shto ya a·paz·*da·*la

Never mind.
   Ничего! ni·chi·*vo*

drugs

наркотика

Do you have a light?
  Дай мне прикурить!   dey mnye pri·ku·*rit'*
Do you want to have a smoke?
  Хочешь покурить?   *kho*·chish' pa·ku·*rit'*
I take … occasionally.
  Я иногда принимаю …   ya i·nag·*da* pri·ni·*ma*·yu …
I don't take drugs.
  Я не принимаю наркотик.   ya nye pri·ni·*ma*·yu nar·*ko*·tik
I'm high.
  Я под кайфом.   ya pat *key*·fam

If the police are talking to you about drugs, see **police**, page 193, for useful phrases.

We've given phrases in the polite *вы* vih form in **asking some-one out**, **pick-up lines** and **rejections**. For the rest of this chapter, phrases are in the informal *ты* tih (you) form only. If you're not sure what this means, see the box on page 106.

asking someone out

приглашения

Where would you like to go (tonight)?
Куда вы хотите пойти   ku·*da* vih kha·*tit*·ye pey·*ti*
(сегодня вечером)?   (si·*vod*·nya *vye*·chi·ram)

Would you like to do something (tomorrow)?
Хотите, пойдём   kha·*tit*·ye peyd·*yom*
куда-нибудь (завтра)?   ku·*da*·ni·but' (*zaf*·tra)

Yes, I'd love to.
С удовольствием.   s u·da·*volst*·vi·yem

Sorry, I can't.
К сожалению, я не могу.   k sa·zhal·*ye*·ni·yu ya nye ma·*gu*

pick-up lines

Would you like a drink?
Хотите выпить со мной?   kha·*tit*·ye *vih*·pit' sa mnoy

What are you having?
Что вы хотите пить?   shto vih kha·*tit*·ye pit'

Can I have a light?
Можно прикурить?   *mozh*·na pri·ku·*rit'*

Let's dance.
Давайте потанцуем.   da·*veyt*·ye pa·tant·*su*·yem

Isn't this place great/terrible?
Здесь классно/   zdyes' *klas*·na/
паршиво, правда?   par·*shih*·va *prav*·da

This isn't how I normally meet people.
Для меня это весьма   dlya min·*ya* e·ta vis'·*ma*
необычный способ   ni·a·*bihch*·nih *spo*·sap
знакомства.   zna·*komst*·va

You look great!
Вы классно выглядите!   vih *klas*·na *vih*·gli·dit·ye

What are they selling? (in a queue)
Что дают?   shto da·*yut*

flower power

Don't give an even number of flowers to your Russian para-
mour, as superstition says this is only suitable for a funeral.
Always give an odd number.

rejections

No, thank you.
Нет, спасибо.   nyet spa·*si*·ba

I'd rather not.
Я не хочу.   ya nye kha·*chu*

I'm here with my girlfriend.
Я здесь с подругой.   ya zdyes' z pa-*dru*-goy

I'm here with my boyfriend.
Я здесь с другом.   ya zdyes' z pa-*dru*-gam

Excuse me, I have to go now.
Извините, мне пора идти.   iz-vi-*nit*-ye mnye pa-*ra* i-*ti*

local talk		
Leave me alone!	Приваливай!	pri-*va*-li-vey
Piss off!	Отъебись!	at-ye-*bis'*

getting closer

I like you very much.
Ты мне очень нравишься.   tih mnye *o*-chin' *nra*-vish'-sa

You're good-looking.
Ты красивый. m   vih kra-*si*-vih
Ты красивая. f   vih kra-*si*-va-ya

You're great.
Ты классный. m   tih *klas*-nih
Ты классная. f   tih *klas*-na-ya

I want to get to know you better.
Мне бы хотелось узнать   mnye bih khat-*ye*-las' uz-*nat*'
о тебе побольше.   a tib-*ye* pa-*bol'*-she

Can I kiss you?
Можно тебя поцеловать?   *mozh*-na tib ya pat-se-la-*vat*'

Do you want to come inside for a while?
Хочешь зайти на время?   *kho*-chish' zey-*ti* na *vryem*-ya

Do you want a massage?
Хочешь, я сделаю   *kho*-chish' ya *zdye*-la-yu
тебе массаж?   tib-*ye* ma-*sash*

Can I stay over?
Можно мне остаться?   *mozh*-na mnye a-*stat'*-sa

sex

Hold me.
Обними меня.
ab·ni·*mi* min·*ya*

Kiss me.
Поцелуй меня.
pat·se·*luy* min·*ya*

I want you.
Я хочу тебя.
ya kha·*chu* tib·*ya*

Let's go to bed.
Давай в постель!
da·*vey* f past·*yel'*

Touch me here.
Трогай меня здесь!
tro·gey min·*ya* zdyes'

Use your tongue.
Языком.
yi·zih·*kom*

Do you like this?
Это тебе нравится?
e·ta tib·*ye* nra·vit·sa

I (don't) like that.
Это мне (не) нравится.
e·ta mnye (nye) nra·vit·sa

I think we should stop now.
Мы должны остановиться!
mih dalzh·*nih* a·sta·na·*vit'*·sa

I won't do it without protection.
Ничего не сделаю
без защиты.
ni·chi·*vo* nye *zdye*·la·yu
byez zash·*chi*·tih

Do you have a (condom)?
У тебя есть (презерватив)?
u tib·*ya* yest' (pri·zir·va·*tif*)

Let's use a (condom).
Одень (презерватив).
ad·*yen'* (pri·zir·va·*tif*)

---

boy talk

He's hot!	Красавец мужчина!	kra·*sa*·vits mush·*chi*·na
He's a babe.	Он красавец.	on kra·*sa*·vits
He's a bastard.	Он сволочь.	on *svo*·lach'
He gets around.	Он блядует.	on *blya*·du·yet

144

She's hot!	Знойная	*znoy*·na·ya
	женщина!	*zhensh*·chi·na
She's a babe.	Она красавица.	a·*na* kra·*sa*·vit·sa
She's a bitch.	Она сука.	a·*na* su·ka
She gets around.	Она блядует.	a·*na blya*·du·yet

It's my first time.
Это мой первый раз. e·ta moy *pyer*·vih ras

Oh my god!
Боже мой! *bo*·zhe moy

That's great.
Это здорово! e·ta *zdo*·ra·va

Don't stop!
Не останавливайся! nye a·sta·*nav*·li·vey·sa

Stop!
Стой! stoy

Faster!	Побыстрее!	pa·bihst·*rye*·ye
Harder!	Посильнее!	pa·siln·*ye*·ye
Slower!	Помеденее!	pa·mid·lin·*ye*·ye
Softer!	Помягче!	pam·*yakh*·che

That was …	Было …	*bih*·la …
amazing	чудесно	chud·*yes*·na
romantic	романтично	ra·man·*tich*·na
wild	дико	*di*·ka

Don't worry, I'll do it myself.
Ничего, сам сделаю. m ni·chi·*vo* ya sam *zdye*·la·yu
Ничего, сама сделаю. f ni·chi·*vo* ya a·*ma zdye*·la·yu

It helps to have a sense of humour.
Чувство юмора *chust*·va *yu*·ma·ra
всегда помогает! fsig·*da* pa·ma·*ga*·yet

Is that why you're single?
И вот почему ты не i vot pa·chi·*mu* tih nye
женат, да? (to man) zhih·*nat* da
И вот почему ты не i vot pa·chi·*mu* tih nye
замужем, да? (to woman) *za*·mu·zhihm da

crumb	Крошка.	*krosh*·ka
my angel	Ангел мой.	*an*·gil moy
my love	Любовь моя.	lyu·*bof*' ma·*ya*
my rabbit	Зайчик мой.	*zey*·chik moy
my sunshine	Солнышко моё.	*sol*·nihsh·ka ma·*yo*
little pigeon	Голубчик. m	ga·*lup*·chik
	Голубушка. f	ga·*lu*·bush·ka

love

любовь

I'm serious about you.
Я серьёзен/серьёзна. m/f ya sir·*yo*·zin/sir·*yoz*·na

I see you in my dreams.
Я вижу тебя во сне. ya vi·*zhu* tib·*ya* va snye

I need you.
Ты мне нужна. (to woman) tih mnye nuzh·*na*
Ты мне нужен. (to man) tih mnye *nu*·zhihn

I love you.
Я люблю тебя. ya lyub·*lyu* tib·*ya*

There is no greater happiness than being close to you.
Нет большего счастья, nyet *bol*'·she·va *shast*·ya
чем близость с тобой. chem *bli*·zast' s ta·*boy*

I'll die without your love!
Я умру без твоей любви! ya um·*ru* byes tva·*yey* lyub·*vi*

Will you ...?	Ты ...?	tih ...
go out	будешь	*bu*·dish
with me	встречаться	fstri·*chat*'·sa
	со мной	sa mnoy
meet my	познакомишься	paz·na·*ko*·mish'·sa
parents	с моими	sa ma·*i*·mi
	родителями	ra·*di*·til·ya·mi
marry me	выйдешь за меня	*vih*·dish' za min·*ya*

problems

We need to talk.
Нам нужно поговорить.   nam *nuzh*·na pa·ga·va·*rit'*

Why are you so sad?
Что тебе так грустно?   shto tib·*ye* tak *grus*·na

I don't feel right.
Мне неловко.   mnye ni·*lof*·ka

You've hurt my feelings.
Ты меня обидел. (to man)   tih min·*ya* a·*bi*·dil
Ты меня обидела. (to woman)   tih min·*ya* a·*bi*·di·la

I need time to think.
Мне нужно время   mnye *nuzh*·na *vryem*·ya
подумать.   pa·*du*·mat'

We'll work it out.
Мы разберёмся.   mih raz·bir·*yom*·sa

We were just too different.
Не сошлись характерами.   nye sash·*lis'* kha·*rak*·ti·ra·mi
(lit: our personalities didn't come together)

small talk

Russians have an extensive range of 'diminutives' – or shortened affectionate forms – for most first names, which are used by friends, family and loved ones. Инна *i*·na (Inna) for example, can be called Иннуся *i*·*nus*·ya (Innusya), Иночка *i*·nach·ka (Innochka), Инка *in*·ka (Inka) or Иннуля *i*·*nul*·ya (Innulya), to name a few variations.

tell it like it is

So you've really *завалился/завалилась* za·va·*lil*·sa/za·va·li·las' m/f (screwed it up), and you desperately need to apologise to your Russian beloved. Here are some phrases to help you in effective grovelling:

I'm a/an ...	Я ... m&f	ya ...
idiot	идиот	i·di·*ot*
fool	дурак	du·*rak*
loser	неудачник	ni·u·*dach*·nik
wanker	пиздобол	piz·da·*bol*
waste of space	обуза	a·*bu*·za

leaving

расставание

I have to leave (tomorrow).
Я (завтра) уезжаю.   ya (*zaf*·tra) u·iz·*zha*·yu

I'll ...	Я буду ...	ya *bu*·du ...
keep in touch	писать	pi·*sat'*
miss you	скучать	sku·*chat'*
visit you	приезжать	pri·yiz·*zhat'*

beliefs & cultural differences

вера и культурные различия

religion

What's your religion?
Какая ваша религия?   ka·*ka*·ya *va*·sha ri·*li*·gi·ya

Are you a believer?
Вы верующий? m   vih *vye*·ru·yu·shi
Вы верующая? f   vih *vye*·ru·yu·sha·ya

I'm not religious.
Я неверующий. m   ya nyev·*ye*·ru·yu·shi
Я неверующая. f   ya nyev·*ye*·ru·yu·sha·ya

I'm (a/an) …	Я …	ya …
atheist	атеист	at·ye·*ist*
agnostic	агностик	ag·*no*·stik
Buddhist	будист m	bu·*dist*
	будистка f	bu·*dist*·ka
Catholic	католик m	ka·*to*·lik
	католичка f	ka·*to*·lich·ka
Christian	христианини m	khri·sti·*a*·nin
	христианка f	khri·sti·*an*·ka
Jewish	еврей m	yev·*ryey*
	еврейка f	yev·*ryey*·ka
Muslim	мусульманин m	mu·sul'·*ma*·nin
	мусульманка f	mu·sul'·*man*·ka
Orthodox	православный m	pra·vas·*luv*·nih
	православная f	pra·vas·*lav*·na·ya

I (don't) believe in …	Я (не) верю в …	ya (nye) *vyer*·yu v …
astrology	астрологию	a·stra·*lo*·gi·yu
fate	судьбу	sud'·*bu*
God	Бога	*bo*·ga
miracles	чудеса	chu·di·*sa*

Can I ... here?	Можно здесь ...?	*mozh*·na zdyes' ...
Where can I ...?	Где можно ...?	gdye *mozh*·na ...
attend mass	ходить к Обедне	kha·*dit*' k ab·*yed*·nye
attend a	ходить к	kha·*dit*' k
service	церковной	tsir·*kov*·ney
	службе	*sluzh*·bye
pray	молиться	ma·*lit*'·sa
worship	поклоняться	pa·klan·*yat*'·sa

cultural differences

культурные различия

Is this a local or national custom?

Это местный или	*e*·ta *myes*·nih *i*·li
народный обычай?	na·*rod*·nih a·*bih*·chey

I didn't mean to do anything wrong.

Я не хотел/хотела	ya nye khat·*yel*/khat·*ye*·la
сделать что-то	*zdye*·lat' *shto*·ta
не правильно. m/f	nye *pra*·vil'·na

I don't want to offend you.

Я не хочу вас обижать.	ya nye kha·*chu* vas a·*bi*·zhat'

I'm not used to this.

Я не привык к этому. m	ya nye pri·*vihk* k *e*·ta·mu
Я не привыкла к этому. f	ya nye pri·*vih*·*kla* k *e*·ta·mu

I'd rather not join in.

Я предпочитаю не	ya prit·pa·chi·*ta*·yu nye
участвовать.	u·*chast*·va·vat'

I'll try it.

Я попробую!	ya pa·*pro*·bu·yu

I'm sorry, it's	Извините, но	iz·vi·*nit*·ye no
against my ...	это не по ...	*e*·ta nye po ...
beliefs	моим	ma·*im*
	верованиям	vye·ra·va·ni·yam
religion	вероучениям	vye·ra·u·*che*·ni·yam
	моей религии	ma·*yey* ri·*li*·gi

When's the gallery/museum open?

В какие часы работает
галерея/музей?

f ka·*ki*·ye chi·*sih* ra·*bo*·ta·yet
ga·lir·*ye*·ya/muz·*yey*

What's in the collection?

Что в коллекции?

shto f kal·*yekt*·sih

It's an exhibition of …

Это выставка …

e·ta *vih*·staf·ka …

What do you think of …?

Как вы думаете о …?

kak vih *du*·ma·it·ye a …

I'm interested in …

Я интересуюсь …

ya in·ti·ri·*su*·yus' …

I like the works of …

Я люблю произведения …

ya lyub·*lyu* pra·iz·vid·*ye*·ni·ya …

It reminds me of …

Это мне напоминает …

e·ta mnye na·pa·mi·*na*·yet …

architecture	архитектура f	ar·khi·tek·*tu*·ra
artwork	произведение n	pra·iz·vid·*ye*·ni·ye
carving	резная работа f	riz·*na*·ya ra·*bo*·ta
design	дизайн m	di·*zeyn*
etching	гравировка f	gra·vi·*rof*·ka
exhibit	выставка f	*vih*·staf·ka
painter	художник m	khu·*dozh*·nik
painting (artwork)	картина f	kar·*ti*·na
painting (technique)	живопись f	*zhih* va·pis'
print	эстамп m	e·*stamp*
sculptor	скульптор m	*skulp*·tar
sculpture	скульптура f	skulp·*tu*·ra
statue	статуя f	*sta*·tu·ya
studio	студия f	*stu*·di·ya
style	стиль m	stil'
technique	техника f	*tyekh*·ni·ka
woodcraft	ремесло n	ri·mis·*lo*

Chagall	Шагал	sha·*gal*
Kandinsky	Кандинский	kan·*din*·ski
Malevich	Малевич	mal·*ye*·vich
Repin	Репин	*rye*·pin
Stepanova	Степанова	sti·*pa*·na·va
Alexander	Александр	a·lik·*sandr*
Petrovsky	Петровский	pi·*trof*·ski

Byzantine style	византийский стиль m	vi·zan·*tih*·ski stil'
classicism	классицизм m	kla·sit·*sihzm*
computer art	компьютерное искусство n	kam·*pyu*·tir·na·ye is·*kust*·va
constructivism	конструктивизм m	kan·struk·ti·*vizm*
expressionism	экспрессионизм m	eks·prye·si·a·*nizm*
futurism	футуризм m	fu·tu·*rizm*
graphic art	графическое искусство n	gra·*fi*·chi·ska·ye is·*kust*·va
icon painting	иконопись f	*i*·kan·a·pis'
impressionism	импрессионизм m	im·pri·si·a·*nizm*
modernism	модернизм m	ma·dir·*nizm*
ornamental china	фарфор m	far·*for*
postmodernism	постмодернизм m	post·ma·dir·*nizm*
religious art	церковное искусство n	tsihr·*kov*·na·ye is·*kust*·va
Renaissance art	искусство эпохи Возрождения n	is·*kust*·va e·*po*·khi vaz·vrazh·*dye*·ni·ya
romanticism	романтицизм m	ra·man·tit·*sizm*
socialist realism	социалисти- ческий реализм m	sat·sih·a·li·*sti*· chi·ski ri·a·*lizm*
suprematism	супрематизм m	su·pri·ma·*tizm*
symbolism	символизм m	sim·va·*lizm*

sporting interests

спортивные интересы

What sport do you …?	… каким видом спорта вы?	… ka·*kim* vi·dam *spor*·ta vih
play	Занимаетесь	za·ni·*ma*·it·yes'
follow	Интересуетесь	in·ti·ri·*su*·it·yes'

I play …	Я играю в …	ya i·*gra*·yu v …
I watch …	Я смотрю …	ya smat·*ryu* …
football (soccer)	футбол	fud·*bol*
ice hockey	хоккей	khak·*yey*
basketball	баскетбол	bas·kid·*bol*
volleyball	волейбол	val·yey·*bol*
tennis	теннис	*tye*·nis

I do/go …	Я занимаюсь …	ya za·ni·*ma*·yus' …
cycling	велоспортом	vye·la·*spor*·tam
gymnastics	гимнастикой	gim·*na*·sti·key
running	бегом	*bye*·gam
to the gym	фитнесом	*fit*·ni·sam

I go …	Я катаюсь на …	ya ka·*ta*·yus' na …
skating	коньках	kan'·*kakh*
skiing	лыжах	*lih*·zhakh

Do you like (football/soccer)?
Вам нравится (футбол)? — vam *nra*·vit·sa (fud·*bol*)

Yes, very much.
Да, очень. — da o·*chin'*

Not really.
Не очень. — nye o·*chin'*

I like watching it.
Я предпочитаю смотреть. — ya prit·pa·chi·*ta*·yu smat·*ryet'*

sports talk		
What a …!	**Какой …!**	ka·*koy* …
goal	гол	gol
hit/kick	удар	u·*dar*
pass	пас	pas
shot	удар	u·*dar*

going to a game

пойти на матч

Would you like to go to a game?
Хотите пойти на матч?   kha·*tit*·ye pey·*ti* na match

Who are you supporting?
За кого вы болеете?   za ka·*vo* vih bal·*ye*·it·ye

Who's …?	**Кто …?**	kto …
playing	играет	i·*gra*·yet
winning	ведёт	vid·*yot*

That was a … game!	**Был … матч!**	bihl … match
bad	плохой	pla·*khoy*
boring	скучный	*skuch*·nih
great	отличный	at·*lich*·nih

playing sport

заниматься спортом

Do you want to play?
Вы хотите играть?   vih kha·*tit*·ye i·*grat'*

Can I join in?
Можно присоединиться?   *mozh*·na pri·sa·ye·di·*nit'*·sa

I'd love to.
С удовольствием!   s u·da·*volst*·vi·yem

I have an injury.
Я ранен/ранена. **m/f**   ya *ra*·nin/*ra*·ni·na

Your/My point.
Ваше/Моё очко.
va·shih/ma·*yo* ach·*ko*

Kick/Pass it to me!
Мне!
mnye

You're a good player.
Вы хорошо играете.
vih kha·ra·*sho* i·*gra*·it·ye

Thanks for the game.
Спасибо за игру.
spa·*si*·ba za i·*gru*

How much does it cost to …?
Сколько стоит играть в …?
skol'·ka *sto*·it i·*grat*' v …

    go bowling   боулинг   *bo*·u·link

    play pool   бильярд   bil·*yart*

Where's the nearest …?
Где здесь …?
gdye zdyes' …

    golf course   корт для гольфа   kort dlya *gol*'·fa

    gym   спортзал   spart·*zal*

    swimming pool   бассейн   bas·*yeyn*

    tennis court   теннисный корт   *tye*·nis·nih kort

Where do you work out?
Где вы занимаетесь фитнесом?
gdye vih za·ni·*ma*·it·yes' *fit*·ni·sam

Do I have to be a member to attend?
Нужно быть членом?
nuzh·na biht' *chlye*·nam

Is there a women-only session?
Есть сессия только для женщин?
yest' *sye*·si·ya *tol*'·ka dlya *zhensh*·chin

Where are the changing rooms?
Где раздевалка?
gdye raz·di·*val*·ka

scoring		
What's the score?	Какой счёт?	ka·*koy* shot
draw/even	ничья	ni·*cha*
match point	матч-пойнт	mach·*poynt*
nil/love	ноль	nol'
nil all	сухой счёт	su·*khoy* shot

What's the charge per ...?	Сколько стоит билет на ...?	skol'·ka sto·it bil·yet na ...
day	день	dyen'
game	игру	i·gru
hour	час	chas
visit	один раз	a·din ras

Can I hire a ...?	Можно взять ... напрокат?	mozh·na vzyat' ... na·pra·kat
ball	мяч	myach
bicycle	велосипед	vi·la·sip·yet
court	корт	kort
racquet	ракетку	rak·yet·ku

football/soccer

футбол

Who plays for (Torpedo)?
Кто играет за (Торпедо)?
kto i·gra·yet za (tarp·ye·do)

He's a great player.
Он классный футболист.
on klas·nih fud·ba·list

He played brilliantly in the match against (Italy).
Он прекрасно играл
против (Италии).
on pri·kras·na i·gral
pro·tif (i·ta·li)

Which team is at the top of the league?
Какая команда –
лидер чемпионата?
ka·ka·ya ka·man·da
li·dir chim·pi·a·na·ta

What a great/terrible team!
Какая прекрасная/
ужасная команда!
ka·ka·ya pri·kras·na·ya/
u·zhas·na·ya ka·man·da

Go (Spartak)!
(Спартак) – чемпион!
(spar·tak) chim·pi·on

Scum!
На мыло!
na mih·la

ball	мяч m	myach
coach	тренер m	*tre*·nir
corner (kick)	корнер m	*kor*·nir
expulsion	удаление с поля n	u·dal·*ye*·ni·ye s *pol*·ya
fan	болельщик m	bal·*yel*'·shik
	болельщица f	bal·*yel*·shit·sa
foul	нарушение n	na·ru·*she*·ni·ye
free kick	свободный удар m	sva·*bod*·nih u·*dar*
goal	гол m	gol
goalkeeper	голкипер m	gol·*ki*·pir
hooligan	хулиган m	khu·li·*gan*
manager	менеджер m	*mye*·nid·zhihr
offside	офсайд m	of·*seyt*
penalty	пенальти m	pi·*nal*'·ti
player	игрок m	i·*grok*
red card	красная карточка f	*kras*·na·ya *kar*·tach·ka
referee	рефери m	ri·fi·*ri*
streaker	стрикер m	*stri*·kir
striker	бомбардир m	bam·bar·*dir*
yellow card	жёлтая карточка f	*zhol*·ta·ya *kar*·tach·ka

Off to see a match? Check out **going to a game**, page 154.

skiing

Is it possible to go ...?	Можно ли покататься на ...?	*mozh*·na li pa·ka·*tat*'·sa na ...
Alpine skiing	горных лыжах	*gor*·nihkh *lih* zhakh
cross-country skiing	обычных лыжах с палками	a·*bihch*·nlhklı *lih*·zhakh s *pal*·ka·mi
snowboarding	сноуборде	sno·u·*bord*·ye
tobogganing	санках	*san*·kakh

How much is a pass?
Сколько стоит проездной? *skol*'·ka *sto*·it pra·izd·*noy*

Can I take lessons?
Можно ли брать уроки? *mozh*·na li brat' u·*ro*·ki

I'd like to hire (a) …	Я бы хотел/ хотела взять … напрокат. m/f	ya bih khat·yel/ khat·ye·la vzyat' … na·pra·kat
boots	ботинки	ba·tin·ki
gloves	перчатки	pir·chat·ki
goggles	лыжные очки	lihzh·nih·ye ach·ki
poles	палки	pal·ki
skis	лыжи	lih·zhih
ski suit	лыжный костюм	lihzh·nih kast·yum

What level is that slope?

Какого уровня сложности этот склон?	ka·ko·va u·rav·nya slozh·na·sti e·tat sklon

Which are the … slopes?	Какие склоны подойдут для … лыжника?	ka·ki·ye sklo·nih pa·dey·dut dlya … lihzh·ni·ka
beginner	начинающего	na·chi·na·yush·chi·va
intermediate	опытного	o·piht·na·va
advanced	многоопытного	mno·ga·o·piht·na·va

What are the conditions like …?	Какие условия для катания на …?	ka·ki·ye u·slo·vi·ya dlya ka·ta·ni·ya na …
at Elbrus	Эльбрусе	el'·brus·ye
on that run	этой трассе	e·tey tras·ye
higher up	высоте	vih·sat·ye

cable car	фуникулёр m	fu·ni·kul·yor
chairlift	подвесной подъёмник m	pad·vis·noy pad·yom·nik
instructor	инструктор m	in·struk·tar
resort	курорт m	ku·rort
ski lift	подъёмник для лыжников m	pad·yom·nik dlya lihzh·ni·kaf
sled	санки f pl	san·ki

hiking

поход

Where can I ...?	Где можно ...?	gdye *mozh*·na ...
buy supplies	купить продукты	ku·*pit'* pra·*duk*·tih
find someone who knows this area	найти кого-нибудь, кто знает местность	nay·*ti* ka·vo·ni·but' kto *zna*·yet *myes*·nast'
get a map	достать карту	da·*stat'* *kar*·tu
hire hiking gear	взять в прокат обмундирование для туризма	vzyat' f pra·*kat'* ab·mun·di·ra·*va*·ni·ye dlya tu·*riz*·ma

Which is the ... route?	Какой маршрут самый ...?	ka·*koy* marsh·*rut* *sa*·mih ...
easiest	лёгкий	*lyokh*·ki
most interesting	интересный	in·tir·*yes*·nih
shortest	быстрый	*bih*·strih

Is the track ...?	Маршрут ...?	marsh·*rut* ...
(well-)marked	(хорошо) помечен	(kha·ra·*sho*) pam·*ye*·chin
open	открыт	at·*kriht*
scenic	сценический	tsih·*ni*·chi·ski

Do we need to take ...?	Нужно взять ...?	*nuzh*·na vzyat' ...
bedding	спальный мешок	*spal'*·nih mi·*shok*
food	еду	ye·*du*
water	воду	*vo*·du

Where can I find the ...?	Где ...?	gdye ...
camping ground	кемпинг	*kyem*·pink
nearest village	ближайшая деревня	bli·*zhay*·sha·ya dir·*yev*·nya
showers	душ	dush
toilets	туалет	tu·al·*yet*

Is it safe?
Безопасно?
bi·za·*pas*·na

Do we need a guide?
Нам нужен проводник?
nam *nu*·zhihn pra·vad·*nik*

How high is the climb?
Как высоко мы поднимимся?
kak vih·sa·*ko* mih pad·*ni*·mim·sa

How long is the trail?
Какова протяжённость маршрута?
ka·ka·*va* prat·ya·*zho*·nast' marsh·*ru*·ta

Is there a hut?
Есть сторожка?
yest' sta·*rosh*·ka

When does it get dark?
Когда темнеет?
kag·*da* tim·*nye*·yet

Where have you come from?
Откуда вы пришли?
ot·*ku*·da vih prish·*li*

How long did it take?
Сколько времени это заняло?
skol'·ka *vrye*·mi·ni e·ta *zan*·ya·la

---

know your gender

Masculine and feminine markers (m and f) in our phrases always show the subject of a sentence – in the phrase *Я бы хотел/хотела ...* m/f ya bih khat·*yel*/khat·*ye*·la (I'd like ...), the m/f refers to the gender of the speaker.

Does this path go to …?
    Эта тропа ведёт к …?   *e*·ta tra·*pa* vid·*yot* k …

Can I go through here?
    Можно пройти?   *mozh*·na pray·ti

Is the water OK to drink?
    Вода питьевая?   va·*da* pi·ti·*va*·ya

I'm lost.
    Я потерялся/потерялась. m/f   ya pa·tir·*yal*·sa/pa·tir·*ya*·las'

weather

What's the weather like (tomorrow)?
    Какая (завтра) погода?   ka·*ka*·ya (*zaf*·tra) pa·*go*·da

It's …

cloudy	Облачно.	*ob*·lach·na
cold	Холодно.	*kho*·lad·na
fine	Прекрасно.	pri·*kras*·na
freezing	Морозный.	ma·*roz*·nih
frozen	Замёрзший.	zam·*yors*·shih
hot	Жарко.	*zhar*·ka
humid	Влажно.	*vlazh*·na
raining	Идёт дождь.	id·*yot* dozhd'
snowing	Идёт снег.	id·*yut* snyek
sunny	Солнечно.	*sol*·nich·na
warm	Тепло.	ti·*plo*
windy	Ветрено.	*vye*·tri·na

Where can I buy a/an …?	Где можно купить …?	gdye *mozh*·na ku·*pit'* …
rain jacket	плащ	plash
umbrella	зонтик	*zon*·tik

flora & fauna

What ... is that?	Что это за ...?	shto e·ta za ...
animal	животное	zhih·vot·na·ye
flower	цветок	tsvi·tok
plant	растение	rast·ye·ni·ye
tree	дерево	dye·ri·va

Is it ...?	Он ...?	on ...
common	обыкновенный	a·bihk·nav·ye·nih
dangerous	опасный	a·pas·nih
endangered	вымирающий	vih·mi·ra·yu·shi
poisonous	ядовитый	yi·da·vi·tih
protected	заповедный	za·pav·yed·nih

What's it used for?

Для чего это использует?   dlya chi·vo e·ta is·pol'·zu·yit

Can you eat the fruit?

Фрукты можно есть?   fruk·tih mozh·na yest'

For geographical and agricultural terms, and names of animals and plants, see the **dictionary**.

local plants, animals & environments

eagle	орёл m	ar·yol
fir	берёза f	bir·yo·za
fox	лиса f	li·sa
larch	лиственница f	list·vi·nit·sa
pine	сосна f	sas·na
polar bear	белый медведь m	bye·lih mid·vyed'
reindeer	северный олень m	sye·vir·nih al·yen'
seal	тюлень m	tyul·yen'
Siberian tiger	сибирский тигр m	si·bir·ski tigr
spruce	ель f	yel'
taiga	тайга f	tey·ga
tundra	тундра f	tun·dra
steppe	степь f	styep'
wolf	волк m	volk

basic language

простые фразы

breakfast	завтрак m	*zaf*·trak
lunch	обед m	ab·*yet*
dinner	ужин m	*u*·zhihn
snack	закуска f	za·*kus*·ka
eat v	есть	yest'
drink v	пить	pit'
Please.	Пожалуйста.	pa·*zhal*·sta
Thank you.	Спасибо.	spa·*si*·ba

I'd like …
Я бы хотел/хотела … m/f   ya bih khat·*yel*/khat·*ye*·la …

I'm starving!
Я умираю с голоду!   ya u·mi·*ra*·yu z *go*·la·du

Enjoy your meal!
Приятного аппетита!   pri·*yat*·na·va a·*pi·ti*·ta

finding a place to eat

где найти ресторан

Dining out in Russia offers various specialist cafés as well as
столовая sta·*lo*·va·ya – a type of cheap and (almost) cheerful
canteen found in stations or market areas. Many stations and
hotels also have small *буфет* buf·*yet* (buffets) or *шведский
стол* shvyet·ski stol (smorgasbords). Some of these eateries do
с собой s sa·*boy* (take away).

snack time

For *уличная пища* u·lich·na·ya *pish·*cha (street food) try a *закусочная* za·*ku*·sach·na·ya (snack bar) like the ones below.

блинная f   *bli*·na·ya
Serves pancakes with savoury or sweet fillings.

бутербродная f   bu·tir·*brod*·na·ya
Prepares small open sandwiches.

закусочная f   za·*ku*·sach·na·ya
Offers miscellaneous snacks such as *кебаб* ki·*bap* (kebab), *пирожок* pi·ra·*zhok* (spicy mutton pie) or *сосиски* sa·*sis*·ki (fried or boiled sausage).

пельменная f   pilm·*ye*·na·ya
Specialises in meat ravioli.

пирожковая f   pi·rash·*ko*·va·ya
Sells deep-fried meat or vegetable turnovers.

чебуречная f   chi·bur·*yech*·na·ya
Cooks Armenian or Georgian spicy, deep-fried mutton pies.

шашлычная f   shash·*lihch*·na·ya
Serves up charcoal-grilled meat kebabs.

Can you recommend a ...?	Вы можете порекомендовать ...?	vih *mo*·zhiht·ye pa·ri·ka·min·da·*vat'* ...
café	кафе	ka·*fe*
canteen	столовую	sta·*lo*·vu·yu
dumpling café	пельменную	pilm·*ye*·nu·yu
kebab café	шашлычную	shash·*lihch*·nu·yu
restaurant	ресторан	ri·sta·*ran*
pastry café	кондитерскую	kan·*di*·tir·sku·yu
snack bar	закусочную	za·*ku*·sach·nu·yu

I'd like to reserve a table for …	Я бы хотел/ хотела заказать столик на … m/f	ya bih khat·yel/ khat·ye·la za·ka·zat' sto·lik na …
two people	двоих	dva·ikh
(eight) o'clock	(восемь) часов	(vo·sim') chi·sof

Are you still serving food?
Кухня открыта?   kukh·nya at·krih·ta

How long is the wait?
Как долго ждать?   kak dol·ga zhdat'

at the restaurant

I'd like (a/the) …, please.	Я бы хотел … m Я бы хотела … f	ya bih khat·yel … ya bih khat·ye·la …
children's menu	детское меню	dyet·ska·ye min·yu
drink list	карту вин	kur·tu vin
half portion	пол-порцию	pol·port·sih·yu
local speciality	местную специальность	myes·nu·yu spit·sih·al'·nast'
menu (in English)	меню (на английском)	min·yu (na an·gli·skam)
nonsmoking	некурящий	nye·kur·yash·chi
smoking	курящий	kur·yash·chi
table for (three)	столик на (троих)	sto·lik na (tra·ikh)
that dish	это блюдо	e·ta blyu·da

What would you recommend?
Что вы рекомендуете?   shto vih ri·ka·min·*du*·it·ye

What's in that dish?
Что входит в это блюдо?   shto *fkho*·dit v e·ta *blyu*·da

What's that called?
Как это называется?   kak e·ta na·zih·*va*·it·sa

Is it self-serve?
Здесь   zdyes'
самообслуживание?   sa·ma·aps·*lu*·zhih·va·ni·ye

Are these complimentary?
Это бесплатно?   e·ta bis·*plat*·na

I'd like it with …	Можно мне с …	*mozh*·na mnye s …
cheese	сыром	*sih*·ram
chilli	перцом	*pyert*·sam
chilli sauce	чили соусом	*chi*·li *sou*·sam
garlic	чесноком	chis·na·*kom*
ketchup	кетчупом	*kyet*·chu·pam
nuts	орехами	ar·*ye*·kha·mi
oil	маслом	*mas*·lam
pepper	перцом	*pyert*·sam
sauce	соусом	*sou*·sam
tomato sauce	кетчупом	*kyet*·chu·pam
vinegar	уксусом	*uk*·su·sam

I'd like it without …	Можно мне без …	*mozh*·na mnye byes …
cheese	сыра	*sih*·ra
chilli	перца	*pyert*·sa
chilli sauce	чили соуса	*chi*·li *sou*·sa
garlic	чеснока	chis·na·*ka*
ketchup	кетчупа	*kyet*·chu·pa
nuts	орехов	ar·*ye*·khaf
oil	масла	*mas*·la
pepper	перца	*pyert*·sa
sauce	соуса	*sou*·sa
tomato sauce	кетчупа	*kyet*·chu·pa
vinegar	уксуса	*uk*·su·sa

For other specific meal requests, see **vegetarian & special meals**, page 181.

For other specific meal requests, see **vegetarian & special meals**, page 181.

---

local brews

компот m   kam·*pot*
A brew of boiled water with fruits and sugar, served either hot or cold.

кефир m   ki·*fir*
Buttermilk served cold as a breakfast drink and recommended as a cure for hangovers.

молочный коктейль m   ma·*loch*·nih kak·*teyl*
'Milk cocktails' – milkshakes made with ice cream and fruit syrup.

морс m   mors
A fresh fruit juice made from blackberries, cranberries or raspberries.

простокваша f   pra·stak·*va*·sha
Fermented sour milk – a traditional Russian elixir for good health.

сбитень m   *zbi*·tin'
A drink made from honey, treacle, cinnamon and mint boiled in water, usually served hot with cakes and biscuits.

If this list doesn't match your menu, yours might be written in lower-case or italics (see the box on page 14).

ЗАКУСКИ	za·*kus*·ki	**Appetisers**
ПЕРВЫЕ БЛЮДА	*pyer*·vih·ye *blyu*·da	**First Courses**
САЛАТЫ	sa·*la*·tih	**Salads**
ВТОРЫЕ БЛЮДА	fta·*rih*·ye *blyu*·da	**Main Courses**
МУЧНЫЕ БЛЮДА	much·*nih*·ye *blyu*·da	**Grain Dishes**
ОВОЩНЫЕ БЛЮДА	a·vash·*nih*·ye *blyu*·da	**Vegetables**
РЫБНЫЕ БЛЮДА	*rihb*·nih·ye *blyu*·da	**Fish**
ДИЧЬ И ПТИЦА	dyich' i *ptit*·sa	**Game & Poultry**
МЯСНЫЕ БЛЮДА	mis·*nih*·ye *blyu*·da	**Meat**
ЯИЧНЫЕ БЛЮДА	yi·*ich*·nih·ye *blyu*·da	**Egg Dishes**
СЫР И ТВОРОГ	sihr i tva·*rok*	**Cheese & Dairy**
ПИРОЖКИ	pi·*rash*·ki	**Pies**
ПЕЛЬМЕНИ	pilm·*ye*·nih	**Dumplings**
ФИРМЕННЫЕ БЛЮДА	*fir*·mi·nih·ye *blyu*·da	**House Specials**
ДОМАШНИЕ БЛЮДА	da·*mash*·ni·ye *blyu*·da	**Home-style Dishes**
НАЦИОНАЛЬНЫЕ БЛЮДА	nat·sih·a·*nal'*·nih·ye *blyu*·da	**National & Ethnic Dishes**
ДИЕТИЧЕСКИЕ БЛЮДА	di·ye·*ti*·chi·ski·ye *blyu*·da	**Special Diets**
СЛАДКИЕ БЛЮДА	*slat*·ki·ye *blyu*·da	**Desserts**
АПЕРИТИВЫ	a·pi·ra·*ti*·vih	**Apéritifs**
НАПИТКИ	na·*pit*·ki	**Drinks**
БЕЗАЛКОГОЛЬНЫЕ НАПИТКИ	bi·zal·ka·*gol'*·nih·ye na·*pit*·ki	**Soft Drinks**
ПИВО	*pi*·va	**Beers**
ШАМПАНСКОЕ	sham·*pan*·ska·ye	**Sparkling Wines & Champagnes**
БЕЛОЕ ВИНО	*bye*·la·ye vi·*no*	**White Wines**
КРАСНОЕ ВИНО	*kras*·na·ye vi·*no*	**Red Wines**
ДЕССЕРТНОЕ ВИНО	di·*sert*·na·ye vi·*no*	**Dessert Wines**
СПИРТНЫЕ НАПИТКИ	spirt·*nih*·ye na·*pit*·ki	**Spirits**
ВОДКА	*vot*·ka	**Vodkas**

at the table

за столом

Please bring (a/the) ...	Принесите, пожалуйста ...	pri·ni·*sit*·ye pa·*zhal*·sta ...
bill	счёт	shot
cloth	тряпку	*tryap*·ku
glass	стакан	sta·*kan*
serviette	салфетку	salf·*yet*·ku
wineglass	рюмку	*ryum*·ku

ashtray
пепельница f
pye·pil'·nit·sa

spoon
ложка f
losh·ka

fork
вилка f
vil·ka

plate
тарелка f
tar·*yel*·ka

knife
нож m
nosh

wineglass
рюмка f
ryum·ka

glass
стакан m
sta·*kan*

table
столик m
sto·lik

eating out

169

talking food

I love this dish.
Это блюдо очень
вкусное.

e·ta *blyu*·da *o*·chin'
fkus·na·ye

I love the local cuisine.
Мне очень нравится
местная кухня.

mnye *o*·chin' *nra*·vit·sa
myes·na·ya *kukhn*·ya

That was delicious!
Было очень вкусно!

bih·la *o*·chin' *fkus*·na

My compliments to the chef.
Похвалу повару!

pakh·va·*lu po*·va·ru

I'm full.
Я наелся. m
Я наелась. f

ya na·*yel*·sa
ya na·*ye*·las'

This is …	Это …	*e*·ta …
(too) cold	(слишком)	(*slish*·kam)
	холодное	kha·*lod*·na·ye
spicy	острое	*o*·stra·ye
superb	великолепное	vi·li·kal·*yep*·na·ye

---

eating in

Russian food is simple, generous, and appetising. A typical
Russian breakfast, for instance, consists of *каша ka*·sha
(buckwheat porridge), *хлеб* khlyep (bread) and *кефир* ki·*fir*
(sour milk).

methods of preparation

способы приготовления

I'd like it …	…, пожалуйста.	… pa·*zhal*·sta
(deep-)fried	(Сильно) Жареное	(*sil'*·na) *zha*·ri·na·ye
grilled	В гриле	v *gril*·ye
rare	Поджаренное	pad·*zha*·ri·na·ye
raw	Сырое	sih·*ro*·ye
steamed	Паровое	pa·ra·*vo*·ye
well-done	Хорошо	kha·ra·*sho*
	прожаренное	pra·*zha*·ri·na·ye
without …	Без …	byez …

nonalcoholic drinks

безалкогольные напитки

… water	… вода f	… va·*da*
boiled	кипячёная	ki·pi·*cho*·na·ya
soda	газированная	ga·zi·*ro*·va·na·ya
(sparkling)	(шипучая)	(shih·*pu*·cha·ya)
mineral	минеральная	mi·ni·*ral'*·na·ya
fruit juice	фруктовый сок m	fruk·*to*·vih sok
lemonade	лимонад m	li·ma·*nat*
soft drink	безалкогольный	bye·zal·ka·*gol'*·nih
	напиток m	na·*pi*·tak
tea …	чай … m	chey …
cup of tea …	чашка чаю … f	*chash*·ka *cha*·yu …
herbal tea …	чай из трав … m	chey is traf …
with lemon	с лимоном	s li·*mo*·nam
with honey	с мёдом	s *myo*·dam
with jam	с вареньем	s var·*ye*·nim

coffee

Getting *кофе kof·ye* (coffee) the way you want it is traditionally difficult in Russia. It's often brewed in pre-mixed batches with milk and/or sugar, so you'd be wise to order *с молоком/сахаром s* ma·la·*kom/sa*·kha·ram (with milk/sugar) or *без молока/сахару byez* ma·la·*ka/sa*·kha·ru (without milk/sugar). Here are some other options for the coffee aficionado.

... coffee	кофе ... n	*kof·ye ...*
cup of ... coffee	чашка кофе ... f	*chash·ka kof·ye ...*
decaffeinated	без кафеина	byes kaf·ye·*i*·na
iced	со льдом	sa ldom
strong	крепкий	*krep·*ki
Turkish	по-турецки	pa·tur·*yets*·ki
weak	слабый	*sla·*bih

alcoholic drinks

алкогольные напитки

brandy	коньяк m	kan·*yak*
champagne	шампанское n	sham·*pan*·ska·ye
cocktail	коктейль m	kak·*teyl*
50/100 grams of ...	пятьдесят/ сто грамм ...	pi·dis·*yat/* sto gram ...
gin	джина	*dzhih*·na
rum	рома	*ro*·ma
sherry	хереса	*khye*·ri·sa
vodka	водки	*vot*·ki
whisky	виски	*vis*·ki
... beer	... пиво n	... *pi*·va
draught	бочковое	*boch*·ka·va·ye
lager	светлое	*svyet*·la·ye
light	лёгкое	*lyokh*·ka·ye
stout	тёмное	*tyom*·na·ye

a ... of beer	... пива n	... *pi*·va
small bottle	маленькая бутылка	*ma*·lin'·ka·ya bu·*tihl*·ka
large bottle	большая бутылка	bal'·*sha*·ya bu·*tihl*·ka
glass	стакан	sta·*kan*
jug	кувшин	kuf·*shihn*
mug	кружка	*krush*·ka
pint	пинта	*pin*·ta

a bottle/glass	бутылка/рюмка	bu·*tihl*·ka/*ryum*·ka
of ... wine	... вина f/f	... vi·*na*
dessert	дессертного	dis·*yert*·na·va
dry	сухого	su·*kho*·va
red	красного	*kras*·na·va
rosé	розового	*ro*·za·va·va
semidry	полусухого	pa·lu·su·*kho*·va
semisweet	полусладкого	pa·lus·*lat*·ka·va
sparkling	шипучего	shih·*pu*·chi·va
sweet	сладкого	*slat*·ka·va
white	белого	*bye*·la·va

not drinking with the locals

When you simply can't take another vodka hangover, you need to know how to fend off the alcohol you'll be so generously served. It's not acceptable to only drink some of what you're given, but you can say *чуть-чуть* chut'·*chut'* (just a little) when your glass is being refilled – that way you're only forced to down half as much. And if your protests are still to no avail, try the moral high ground of *Я лечусь от алкоголя* ya li·*chus'* at al·ka·*gol'*·ya (I'm a recovering alcoholic). The praise you'll earn from this confession will add a lovely touch of irony to your drinking tales when you get home …

in the bar

в баре

A lot of public drinking happens in a *кафе* ka·*fe* (café), *ресторан* ri·sta·*ran* (restaurant) or *бар* bar (bar). Russians can also be found in the local *трактир* trak·*tir*, which is more like a typical pub, or in a *пивная* piv·*na*·ya (tavern). During the Soviet era the *пивная* was where you'd line up to collect your ration of vodka, and it's still considered the place to go to get under the table fast.

Can you recommend a …?	Вы можете порекомен- довать …?	vih *mo*·zhiht·ye pa·ri·ka·*min*· da·*vat'* …
bar	бар	bar
pub	трактир	trak·*tir*
tavern	пивную	piv·*nu*·yu

Is anyone serving?
    Кто здесь подаёт?   kto zdyes' pa·da·*yot*

I'm next.
    Я следующий. m   ya *slye*·du·yu·shi
    Я следующая. f   ya *slye*·du·yu·sha·ya

I'll have …
    …, пожалуйста.   … pa·*zhal*·sta

Same again, please.
    Ещё то же самое!   ye·*sho* to zhe sa·ma·ye

No ice, thanks.
    Безо льда.   *bye*·za lda

Let's have a drink!
    Давайте выпьем!   da·*veyt*·ye *vih*·pim

My round.
    Я угощаю.   ya u·ga·*sha*·yu

What would you like?
    Что вы хотите?   shto vih kha·*ti*·tye

I don't drink alcohol.
    Я не пью спиртного.   ya nye pyu spirt·*no*·va

How much is that?
    Сколько с нас?   *skol'*·ka s nas

Do you have any cold drinks?
    У вас есть холодное?   u vas yest' kha·*lod*·na·ye

shouting match

It's bad form to try to split the bill for meals when eating out, so fight to pay for everyone – say *Уберите деньги, я угощаю!* u·bi·*rit*·ye *dyen'*·gi ya u·ga·*sha*·yu, which means 'Put your money away, it's my shout'. If you lose, return the compliment later.

drinking up

This is hitting the spot.
Это как раз! · e·ta kak ras

I feel fantastic!
Я чувствую себя отлично! · ya *chust*·vu·yu sib·*ya* at·*lich*·na

Do you respect me?
Ты меня уважаешь? inf · tih min·*ya* u·va·*zha*·yesh'

I think I've had one too many.
Я напился/напилась. m/f · ya na·*pil*·sa/na·*pi*·las'

I'm feeling drunk.
Я пьяный/пьяная. m/f · ya *pya*·nih/*pya*·na·ya

I'm pissed.
Я мертвецки пьяный. m · ya mirt·*vyet*·ski *pya*·nih
Я мертвецки пьяная. f · ya mirt·*vyet*·ski *pya*·na·ya

I'm going to throw up.
Меня будет мутить. · min·*ya* *bu*·dit mu·*tit*'

Where's the toilet?
Где туалет? · gdye tu·al·*yet*

your weight in alcohol

Russians measure their spirits in grams, not shots. The equivalent of a shot is *пятьдесят грамм* pi·dis·*yat* gram (50g), and a double is about *сто грамм* sto gram (100g). If you don't want to order a whole bottle of spirits at a restaurant or bar, you can order by weight – a common amount to share over a meal is *двести грамм* dvye·sti gram (200g).

vodka

The clichéd Russian drink is, of course, *водка vot·ka* – your average Russian drinks more than a bottle of 'little water' per week. Vodka is perfect, according to the locals, when chilled to 10°C and sculled by the *пятьдесят* pit'·dis·*yat* (50 gram shot). Mixing or sipping vodka is considered both cowardly and in poor form. When toasting with vodka or *самогон* sa·ma·*gon* (home-made vodka), say *Пей до дна!* pyey da dna (Drink to the bottom!) then empty your glass. Beware – you need to do this for every toast. A bottle of vodka is traditionally shared between three, so if there are only two of you, you can ask a potential drinking partner *Третьим будешь?* trye·tim bu·dish' (Will you be the third?).

Vodka is considered the universal remedy, guaranteed to cure everything from the common cold to a hangover. You'll also see Russians participating in a bread-and-vodka ritual. To try it yourself, get a *пятьдесят* and a piece of *хлеб чёрный* khlyep *chor*·nih (rye bread). Breathe in and out quickly, bringing your food to the tip of your nose in a kind of blessing. Down your vodka in one shot, and eat your food.

Here are some vodkas available in Russia. *Пей до дна!*

vodka ...	водка ... f	*vot*·ka ...
with apple	яблочная	*ya*·blach·na·ya
with ash berries	рябиновка	rya·*bi*·naf·ka
with caraway	тминная	*tmi*·na·ya
with cinnamon, lemon & bison grass	зубровка	zu·*brof*·ka
'Hunter's vodka' (with peppers, berries, ginger & cloves)	охотничья	a·*khot*·ni·cha
with lemon	лимонная	li·*mo*·na·ya
with pepper	перцовка	pirt·*sof*·ka
Moskovskaya (with sodium bicarbonate)	московская	mas·*kof*·ska·ya
Stolichnaya (with infused sugar)	столичная	sta·*lich*·na·ya

I'm tired, I'd better go home.
  Я устал/устала,   ya u·*stal*/u·*sta*·la
  пора идти домой. m/f   pa·*ra* i·*ti* da·*moy*

Can you call a taxi for me?
  Закажите мне такси.   za·ka·*zhih*·t·ye mnye tak·*si*

I don't think you should drive.
  Вы не должны   vih nye dalzh·*nih*
  водить машину.   va·*dit'* ma·*shih*·nu

I have a hangover.
  Я с похмелья.   ya s pakh·*myel*·ya

Beer is bad for you!
  Пиво тебе вредно! inf   *pi*·va tyib·*ye vryed*·na

---

buying food

What's the local speciality?
Что типично местное? — shto ti·*pich*·na *myes*·na·ye

What's that?
Что это? — shto *e*·ta

Can I taste it?
Дайте мне попробовать! — *deyt*·ye mnye pa·*pro*·ba·vat'

Can I have a bag, please?
Дайте, пожалуйста, пакет. — *deyt*·ye pa·*zhal*·sta pak·*yet*

I don't need a bag, thanks.
Пакет не нужен. — pak·*yet* nye *nu*·zhihn

How much (is a kilo of cheese)?
Сколько стоит (кило сыра)? — *skol'*·ka *sto*·it (ki·*lo* sih·ra)

I'd like (a) …	Дайте …	*deyt*·ye …
ten	десяток	dis·*ya*·tak
(200) grams	(двести) грамм	(*dvye*·sti) gram
half a kilo	полкило	pol·ki·*lo*
(two) kilos	(два) кило	(dva) ki·*lo*
bottle	бутылку	bu·*tihl*·ku
jar/tin	банку	*ban*·ku
packet	пакет	pak·*yet*
piece	кусок	ku·*sok*
(three) pieces	(три) куска	(tri) kus·*ka*
slice	ломтик	*lom*·tik
(six) slices	(шесть) ломтика	(shest') *lom*·ti·ka
(just) a little	(только) немного	(*tol'*·ka) nim·*no*·ga
more	ещё	yi·*sho*
some …	немного …	nim·*no*·ga …
that one	то	to
this one	это	*e*·ta

Less.	Меньше.	*myen'*·shih
A bit more.	Ещё немного.	yi·*sho* nim·*no*·ga
Enough.	Достаточно.	da·*sta*·tach·na

Do you have ...?	У вас есть ...?	u vas yest' ...
anything	что-нибудь	*shto*·ni·but'
cheaper	подешевле	pa·di·*shev*·lye
other kinds	другие	dru·*gi*·ye

Where can I find the ... section?	Где продают ...?	gdye pra·da·*yut* ...
bread	хлеб	khlyep
dairy	молоко	ma·la·*ko*
dried goods	сушёные продукты	su·*sho*·nih·ye pra·*duk*·tih
fish	рыбу	*rih*·bu
frozen goods	замороженные продукты	za·ma·*ro*·zhih·nih·ye pra·*duk*·tih
fruit & vegetable	овощи и фрукты	*o*·va·shi i *fruk*·tih
meat	мясо	*mya*·sa

cooking utensils

приборы

Could I please borrow a ...?	Можно взять ...?	*mozh*·na vzyat' ...
frying pan	сковороду	ska·va·ra·*du*
knife	нож	nosh
samovar	самовар	sa·ma·*var*
saucepan	кастрюлю	kast·*ryul*·yu

For more cooking implements, see the **dictionary**.

vegetarian & special meals
вегетарианские и особые блюда

ordering food

Is there a ... restaurant nearby?	Здесь есть ... ресторан?	zdyes' yest' ... ri·sta·*ran*
halal	халал	kha·*lal*
kosher	кошерный	ka·*sher*·nih
vegetarian	вегетарианский	vi·gi·ta·ri·*an*·ski
Could you prepare a meal without ...?	Вы могли бы приготовить блюдо без ...?	vih ma·*gli* bih pri·ga·*to*·vit' *blu*·da byez ...
I don't eat ...	Я не ем ...	ya nye yem ...
butter	масла	*mas*·la
eggs	яиц	*ya*·its
fish	рыбы	*rih*·bih
fish stock	рыбного бульона	*rihb*·na·va bu·*lo*·na
meat stock	мясного бульона	myas·*no*·va bu·*lo*·na
oil	масла	*mas*·la
pork	свинины	svi·*ni*·nih
poultry	птицы	*ptit*·sih
red meat	мяса	*mya*·sa

give the man meat

Vegetarians could have a hard time outside of the big cities – most Russians consider that they haven't eaten at all unless meat appears in their meal. It's advised that you don't goad meat-eaters with statements like Мясник, как вам не стыдно! myas·*nik* kak vam nye *stihd*·na (Butcher, have you no shame?).

cured/salted	солёный	*sal·yo·*nih
dried	сушёный	*su·sho·*nih
fresh	свежий	*svye·*zhih
frozen	замороженный	*za·ma·ro·*zhih·nih
marinated	маринованный	*ma·ri·no·va·*nih
smoked	копчёный	*kap·cho·*nih
stuffed	фаршированный	*far·shih·ro·va·*nih

Is this …?	Это …?	*e·*ta …
decaffeinated	без кофеина	byes kaf·ye·*i·*na
free of animal produce	без животных продуктов	byes zhih·*vot·*nihkh pra·*duk·*taf
free-range	от курицы, живущей на свободном выгуле	at *ku·*rit·sih zhih·*vush·*chey na sva·*bod·*nam *vih·*gu·li
genetically modified	генетически модифицировано	gi·ni·*ti·*chi·ski mo·di·fit·*sih·*ra·va·na
gluten-free	без клейковины	byes kli·ka·*vi·*nih
low-fat	маложирно	ma·la·*zhihr·*na
low in sugar	с низким содержанием сахара	s *nis·*kim sa·dir·*zha·*ni·yem *sa·*kha·ra
organic	органически	ar·ga·*ni·*chi·ski
salt-free	без соли	byes *so·*li

I love animals so I don't eat them.

Я люблю животных, поэтому я не ем их.	ya lyub·*lyu* zhih·*vot·*nihkh pa·*e·*ta·mu ya nye yem ikh

Meat is murder.

Мясо есть убийство.	*mya·*sa yest' u·*bist·*va

special diets & allergies

особые диеты и аллергии

I'm on a special/strict diet.
Я на особенной/
строгой диете.

ya na a·*so*·bi·ney/
stro·gey di·*yet*·ye

I'm (a) ...	Я ...	уа ...
Buddhist	буддист m	bu·*dist*
	буддистка f	bu·*dist*·ka
Hindu	индус/индуска m/f	in·*dus*/in·*dus*·ka
Jewish	еврей/еврейка m/f	yiv·*ryey*/yiv·*ryey*·ka
Muslim	мусульманин m	mu·sul'·*ma*·nin
	мусульманка f	mu·sul'·*man*·ka
vegan	веган/веганка m/f	*vye*·gan/*vye*·gan·ka
vegetarian	вегетарианец m	vi·gi·ta·ri·*a*·nits
	вегетарианка f	vi·gi·ta·ri·*an*·ka

vegetarian & special meals

183

I'm allergic to ...	У меня	u min·ya
	аллергия на ...	a·lir·gi·ya na ...
crustaceans	ракообразных	ra·ka·a·braz·nihkh
dairy produce	молочные	ma·loch·nih·ye
	продукты	pra·duk·tih
eggs	яйца	yeyt·sa
gelatine	желатин	zhih·la·tin
gluten	клейковину	klyey·ka·vi·nu
honey	мёд	myot
molluscs	моллюсков	mal·yu·skaf
MSG	МНГ	em·en·ge
nuts	орехи	ar·ye·khi
peanuts	арахисы	a·ra·khi·sih
seafood (general)	морепродукты	mor·ye·pra·duk·tih

talk to the animals

To form a stronger bond with Russian animal life, try these phrases ...

Quiet!	Молчать!	mal·chat'
Stand!	Стоять!	sta·yat'
Sit!	Сидеть!	sid·yet'
Shake hands!	Дай лапу!	day la·pu
Here (boy/girl)!	Сюда, сюда!	syu·da syu·da
What a nice	Какая милая	ka·ka·ya mi·la·ya
cat/dog!	кошка/собака!	kosh·ka/sa·ba·ka

Don't be tempted to use these ones with people ...

| Puss puss! | Кис кис кис! | kis·kis·kis |
| Give us a kiss! | Ну, поцелуй меня! | nu pat·se·luy min·ya |

culinary reader

кулинарный словарь

This miniguide to Russian cuisine is designed to help you get the most out of your gastronomic experience by providing you with food terms that you may see on menus. Nouns have their gender indicated by ⓜ, ⓕ or ⓝ, while adjectives are given in the masculine form only. Both nouns and adjectives are provided in the nominative case. For an explanation of case, and how to form feminine and neuter adjectives, see the **phrasebuilder**, pages 17 & 18.

> This **culinary reader** has been ordered according to the Cyrillic alphabet, shown below in both roman and italic text:
>
> Аа Бб Вв Гг Дд Ее Ёё Жж Зз Ии Йй Кк Лл Мм Нн Оо Пп
> *Аа Бб Вв Гг Дд Ее Ёё Жж Зз Ии Йй Кк Лл Мм Нн Оо Пп*
>
> Рр Сс Тт Уу Фф Хх Цц Чч Шш Щщ Ъъ Ыы Ьь Ээ Юю Яя
> *Рр Сс Тт Уу Фф Хх Цц Чч Шш Щщ Ъъ Ыы Ьь Ээ Юю Яя*

А

абрикос ⓜ a·bri·*kos* apricot
авсень ⓜ af·*syen'* beef or pork brain & tongue cooked with vegetables & spices
авюторга ⓕ av·yu·*tor*·ga pickled mullet
азербайджанский плов ⓜ a·zir·bey·*dzhan*·ski plof Azerbaijan pilau with almonds, sesame seeds & ginger
азу из говядины ⓝ a·zu iz gav·*ya*·di·nih beef stew with vegetables & spices
антрекот ⓜ an·tri·*kot* entrecôte (boned sirloin steak)
апельсин ⓜ a·pil'·*sin* orange
апельсиновый сок ⓜ a·pil'·*si*·na·vih sok orange juice
арахис ⓜ a *ra* khis peanut
арбуз ⓜ ar·*bus* melon • rockmelon • watermelon

Б

бабка ⓕ *bap*·ka baked meat & potato • cake
— **ромовая** ⓕ *ro*·ma·va·ya rum cake
— **яблочная** ⓕ *ya*·blach·na·ya apple cake
баклажан ⓜ ba·kla·*zhan* aubergine • eggplant
— **в сметане** f smi·*tan*·ye fried eggplant & onions with sour cream
— **фаршированный** far·shih·*ro*·va·nih eggplant stuffed with vegetables
балык сорпа ⓕ ba·*lihk* sor·pa stew of mutton, sheep tail fat, rice & sour milk
банан ⓜ ba·*nan* banana
баранина ⓕ ba·*ra*·ni·na lamb • mutton
булочка ⓕ *bu*·lach·ka bread rolls
бекон ⓜ bi·*kon* bacon
бефстроганов ⓜ bif·stra·ga·*nof* beef stroganoff – braised beef with sour cream & mushrooms
биточки ⓕ pl bi·*toch*·ki meatballs, often served in tomato sauce
бифштекс ⓜ bif·*shteks* steak – usually glorified hamburger filling
блинчики ⓜ pl blin·*chi*·ki pancakes – either rolled around meat or cheese & or filled with jam or another sweet filling
— **с мясом** s *mya*·sam pancakes & meat
блины ⓜ pl bli·*nih* buckwheat pancakes
— **картофельные с икрой** kar·to·fil'·nih·ye s i·*kroy* potato pancakes with red caviar
— **со сметаной** sa smi·*ta*·ney baked pancakes with sour cream
бобовые ⓝ pl ba·*bo*·vih·ye legumes
борщ ⓜ borsh beetroot soup with vegetables & meat
— **зелёный** zil·*yo*·nih green beetroot soup with sorrel & sour cream

culinary reader

185

— **московский** mas·*kof*·ski *Moscow beetroot soup with beef & frankfurters*

— **постный** *post*·nih *meatless beetroot soup*

— **украинский** u·kra·*in*·ski *Ukrainian beetroot soup with vegetables*

ботвинья ⓕ bat·*vi*·nya *fish soup with green vegetables & kvass*

брокколи ⓝ bro·*ka*·li *broccoli*

брусника ⓕ brus·*ni*·ka *cranberries*

брынза ⓕ *brihn*·za *salty white cheese*

бульон ⓜ bu·*lon chicken broth*

В

в гриле v *gril*·ye *grilled*

в сметане f smi·*tan*·ye *in sour cream*

в томате f ta·*mat*·ye *in tomato*

варево ⓝ *va*·ri·va *liquid dishes*

вареники ⓝ pl var·*ye*·ni·ki *dumplings with berries inside, then topped with sugar*

— **с картофелем** s kar·*to*·fil·yem *fried potato* **вареники**

варёное мясо порусски ⓝ var·*yo*·na·ye *mya*·sa pa·*rus*·ki *Russian-style boiled beef*

варёный var·*yo*·nih *boiled • poached*

варенье ⓝ var·*yen*·ye *jam • fruit cooked in sugar*

ватрушки pl vat·*rush*·ki *pastries with cottage cheese & sour cream*

вегетарианский vi·gi·ta·ri·*an*·ski *vegetarian*

вермишель ⓕ vir·mi·*shel' noodles*

ветчина ⓕ vit·chi·*na ham*

взвар ⓜ vzvar *vegetable or herb sauce*

винегрет ⓜ vi·nig·*ryet 'winter salad' — potato, carrot, beetroot, onion & pickles*

виноград ⓜ vi·na·*grat grapes*

вишня ⓕ *vish*·nya *cherry*

вырезка по-таёжному *vih*·ris·ka pa·ta·*yozh*·na·mu *cubed steak with herbs*

Г

говядина ⓕ gav·*ya*·di·na *beef*

гоголь-моголь ⓜ *go*·gal' *mo*·gal' *whipped egg yolks with alcohol & sugar*

голубь ⓜ *go*·lub' *pigeon*

голубцы ⓜ pl ga·lub·*tsih cabbage rolls stuffed with meat & rice*

— **вегетарианские** vi·gi·ta·ri·*an*·ski·ye *cabbage rolls with mushrooms & carrots*

горох ⓜ ga·*rokh peas*

гребешки ⓜ pl gri·*bish*·ki *scallops*

гренки ⓜ pl grin·*ki toast fried in butter*

грецкий орех ⓜ *gryets*·ki ar·*yekh walnut*

грибы ⓜ pl gri·*bih mushrooms*

— **в сметане** f smi·*tan*·ye *mushrooms baked in sour cream*

груша ⓕ *gru*·sha *pear*

гурьевская каша ⓕ gur·*yef*·ska·ya *ka*·sha *porridge with caramelised nuts & fruits*

гусь ⓜ gus' *goose*

Д

дары моря ⓜ pl da·*rih mor*·ya *seafood*

дзеренина ⓕ dzir·ye·*ni*·na *wild goat cutlets, served with fried potatoes, mushrooms & pickled fruits*

деруны ⓜ pl dra·ru·*nih Ukrainian potato pancakes with cream & preserves*

драники ⓕ *dra*·ni·ki *potato pancakes*

драчона ⓕ dra·*cho*·na *baked egg & milk mix served with parsley*

дыня ⓕ *dihn*·ya *melon*

Ж

жаренина ⓕ zha·ri·*ni*·na *potatoes baked in milk & buckwheat*

жареница ⓕ zha·ri·*nit*·sa *fish pie*

жареный *zha*·ri·nih *fried • roasted*

— **поросёнок** ⓜ pa·ras·*yo*·nak *roasted suckling pig*

жаркое ⓝ zhar·*ko*·ye *meat or poultry stewed in a clay pot*

— **из медвежатины** is mid·vi·*zha*·ti·na *bear-meat stew*

— **по-домашнему** pa·da·*mash*·ni·mu *'home-style' meat stew with vegetables*

харчо ⓜ zhar·*cho Georgian lamb soup with cherries, walnuts, rice & vegetables*

житня ⓕ *zhiht*·nya *rye porridge*

жюльен куриный в кокотницах ⓜ zhyul'·*yen* ku·*ri*·nih f ka·*kot*·ni·tsakh *chicken, mushroom & Swiss cheese bake*

З

зайчатина ⓕ zey·*cha*·ti·na *rabbit meat*

запеканка ⓕ za·pi·*kan*·ka *pie of cottage cheese, semolina, sour cream & raisins*

запечённый za·pi·*cho*·nih *baked*

заяц ⓜ *za*·yits *hare*

зелень ⓕ *zye*·lin' *greens • herbs*

земляника ⓕ zim·li·*ni*·ka *wild strawberries*

зразы картофельные ⓕ pl *zra*·zih kar·to·*fil'*·nih·ye *boiled potatoes mixed with mince & fried in small cakes*

И

изюм ⓜ *iz·yum* raisins

икра ⓕ *i·kra* caviar
— **баклажанная** *ba·kla·zha·na·ya*
eggplant caviar – baked eggplant blended
with tomato & onion (like baba ghanooj)
— **красная** *kras·na·ya* red caviar (salmon)
— **чёрная** *chor·na·ya*
black caviar (sturgeon)

индейка ⓕ *in·dyey·ka* turkey

инжир ⓜ *in·zhihr* figs

К

кабачок ⓜ *ka·ba·chok* courgette • zucchini

казахский плов ⓜ *ka·zakh·ski plof*
pilau with lamb, carrots & apricots

какао ⓝ *ka·ka·o* milky cocoa

кальмары ⓜ pl *kal'·ma·rïa* squid

капуста ⓕ *ka·pu·sta* sauerkraut
— **с помидорами** *s pa·mi·do·ra·mi*
cabbage with thickened tomato sauce

карп ⓜ *karp* carp

карри ⓜ *ka·ri* curry

картофель ⓜ *kar·to·fil'* potato
— **в мундире** *v mun·dir·ye*
baked jacket potatoes
— **фаршированный грибами**
far·shih·ro·va·nih gri·ba·mi
potatoes stuffed with mushroom & onion,
drizzled with sour cream then baked

картофлянки ⓜ pl *kar·tof·lyan·ki*
baked potato dumplings

картошка ⓕ *kar·tosh·ka* potato

картошник ⓜ *kar·tosh·nik*
potatoes boiled, mixed with cheeses,
cream & baking powder then baked

катык ⓜ *ka·tihk* fermented clotted milk

каша ⓕ *ka·sha* buckwheat porridge
— **сименуха** *si·mi·nu·kha*
porridge with mushrooms, eggs & onions

каштан ⓜ *kash·tan* chestnut

квас ⓜ *kvas* kvass – a beer-like drink
made from sugar & rye flour

квашеная капуста ⓕ *kva·shih·na·ya*
ka·pu·sta pickled cabbage • sauerkraut

кешью ⓜ *kye·shu* cashew

кисель ⓜ *kis·yel'* fruit jelly

кишмиш ⓜ *kish·mish* sultana

клубника ⓕ *klub·ni·ka* strawberry

клёцки ⓜ pl *klyots·ki* dumplings

коза ⓕ *ka·za* goat

козинаки ⓜ pl *ka·zi·na·ki*
walnut honey toffee

колбаса ⓕ *kal·ba·sa* salami • sausage
— **копчёная** *kap·cho·na·ya*
smoked sausage

компот ⓜ *kam·pot* fruit in syrup

копчёный *kap·cho·nih* smoked

корица ⓕ *ka·rit·sa* cinnamon

котлета ⓕ *kat·lye·ta* ground meat croquette
— **пожарская** *pa·zhar·ska·ya*
croquette with minced chicken or turkey
— **по-киевски** *pa·ki·if·ski* chicken Kiev –
rolled boneless chicken, stuffed with
butter, crumbed & deep-fried

крабы ⓜ pl *kra·bih* crab

красная рыба ⓕ *kras·na·ya rïh·ba* red fish

красная смородина ⓕ
kras·na·ya sma·ro·di·na redcurrant

креветка ⓕ *kriv·yet·ka* prawn

креветки pl *kriv·yet·ki* shrimp

кровавый *kra·va·vih* rare (food)

кролик ⓜ *kro·lik* rabbit

кукуруза ⓕ *ku·ku·ru·za* corn

кулебяка ⓕ *ku·lib·ya·ka* pastry filled with
cabbage, eggs & herbs • salmon cooked
in wine with rice, rice & vegetables

кулич ⓜ *kul·yich*
Easter cake with raisins & nutmeg

курица ⓕ *ku·rit·sa* chicken

курник ⓜ *kur·nik* pancakes filled with rice
& egg, chicken or mushrooms, then baked

кэрри ⓜ *ke·ri* curry

Л

лайм ⓜ *leym* lime

лапша ⓕ *lap·sha* chicken noodle soup

латкес ⓜ *lat·kis*
fried pancakes with pumpkin or squash

лесной орех ⓜ *lis·noy ar·yekh* hazelnut

лещ ⓜ *lyesh* bream

лимон ⓜ *li·mon* lemon

лобио ⓝ *lo·bi·o* spiced bean stew with
capsicum & tomato

лососина ⓕ *la·sa·si·na* salmon

лосось ⓜ *lo·sos'* salmon

лук ⓜ *luk* onions

лук-порей ⓜ *luk·pa·rey* leek

люля-кебаб ⓜ *lyul·ya·ki·bap*
ground lamb sausages

М

майонез ⓜ *ma·yan·yez* mayonnaise

малина ⓕ *ma·li·na* raspberry

манная каша ⓕ *ma·na·ya ka·sha*
porridge with semolina

манты ① pl man·tih steamed, palm-sized version of meat dumplings
мариованый ma·ri·no·va·nih marinated
маринованные грибы ① pl ma·ri·no·va·nih·ye gri·bih pickled mushrooms
маринованный ma·ri·no·va·nih pickled
маслины ① pl mas·li·nih olives
масло ⑪ mas·la butter • oil
мёд ⑪ myot honey
медвежатина ① mid·vi·zha·ti·na bear
мёдивник ⑪ myo·div·nik honey cake with raisins
медовуха ① mi·da·vu·kha honey kvass
мидия ① mi·di·ya mussel
миндаль ⑪ min·dal' almond
молоко ⑪ ma·la·ko milk
морковь ① mar·kof' carrot
мороженое ⑪ ma·ro·zhih·na·ye ice cream
мясной фарш ⑪ mis·noy farsh mince
мясное ассорти ⑪ mis·no·ye a·sar·ti selection of cold meats
мясо ⑪ mya·sa meat
— **по-сибирски** pa·si·bir·ski Siberian-style beef topped with cheese
мята ① mya·ta mint

О

овощи ⑪ pl o·va·shi vegetables
овощная окрошка ① a·vash·na·ya a·krosh·ka cold vegetable soup with potatoes, carrots, turnips & radish
овощной пирог ⑪ a·vash·noy pi·rok vegetable pie with cabbage, mushrooms, cream cheese & eggs
овощной плов ⑪ a·vash·noy plof vegetable pilau
овсянка ① af·syan·ka oats
овёс ⑪ av·yos oats
огурец ⑪ a·gur·yets cucumber
огурцы ⑪ pl a·gurt·sih pickles
окрошка ① a·krosh·ka soup of cucumber, sour cream, potato, egg, meat & kvass
окунь ⑪ o·kun' perch
оладьи из тыквы ⑪ pl a·la·di is tihk·vih pumpkin fritters
оладьи ① pl a·la·di fritters topped with syrup or sour cream, often fried with fruit
оленина ① a·li·ni·na venison
оливка ① a·lif·ka olive
оливковое масло ⑪ a·lif·ka·va·ye mas·la olive oil

оливье ⑪ a·li·vye 'Olivier salad' – meat & vegetables with sour cream
омуль ⑪ o·mul' salmon-like fish
орех ⑪ ar·yekh nut
осетрина ① a·si·tri·na sturgeon
— **отварная** at·var·na·ya poached sturgeon
— **с грибами** z gri·ba·mi sturgeon with mushrooms
— **с майонезом** s ma·yan·ye·zam sturgeon with mayonnaise
отбивная ① at·biv·na·ya beef or pork steak
отварной at·var·noy boiled • poached

П

палтус ⑪ pal·tus halibut
папоротник ⑪ pa·pa·rat·nik fern tips
паровый pa·ra·vih steamed
пасха ① pas·kha Easter cake made from cottage cheese, nuts & candied fruits
патока ① pa·ta·ka treacle
паштет ⑪ pasht·yet meat paste similar to liver sausage
персик ⑪ pyer·sik peach
перец ⑪ pye·rits black pepper • capsicum
пельмени ⑪ pl pilm·ye·ni meat dumplings
петрушка ① pi·trush·ka parsley
печёный pi·cho·nih baked
печень ① pye·chin' liver
пирог ⑪ pi·rok pie
— **из тыквы** ⑪ pi·rok is tihk·vih pumpkin pie – baked whole pumpkin filled with rice, apples, raisins & cherries
пирожное ⑪ pi·rozh·na·ye biscuits • pastries • small cakes
печёная тыква ① pi·cho·na·ya tihk·va baked pumpkin with eggs & almonds
печенье ⑪ pi·chen·ye biscuit • cookie • cracker
пирожки ⑪ pl pi·rash·ki spicy, deep-fried mutton pies
— **картофельные** kar·to·fil'·nih·ye potato pies
— **с капустой** s ka·pus·toy meat & cabbage pies
плов ⑪ plof pilau – rice with mutton
— **из кролика** ⑪ is kro·li·ka rabbit pilau
поджарка ① pad·zhar·ka roast meat, usually beef or pork
помидор ⑪ pa·mi·dor tomato
пончики ⑪ pl pon·chi·ki sugared doughnuts
почки ① pl poch·ki kidneys
— **в мадере** v mad·yer·ye kidneys in Madeira wine & sour cream sauce

простокваша ① pra·stak·*va*·sha *sour milk*
пряник ⓜ *prya*·nik *gingerbread*
птица ① *ptit*·sa *poultry*
пшённая каша с черносливом ①
  psho·na·ya *ka*·sha s chir·na·*sli*·vam
  millet porridge with prunes

Р

рагу ⓜ ra·*gu* *stew*
рассольник ⓜ ra·*sol*'·nik
  soup with chopped pickles & kidney
расстегай ⓜ ra·sti·*gey* *small pies*
редиска ① ri·*dis*·ka *radish*
рис ⓜ ris *rice*
рисовая запеканка ① *ri*·sa·va·ya
  za·pi·*kan*·ka *porridge with rice & cheese*
рыба ① *rih*·ba *fish*
  — **солёная** sal·*yo*·na·ya *salted fish*
рыбное ассорти ⓜ *rihb*·na·ye a·sar·*ti*
  selection of cold fish delicacies

С

салат ⓜ sa·*lat* *salad – usually tomato,*
  onion & cucumber
  — **из капусты** is ka·*pus*·tih
  cabbage, apple & carrot salad
  — **из картофеля** is kar·to·*fil*·ya
  potato salad with onions & mayonnaise
  — **из помидоров** is pa·mi·*do*·raf
  tomato salad
  — **из огурцов** iz a·gurt·*sof*
  cucumber salad
  — **из редиса** is ri·*di*·sa
  radish & onion salad
  — **из яиц** iz *ya*·its *egg salad with*
  mayonnaise, garlic, pimiento & scallion
  — **оливье** a·liv·*ye see* **оливье**
  — **столичный** sta·*lich*·nih
  vegetable, beef, potato & egg salad
самбук ⓜ sam·*buk* *plum & sugar mousse*
самса ① *sam*·sa *baked walnut parcels*
сардина ① sar·*di*·na *sardine*
сардины с лимоном ① pl sar·*di*·nih s
  li·*mo*·nam *sardines with lemon*
сахар ⓜ *sa*·khar *sugar*
сациви ⓜ sat·*sih*·vi *chicken in walnut sauce*
свёкла ① *svyol*·ka *beetroot*
свинина ① svi·*ni*·na *pork*
севрюга ① sev·*ryu*·ga *sturgeon*
селёдка ① sil·*yot*·ka *pickled herrings*
  — **под шубой** pat *shu*·bey *'herrings in*
  sheepskin coats' – salad with herring,
  potato, beet, carrot & mayonnaise

сельдерей ⓜ sil'·dir·*yey* *celery*
сельдь ① syelt' *herring*
сёмга ① *syom*·ga *salmon*
  — **копчёная** kap·*cho*·na·ya
  smoked salmon
сименуха ① si·mi·*nu*·kha
  porridge with mushrooms
скумбрия ① *skum*·bri·ya *mackerel*
слива ① *sli*·va *plum*
сливки ① pl *slif*·ki *cream*
сметана ① smi·*ta*·na *sour cream*
сметаник ⓜ smi·*ta*·nik
  pie with almonds, berries & jam
соевый соус ⓜ *so*·i·vih *sou*·us *soy sauce*
солёные огурцы ①
  sal·*yo*·nih·ye a·gurt·*sih* *pickled cucumber*
солёный sal·*yo*·nih *cured · salted*
  — **арбуз** ⓜ ar·*bus* *pickled watermelon*
солёные грибы ⓜ pl sal·*yo*·nih·ye gri·*bih*
  marinated mushrooms
солянка ① sal·*yan*·ka
  'salted' soup – meat or fish soup with
  salted cucumbers & other vegetables
  — **мясная** myas·*na*·ya
  'salted' soup with meat
  — **рыбная** *rihb*·na·ya
  'salted' soup with fish
сосиски ① pl sa·*sis*·ki *fried/boiled sausages*
соус ⓜ *sou*·us *sauce*
судак ⓜ su·*dak* *pikeperch*
суп ⓜ sup *soup*
  — **вермишелевый** vir·mi·*shel*·i·vih
  noodle soup
  — **грибной** grib·*noy*
  mushroom soup with vegetables
  — **с мясом** s *mya*·sam *soup with meat*
  — **с рыбой** s *rih*·bey *soup with fish*
  — **с фрикадельками**
  s fri·kad·*yel*'·ka·mi *soup with meatballs*
сыр ⓜ sihr *cheese*
сырники ① pl *sihr*·ni·ki *cottage cheese fritters*

Т

табака ① ta·ba·*ka*
  seasoned chicken (fried or grilled)
творог ⓜ *tva*·rok *cottage cheese*
телятина ① til·*ya*·ti·na *veal*
тефтели ① pl *tyef*·ti·li *meatballs*
толма ① *tol*·ma
  dolma – meat & rice stuffed in vine leaves
торт ⓜ tort *large cake*
требуха ① tri·bu·*kha* *tripe*
треска ① tris·*ka* *trout*

тунец Ⓜ tun·*yets* tuna
турецкий горох Ⓜ tu·*rets*·ki ga·*rokh* chickpea
туря Ⓕ tur·ya sauerkraut mixed with bread & onion then covered with kvass
тушёный tu·*sho*·nih stewed
тыква Ⓕ *tihk*·va pumpkin

У

устрица Ⓕ *ust*·rit·sa oyster
утка Ⓕ *ut*·ka duck
уха Ⓕ u·*kha* fish soup with potato & carrot
ушное Ⓝ ush·*no*·ye stew

Ф

фаршированный far·shih·*ro*·va·nih stuffed
фасоль Ⓕ fa·*sol'* bean
финики Ⓜ pl fi·ni·ki dates
фисташка Ⓕ fis·*tash*·ka pistachio
форель Ⓕ far·*yel'* trout
форшмак Ⓜ farsh·*mak* baked liquefied beef & lamb with herrings soaked in milk
фри fri fried
фруктовый торт Ⓜ fruk·*to*·vih tort fruit cake with raisins, almonds, apricots, candied fruits & sherry
фрукты Ⓜ pl *fruk*·tih fruit

Х

хачапури Ⓜ kha·cha·*pu*·ri rich, cheesy bread
хаш Ⓜ khash tripe soup
херес Ⓜ *khye*·ris sherry
хинкали Ⓜ pl khin·*ka*·li lamb dumplings
хлеб Ⓜ khlyep bread
— **белый** *bye*·lih white bread
— **чёрный** *chor*·nih black rye bread
— **с фруктами** s *fruk*·ta·mi rye bread with fruit
— **ячменно-пшеничный** yach·*mye*·na·pshe·*nich*·nih wheat & barley bread
хрен Ⓜ khryen horseradish

Ц

цветная капуста Ⓕ tsvit·*na*·ya ka·*pu*·sta cauliflower
— **с картофелем** Ⓕ s kar·*to*·fil·yem baked cauliflower & potato dish
цыплёнок табака Ⓜ tsihp·*lyo*·nak ta·ba·*ka* Caucasian-style grilled chicken
цитрусовый джем Ⓜ *tsih*·tra·sa·vey dzhem marmalade

Ч

чахохбили Ⓜ pl cha·*khokh*·bi·li steamed dumplings
черешня Ⓕ chir·*yesh*·nya cherry
чёрная редька Ⓕ *chor*·na·ya ryet'·ka black radish
чёрная смородина Ⓕ *chor*·na·ya sma·ro·di·na blackcurrant
черника Ⓕ chir·*ni*·ka blackberries
чернослив Ⓜ chir·nas·*lif* prunes
чебуреки Ⓜ pl chi·bur·*ye*·ki fried beef & pork dumplings
чров плав Ⓜ chrof plof rice pilau with dried fruit & nuts
чучкелла Ⓕ chuch·*kye*·la looped, sugar-coated grape and walnut candies

Ш

шаверма Ⓕ shav·*yer*·ma shawarma – rotisserie meat served in pita bread
шаурма Ⓕ *sha*·ur·ma see **шаверма**
шашлык Ⓜ shash·*lihk* skewered meat
шишки Ⓜ pl *shihsh*·ki cedar nuts
шницель Ⓜ *shnit*·sel' Wiener schnitzel
шоколад Ⓜ sha·ka·*lat* chocolate
шпинат Ⓜ shpi·*nat* spinach
— **по-армянски** pa·arm·*yan*·ski Armenian spinach – baked fried spinach with milk, cheese & eggs
шпроты Ⓜ pl *shpro*·tih sprats (like herring)

Щ

щавель Ⓜ shav·*yel'* sorrel
щи Ⓜ pl shi fresh or pickled cabbage soup, usually with meat & potato
— **постные** *post*·nih·ye cabbage soup without meat
— **с грибами** z gri·*ba*·mi cabbage soup with mushrooms
щука Ⓕ *shu*·ka pike

Я

яблоко Ⓝ *ya*·bla·ka apple
яблочный пирог Ⓜ *ya*·blach·nih pi·*rok* apple pie
ягоды Ⓕ pl *ya*·ga·dih berries
язык с гарниром Ⓜ yi·*zihk* z gar·*ni*·ram tongue with garnish
яйцо Ⓝ yiyt·*so* egg
— **всмятку** fsmyat·ku soft-boiled egg
— **крутое** kru·*to*·ye hard-boiled egg
яичница Ⓕ ya·*ich*·nit·sa fried egg

emergencies

скорая помощь

Help!	Помогите!	pa·ma·*gi*·tye
Stop!	Прекратите!	pri·kra·*ti*·tye
Go away!	Идите отсюда!	i·*dit*·ye at·*syu*·da
Thief!	Вор!	vor
Fire!	Пожар!	pa·*zhar*
Watch out!	Осторожно!	a·sta·*rozh*·na

Call the police!
Вызовите милицию!   *vih*·za·vit·ye mi·*lit*·sih·yu

Call a doctor!
Вызовите врача!   *vih*·za·vit·ye vra·*cha*

Call an ambulance!
Вызовите скорую помощь!   *vih*·za·vit·ye *sko*·ru·yu *po*·mash'

signs

These signs are provided in upper-case letters. If you have trouble reading a sign, it might be in lower-case or italics (see the box on page 14 for details).

БОЛЬНИЦА	*bal'*·nit·sa	**Hospital**
МИЛИЦИЯ	mi·*lit*·sih·ya	**Police**
ОТДЕЛЕНИЕ	a·dil·*ye*·ni·ye	**Police Station**
МИЛИЦИИ	mi·*lit*·sih	
СКОРАЯ	*sko*·ra·ya	**Emergency**
ПОМОЩЬ	*po*·mash'	**Department**

essentials

191

It's an emergency.
Это срочно!   *e*·ta *sroch*·na

There's been an accident.
Произошёл несчастный   pra·i·za·*shol* nye·*shas*·nih
случай.   *slu*·chey

Could you please help?
Помогите, пожалуйста!   pa·ma·*git*·ye pa·*zhal*·sta

Can I use your phone?
Можно воспользоваться   *mozh*·na vas·*pol'*·za·vat'·sa
телефоном?   ti·li·*fo*·nam

I need to make	Мне нужно	mnye *nuzh*·na
a phone call …	позвонить …	paz·va·*nit'* …
as soon as	как можно	kak *mozh*·na
possible	скорее	skar·*ye*·ye
at the next stop	на следующей	na *slye*·du·yu·shey
	остановке	as·ta·*nof*·kye

I'm lost.
Я потерялся. m   ya pa·tir·*yal*·sa
Я потерялась. f   ya pa·tir·*ya*·las'

Where are the toilets?
Где здесь туалет?   gdye zdyes' tu·al·*yet*

Is it safe …?	… безопасно?	… bye·za·*pas*·na
at night	Ночью	*no*·chu
for gay people	Для геев	dlya *gye*·yef
for travellers	Для путешест-	dlya pu·ti·*shest*·
	венников	vi·ni·kaf
for women	Для женщин	dlya *zhen*·shin
on your own	Одному m	ad·na·*mu*
	Одной f	ad·*noy*

police

Where's the police station?
Где милицейский участок?   gdye mi·lit·*sey*·ski u·*cha*·stak

Are there police on this train?
В этом поезде
есть милиция?   v *e*·tam *po*·iz·dye
yest' mi·*lit*·sih·ya

I want to report an offence.
Я хочу заявить
в милицию.   ya kha·*chu* za·ya·*vit'*
v mi·*lit*·sih·yu

It was him.
Это сделал он!   *e*·ta *zdye*·lal on

It was her.
Это сделала она!   *e*·ta *zdye*·la·la a·*na*

I have insurance.
У меня есть страховка.   u min·*ya* yest' stra·*khof*·ka

My ... was/were stolen.	У меня украли ...	u min·*ya* u·*kra*·li ...
I've lost my ...	Я потерял ... m	ya pa·tir·*yal* ...
	Я потеряла ... f	ya pa·tir·*ya*·la ...
backpack	рюкзак	ryug·*zak*
bags	багаж	ba·*gash*
credit card	кредитную карточку	kri·*dit*·nu·yu *kar*·tach·ku
handbag	сумку	*sum*·ku
jewellery	драгоценности	dra·gat·*se*·na·sti
money	деньги	*dyen'*·gi
papers	документы	da·kum·*yen*·tih
travellers cheques	дорожные чеки	da·*rozh*·nih·ye *che*·ki
passport	паспорт	*pas*·part
wallet	бумажник	bu·*mazh*·nik

I've been … He/She has been …	Меня … Его/Её …	min·*ya* … yi·*vo*/yi·*yo* …
assaulted	побили	pa·*bi*·li
raped	изнасиловали	iz·na·*si*·la·va·li
robbed	ограбили	a·*gra*·bi·li
He tried to … me. She tried to … me.	Он пытался … меня. Она пыталась … меня.	on pih·*tal*·sa … min·*ya* a·*na* pih·*ta*·las' … min·*ya*
assault	напасть на	na·*past*' na
rape	изнасиловать	iz·na·*si*·la·vat'
rob	ограбить	a·*gra*·bit'

the police may say …

Вас осудят за … Его/Её осудят за …	vas a·*sud*·yat za … yi·*vo*/yi·*yo* a·*sud*·yat za …	You're charged with … He/She is charged with …
насилие	na·*si*·li·ye	assault
нарушение покоя	na·ru·*she*·ni·ye pa·*ko*·ya	disturbing the peace
хранение (запрещённых предметов)	khran·*ye*·ni·ye (za·pri·*sho*·nihkh prid·*mye*·taf)	possession (of illegal substances)
безвизовый въезд	byez·*vi*·za·vih vyest	not having a visa
просроченную визу	pras·*ro*·chi·nu·yu *vi*·zu	overstaying a visa
воровство в магазине	va·*rafst*·vo v ma·ga·*zin*·ye	shoplifting
ограбление	a·grab·*lye*·ni·ye	theft
Это штраф за …	*e*·ta shtraf za …	It's a … fine.
нарушение правил парковки	na·ru·*she*·ni·ye *pra*·vil par·*kof*·ki	parking
превышение скорости	pri·vih·*she*·ni·ye *sko*·ra·sti	speeding

What am I accused of?
В чём меня обвиняют?   f chom min·*ya* ab·vin·*ya*·yut

I didn't do it.
Я этого не делал. m   ya e·ta·va nye *dye*·lal
Я этого не делала. f   ya e·ta·va nye *dye*·la·la

I didn't realise I was doing anything wrong.
Я не знал/знала, что   ya nye znal/*zna*·la shto
я делаю что-то   ya *dye*·la·yu *shto*·ta
неправильно. m/f   nye·*pra*·vil'·na

I'm sorry.
Извините, пожалуйста.   iz·vi·*nit*·ye pa·*zhal*·sta

Can I pay an on-the-spot fine?
Можно заплатить   *mozh*·na za·pla·*tit'*
штраф на месте?   shtraf na *mye*·stye

I want to contact my embassy/consulate.
Я хочу обратиться в своё   ya kha·*chu* a·bra·*tit'*·sa f sva·*yo*
посольство/консульство.   pa·*solst*·va/kan·sulst·*vo*

Can I make a phone call?
Можно позвонить?   *mozh*·na paz·va·*nit'*

Can I have a lawyer (who speaks English)?
Мне нужен адвокат   mnye *nu*·zhihn ad·va·*kat*
(говорящий на   (ga·var·*ya*·shi na
английском языке).   an·*gli*·skam ya·zihk·*ye*)

This drug is for personal use.
Это лекарство для   e·ta li·*karst*·va dlya
личного пользования.   *lich*·na·va *pol'*·za·va·ni·ya

I have a prescription for this drug.
У меня есть рецепт   u min·*ya* yest' rit·*sept*
на это лекарство.   na e·ta li·*karst*·va

I (don't) understand.
Я (не) понимаю.   ya (nye) pa·ni·*ma*·yu

Now that you're in Russia, it's the perfect time to act out your fantasies and play *Бонд, Джеймс Бонд* bont, dzheyms bont (Bond, James Bond).

Just a drink. A martini. Shaken not stirred.

Просто выпить.	*pro*·sta *vih*·pit'
Мартини.	mar·*ti*·ni
И встряхните его	i fstryakh·*nit*·ye yi·*vo*
получше, не	pa·*luch*·she nye
размешивайте.	raz·*mye*·shih·veyt·ye

Speaking of sick minds, tell me, which lunatic asylum did they get you out of?

Говоря о	ga·var·*ya* a
сумасшедших,	su·ma·*shed*·shihkh
скажите, из какой	ska·*zhiht*·ye is ka·*koy*
психбольницы они вас	psikh·bal'·*nit*·sih a·*ni* vas
вытащили?	*vih*·tash·chi·li

Your plans for world domination are sadly mistaken.

Ваши планы	*va*·shih *pla*·nih
установления	u·sta·nav·*lye*·ni·ya
мирового контроля –	mi·ra·*vo*·va kan·*trol*·ya
жалкая иллюзия.	*zhal*·ka·ya il·*yu*·zi·ya

And from the collected apocrypha of *ноль ноль семь* nol' nol' syem' (007) …

So we meet again, Mr XXX, but this time the advantage is mine.

Ну вот мы и снова	nu vot i mih *sno*·va
встретились,	*fstrye*·ti·lis'
г-н Икс Икс Икс,	ga·spa·*din* iks·iks·*iks*
но на этот раз	no na *e*·tat ras
преимущество	pri·i·*mush*·chist·va
на моей стороне.	na ma·*yey* sta·ran·ye

doctor

врач

Where's the nearest …?	Где здесь …?	gdye zdyes' …
dentist	зубной врач	zub·*noy* vrach
doctor	врач	vrach
emergency department	палата скорой помощи	pa·*la*·ta *sko*·rey *po*·ma·shi
hospital	больница	bal'·nit·sa
medical centre	поликлиника	pa·li·*kli*·ni·ka
optometrist	оптик	*op*·tik
(night) pharmacist	(ночная) аптека	(nach·*na*·ya) ap·*tye*·ka

I need a doctor (who speaks English).
Мне нужен врач, (говорящий на английском языке).
mnye *nu*·zhihn vrach (ga·var·*ya*·shi na an·*gli*·skam ya·zihk·*ye*)

Could I see a female doctor?
Можно записаться на приём к женщине-врачу?
mozh·na za·pi·*sat'*·sa na pri·*yom* k *zhen*·shin·ye·vra·*chu*

Could the doctor come here?
Врач может прийти ко мне?
vrach *mo*·zhiht pri·*ti* ka mnye

Is there an after-hours number?
Есть круглосуточный номер?
yest' kru·gla·*su*·tach·nih *no*·mir

I've run out of my medication.
У меня кончилось лекарство.
u min·*ya* kon·chi·las' li·*karst*·va

This is my usual medicine.

Я обычно принимаю
это лекарство.

ya a·*bihch*·na pri·ni·*ma*·yu
e·ta li·*karst*·va

My child weighs (20 kilos).

Мой ребёнок весит
(двадцать кило).

moy rib·*yo*·nak *vye*·sit
(*dvat*·sat' ki·*lo*)

What's the correct dosage?

Какова правильная доза?

ka·ka·*va pra*·vil'·na·ya *do*·za

I don't want a blood transfusion.

Я не хочу, чтобы мне
переливали кровь.

ya nye kha·*chu shto*·bih mnye
pi·ri·li·*va*·li krof'

---

the doctor may say ...

Что вас беспокоит? shto vas bis·pa·*ko*·it	**What's the problem?**
Где болит? gdye ba·*lit*	**Where does it hurt?**
Есть температура? yest' tim·pi·ra·*tu*·ra	**Do you have a temperature?**
Как давно у вас это состояние? kag dav·*no* u vas e·ta sa·sta·*ya*·ni·ye	**How long have you been like this?**
У вас это было раньше? u vas e·ta *bih*·la ran'·she	**Have you had this before?**
Как долго вы путешествуете? kag *dol*·ga vih pu·ti·*shest*·vu·it·ye	**How long are you travelling for?**

Вы ...?	vih ...	**Do you ...?**
пьёте	*pyot*·ye	**drink**
курите	*ku*·rit·ye	**smoke**
употребляете	u·pa·trib·*lya*·it·ye	**take drugs**
наркотики	nar·*ko*·ti·ki	

the doctor may say ...

Вы сексуально активны? vih syeks·u·*al*·na ak·*tiv*·nih	**Are you sexually active?**
У вас был незащищённый половой контакт? u vas bihl nye·za·shi·*sho*·nih pa·la·*voy* kan·*takt*	**Have you had unprotected sex?**
Вы принимаете лекарство? vih pri·ni·*ma*·it·ye li·*karst*·vo	**Are you on medication?**
У вас есть аллергия на что-нибудь? u vas yest' a·lir·*gi*·ya na *shto*·ni·but'	**Are you allergic to anything?**
Я вас направлю в больницу. ya vas na·prav·*lyu* v *bol'*·nit·su	**You need to be admitted to hospital.**
Сходите к врачу, когда приедете домой. skha·*dit*·ye k vra·*chu* kag·*da* pri·ye·dit·ye da·*moy*	**You should have it checked when you go home.**
Вы должны возвратиться домой. vih dalzh·*nih* vaz·vra·*tit'*·sa da·*moy*	**You should return home.**
Ничего серьёзного. ni·chi·*vo* sir·*yoz*·na·va	**Nothing to worry about.**

Please use a new syringe.
Новым шприцом,
пожалуйста.

no·vihm *shprit*·sam
pa·*zhal*·sta

I have my own syringe.
У меня свой шприц.

u min·*ya* svoy shprits

Is the water safe to drink?
Вода питьевая?

va·*da* pi·ti·*va*·ya

health

199

I've been vaccinated against …	Мне делали прививку против …	mnye *dye*·la·li pri·*vif*·ku *pro*·tif …
He/She has been vaccinated against …	Ему/Ей делали прививку против …	yi·*mu*/yey *dye*·la·li pri·*vif*·ku *pro*·tif …
hepatitis A/B/C	гепатита A/B/C	gi·pa·*ti*·ta a/be/tse
tetanus	столбняка	stalb·nya·*ka*
typhoid	брюшного тифа	bryush·*no*·va *ti*·fa
I need new …	Мне нужны …	mnye nuzh·*nih* …
contact lenses	контактные линзы	kan·*takt*·nih·ye *lin*·zih
glasses	очки	ach·*ki*

My prescription is …
Мой рецепт …   moy rit·*sept* …

How much will it cost?
Сколько это стоит?   *skol'*·ka *e*·ta *sto*·it

Can I have a receipt for my insurance?
Можно квитанцию для моей страховки?   *mozh*·na kvi·*tant*·sih·yu dlya ma·*yey* stra·*khof*·ki

symptoms & conditions

симптомы

I'm (very) sick.
Я (очень) болею.   ya (*o*·chin') bal·*ye*·yu

My friend is sick.
Мой приятель болеет. m   moy pri·*yat*·yel' bal·*ye*·yet
Моя приятельница болеет. f   ma·*ya* pri·*yat*·yel'·nit·sa bal·*ye*·yet

My child is sick.
    Мой ребёнок болеет.   moy rib·*yo*·nak bal·*ye*·yet

He's been injured.
    Он ушибся.   on u·*shihp*·sa

She's been injured.
    Она ушиблась.   a·*na* u·*shihb*·las'

He/She is   У него/неё …   u nyi·*vo*/nyi·*yo* …
having a/an …
    allergic reaction   аллергическая   a·lir·*gi*·chi·ska·ya
                               реакция   ri·*akt*·sih·ya
    asthma attack   астматическая   ast·ma·*ti*·chi·ska·ya
                               реакция   ri·*akt*·sih·ya
    epileptic fit   эпилептический   e·pi·lip·*ti*·chi·ski
                               припадок   pri·*pa*·dak
    heart attack   сердечный   sird·*yech*·nih
                               приступ   *pri*·stup

He/She has been …
    vomiting   Его/Её тошнило.   yi·*vo*/yi·*yo* tash·*ni*·la
    bitten   У него/У неё укус.   u nyi·*vo*/nyi·*yo* u·*kus*

I feel …
    anxious   У меня не в   u min·*ya* nye f
                               порядке нервы.   par·*yat*·kye *nyer*·vih
    depressed   У меня   u min·*ya*
                               депрессия.   dip·*rye*·si·ya
    dizzy   У меня кружится   u min·*ya* kru·zhiht·sa
                               голова.   ga·la·*va*
    hot and cold   У меня приступ   u min·*ya* pri·stup
                               лихорадки.   li·kha·*rat*·ki
    nauseous   Меня тошнит.   min·*ya* tash·*nit*
    shivery   У меня озноб.   u min·*ya* az·*nop*
    weak   У меня слабость.   u min·*ya* sla·bast'

I feel …   Я чувствую   ya *chust*·vu·yu
                               себя …   sib·*ya* …
    better   получше   pa·*luch*·she
    strange   плохо   *plo*·kha
    worse   похуже   pa·*khu*·zhe

It hurts here.
Здесь болит.   zdyes' ba·*lit*

I'm dehydrated.
У меня обезвоживание   u min·*ya* a·bis·*vo*·zhih·va·ni·ye
организма.   ar·ga·*niz*·ma

I can't sleep.
Мне не спится.   mnye nye *spit*·sa

I think it's the medication I'm on.
Это наверно от лекарства,   *e*·ta nav·*yer*·na at li·*karst*·va
которое я принимаю.   ka·*to*·ra·ye ya pri·ni·*ma*·yu

I'm on medication for …
Я принимаю лекарство от …   ya pri·ni·*ma*·yu li·*karst*·va at …

He/She is on medication for …
Он/Она принимает   on/a·*na* pri·ni·*ma*·yet
лекарство от …   li·*karst*·va at …

I have (a/an) …
У меня …   u min·*ya* …

He/She has (a/an) …
У него/неё …   u nyi·*vo*/nyi·*yo* …

AIDS	СПИД m	spit
asthma	астма f	*ast*·ma
cold	простуда f	pra·*stu*·da
constipation	запор m	za·*por*
cough	кашель m	*ka*·shel'
diabetes	диабет m	di·ab·*yet*
diarrhoea	понос m	pa·*nos*
encephalitis	энцефалит m	ent·sih·fa·*lit*
fever	температура f	tim·pi·ra·*tu*·ra
flu	грипп m	grip
headache	головная боль f	ga·lav·*na*·ya bol'
hypothermia	гипотермия f	gi·pa·tir·*mi*·ya
Lyme disease	болезнь Лайма f	bal·*yezn*' *ley*·ma
nausea	тошнота f	tash·na·*ta*
pain	боль f	bol'
rabies	бешенство m	*bye*·shihnst·va
sore throat	болит горло	ba·*lit gor*·la
ticks	клещи m pl	*klye*·shi

allergies

I have a skin allergy.
    У меня кожная аллергия.   u min·*ya kozh*·na·ya a·lir·*gi*·ya

I'm allergic to ...	У меня аллергия на...	u min·*ya* a·lir·*gi*·ya na ...
He/She is allergic to ...	У него/неё аллергия на ...	u nyi·*vo*/nyi·*yo* al·*yer*·*gi*·ya na ...
antibiotics	антибиотики	an·ti·bi·o·ti·ki
anti-inflammatories	противо-воспалительные препараты	pra·ti·va·va·spa·*li*·til'·nih·ye pri·pa·*ra*·tih
aspirin	аспирин	a·spi·*rin*
bees	пчелиный укус	pchi·*li*·nih *u*·kus
codeine	кодеин	kad·ye·*in*
penicillin	пеницилин	pi·nit·*sih*·lin
pollen	пыльцу	pihlt·*su*
sulphur-based drugs	серные препараты	*syer*·nih·ye pri·pa·*ra*·tih

inhaler	ингалятор m	in·gal·*ya*·tar
injection	инъекция f	in·*yekt*·sih·ya
antihistamines	антигистаминные средства n pl	an·ti·gi·sta·*mi*·nih·ye *sryets*·tva

For food-related allergies, see **special diets & allergies**, page 183.

---

swinging singles

No, the single consonants in our pronunciation guide aren't there by mistake. You'll see f or v for the letter в, k for к and s or z for с.

health

women's health

(I think) I'm pregnant.

(Я думаю, что)   (ya *du*·ma·yu shto)
Я беременна.   ya bir·*ye*·mi·na

I'm on the pill.

Я принимаю   ya pri·ni·*ma*·yu
противозачаточные   pra·ti·va·za·*cha*·tach·nih·ye
таблетки.   tab·*lyet*·ki

I haven't had my period for (six) weeks.

У меня (шесть) недель   u min·*ya* (shest') nid·*yel*'
задержка.   zad·*yersh*·ka

I've noticed a lump here.

У меня здесь опухоль.   u min·*ya* zdyes' *o*·pu·khal'

Do you have something for (period pain)?

У вас есть что-нибудь от   u vas yest' *shto*·ni·but' at
(боли при менструации)?   (*bo*·li pri mins·tru·*at*·sih)

I have a …	У меня	u min·*ya*
infection.	воспаление …	vas·pal·*ye*·ni·ye …
urinary tract	мочевого	ma·chi·*vo*·va
	канала	ka·*na*·la
yeast	влагалища	vla·*ga*·li·sha

I need (a/the) …	Я хочу …	ya kha·*chu* …
pregnancy	анализ на	a·*na*·lis na
test	беременность	bir·*ye*·mi·nast'
contraception	противо-	pra·ti·va·
	зачаточные	za·*cha*·tach·nih·ye
	средства	*sryets*·tva
morning-after	утреннюю	*ut*·rin·yu·yu
pill	таблетку	tab·*lyet*·ku

the doctor may say ...

Вы употребляете противо-зачаточные средства? vih u·pa·trib·*lya*·it·ye pra·ti·va-za·*cha*·tach·nih·ye *sryets*·tva	**Are you using contraception?**
У вас есть месячные? u vas yest' *mye*·sich·nih·ye	**Are you menstruating?**
Вы беременны? vih bir·*ye*·mi·nih	**Are you pregnant?**
Когда были последние месячные? kag·*da* bih·li pa·*sled*·ni·ye *mye*·sich·nih·ye	**When did you last have your period?**
Вы беременны. vih bir·*ye*·mi·nih	**You're pregnant.**

alternative treatments

альтернативная медицина

I don't use (Western medicine).
Я не употребляю
(западную медицину).
ya nye u·pa·trib·*lya*·yu
(*za*·pad·nu·yu mi·dit·*sih*·nu)

I prefer (complementary medicine).
Я предпочитаю
(альтернативную
медицину).
ya prit·pa·chi·*ta*·yu
(al'·tir·na·*tiv*·nu·yu
mi·dit·*sih*·nu)

Can I see someone who practises ...?	Можно видеть кого-нибудь, который занимается ...?	*mozh*·na *vid*·yet' ka·*vo*·ni·but' ka·*to*·rih za·ni·*ma*·it·sa ...
acupuncture	акупунктурой	a·ku·punk·*tu*·rey
naturopathy	натуропатией	na·tu·ra·*pa*·ti·yey
reflexology	рефлексологией	ri·fleks·a·*lo*·gi·yey
reiki	рейки	*ryey*·ki

parts of the body

тело

My ... hurts.
У меня болит ...
u min·*ya* ba·*lit* ...

I can't move my ...
Я не могу двигать ...
ya nye ma·*gu dvi*·gat' ...

I have a cramp in my ...
У меня судорога в ...
u min·*ya su*·da·ra·ga v ...

My ... is swollen.
У меня распух ...
u min·*ya* ras·*pukh* ...

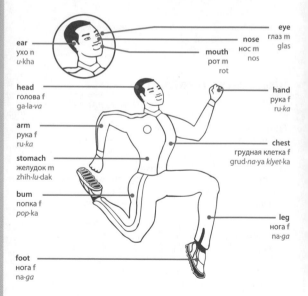

ear
ухо n
u·kha

eye
глаз m
glas

nose
нос m
nos

mouth
рот m
rot

head
голова f
ga·la·*va*

hand
рука f
ru·*ka*

arm
рука f
ru·*ka*

chest
грудная клетка f
grud·*na*·ya *klyet*·ka

stomach
желудок m
zhih·*lu*·dak

bum
попка f
pop·ka

leg
нога f
na·*ga*

foot
нога f
na·*ga*

For other parts of the body, see the **dictionary**.

pharmacist

аптека

I need something for (a headache).
Мне нужно что-нибудь от (головной боли).
mnye *nuzh*·na *shto*·ni·bud' at (ga·lav·*noy* bo·li)

Do I need a prescription for (antibiotics)?
Для (антибиотиков) нужен рецепт?
dlya (an·ti·bi·o·ti·kaf) *nu*·zhihn rit·*sept*

I have a prescription.
У меня есть рецепт.
u min·*ya* yest' rit·*sept*

How many times a day?
Сколько раз в день?
skol'·ka raz v dyen'

antiseptic	антисептик m	an·tis·*yep*·tik
contraceptives	противо-зачаточные средства n pl	pra·ti·va-za·*cha*·tach·nih·ye *sryets*·tva
painkillers	болеутоляющие n pl	bo·li·u·tal·*ya*·yu·shi·ye
thermometer	термометр f	tir·*mo*·mitr
rehydration salts	нюхательная соль m	*nyu*·kha·til'·na·ya sol'

For more pharmaceutical items, see the **dictionary**.

dentist

I have a ...	У меня ...	u min·ya ...
broken tooth	сломался зуб	sla·mal·sa zup
cavity	дыра в зубе	dih·ra v zub·ye
toothache	болит зуб	ba·lit zup

I've lost a filling.
У меня выпала пломба.　　　　u min·ya vih·pa·la plom·ba

My dentures are broken.
Я сломал протез. m　　　　ya sla·mal prat·yes
Я сломала протез. f　　　　ya sla·ma·la prat·yes

My gums hurt.
У меня болят дёсны.　　　　u min·ya bal·yat dyos·nih

I don't want it extracted.
Я не хочу удалять зуб.　　　　ya nye kha·chu u·dal·yat' zup

Please give me an anaesthetic.
Обезбольте, пожалуйста.　　　　a·biz·bolt·ye pa·zhal·sta

Ouch!
Ой!　　　　　　　　　　oy

---

the dentist may say ...

Откройте рот.	at·kroyt·ye rot	**Open wide.**
Кончил! m	kon·chil	**I've finished!**
Кончила! f	kon·chi·la	
удалить	u·da·lit'	**extract**
укол m	u·kol	**injection**
временно	vrye·mi·na	**temporary**

Russian nouns in the **dictionary** have their gender indicated by ⓜ, ① or ⓝ. If it's a plural noun you'll also see pl. When a word that could be either a noun or a verb has no gender indicated, it's a verb. For added clarity, certain words are marked as adjectives a or verbs v. Adjectives, however, are given in the masculine form only. Both nouns and adjectives are provided in the nominative case only. For information on case and gender, refer to the **phrasebuilder**.

Verbs are mostly given in two forms: perfective and imperfective. See the **phrasebuilder** for an explanation of these terms and when to use which form. The two forms are separated by a slash with the imperfective form given first. For example, the verb 'walk' has the forms гулять/погулять gul·*yat'*/pa·gul·*yat'* – the first one is the imperfective form and the second the perfective. If we've only given one verb form, this means it's used for both perfective and imperfective.

A

aboard на борту na bar·*tu*
abortion аборт ⓜ a·*bort*
about около *o*·ka·la
above над nat
abroad за границей za gra·*nit*·sey
acid rain кислый дождь ⓜ *kis*·lih dosht'
accident авария ① a·*va*·ri·ya
accommodation помещение ⓝ
    pa·mi·*she*·ni·ye
account (bank) счёт ⓜ shot
across через *che*·ris
activist активист ⓜ ak·ti·*vist*
actor актёр/актриса ⓜ/① akt·*yor*/ak·*tri*·sa
adaptor адаптер ⓜ a·*dap*·tir
addiction привычка ① pri·*vihch*·ka
address адрес ⓜ *a*·dris
administration администрация ①
    ad·mi·nist·*rat*·sih·ya
admission (price) вход ⓜ fkhot
admit впускать/впустить
    fpu·*skat'*/fpu·*stit'*
adult взрослый/взрослая ⓜ/①
    vzros·lih/vzros·*la*·ya
advertisement реклама ① ri·*kla*·ma
advice совет ⓜ sav·*yet*
(be) afraid бояться ba·*yat'*·sa
after после *pos*·lye
(this) afternoon (сегодня) днём
    (si·*vod*·nya) dnyom

aftershave одеколон ⓜ a·di·ka·*lon*
again ещё раз yi·*sho* ras
age возраст ⓜ *voz*·rast
(three days) ago (три дня) тому назад
    (tri dnya) ta·*mu* na·*zat*
agree соглашаться/согласиться
    sa·gla·*shat'*·sa/sa·gla·*sit'*·sa
agriculture сельское хозяйство ⓝ
    syel'·ska·ye khaz·*yeyst*·va
ahead вперёд fpir·*yot*
AIDS СПИД ⓜ spit
air воздух ⓜ *voz*·dukh
air conditioning кондиционирование ⓝ
    kan·dit·sih·a·*ni*·ra·va·ni·ye
airline авиакомпания ①
    a·vi·a·kam·*pa*·ni·ya
airmail авиапочта ① a·vi·a·*poch*·ta
airplane самолёт ⓜ sa·mal·*yot*
airport аэропорт ⓜ a·e·ra·*port*
airport tax налог на вылет ⓜ
    na·*lok* na *vih*·lit
aisle (on transport) проход ⓜ
    pra·*khot*
alarm clock будильник ⓜ bu·*dil'*·nik
alcohol алкоголь ⓜ al·ka·*gol'*
all все ⓜ&①&ⓝ pl fsye
allergy аллергия ① al·*yer*·gi·ya
almond миндаль ⓜ min·*dal'*
almost почти pach·*ti*
alone один/одна ⓜ/① a·*din*/ad·*na*
already уже u·*zhe*

also тоже *to-*zhih
altar алтарь ⓜ al-*tar'*
altitude высота ⓕ vih-sa-*ta*
always всегда fsig-*da*
ambassador посол ⓜ pa-*sol*
amber янтарь ⓜ yin-*tar'*
ambulance скорая помощь ⓕ
   *sko-*ra-ya po-*mash*
America Америка ⓕ a-*mye-*ri-ka
anaemia анемия ⓕ an-*ye-*mi-ya
anarchist анархист/анархистка ⓜ/ⓕ
   a-nar-*khist/*a-nar-*khist-*ka
ancient древний *dryev-*ni
and и i
angry сердитый sir-*di-*tih
animal животное ⓝ zhih-*vot-*na-ye
ankle лодыжка ⓕ la-*dihsh-*ka
another ещё один/одна ⓜ/ⓕ
   yi-*sho* a-*din/*ad-*na
answer ответ ⓜ at-*vyet*
ant муравей ⓜ mu-rav-*yey*
antibiotics антибиотики ⓟ pl
   an-ti-bi-*o-*ti-ki
antinuclear противоядерный
   pra-ti-va-*ya-*dir-nih
antique антиквариат ⓜ an-*tik-*var-*yat*
antiseptic антисептик ⓜ an-tis-*yep-*tik
any любой lyu-*boy*
apartment квартира ⓕ kvar-*ti-*ra
appendix аппендикс ⓜ ap-*yen-*diks
apple яблоко ⓝ *yab-*la-ka
appointment встреча ⓕ *fstre-*cha
apricot абрикос ⓜ a-bri-*kos*
April апрель ⓜ ap-*ryel'*
archaeological археологический
   ar-khi-a-la-*gi-*chi-ski
architect архитектор ⓜ ar-khit-*yek-*tar
architecture архитектура ⓕ
   ar-khi-tik-*tu-*ra
Arctic Ocean Арктический океан ⓜ
   ark-*ti-*chi-ski a-ki-*an*
argue спорить *spo-*rit'
arm рука ⓕ ru-*ka*
arrest арестовывать/арестовать
   a-ri-sto-vih-*vat'/*a-ri-sta-*vat'*
arrivals прибытие ⓝ pri-*bih-*ti-ye
arrive приезжать/приехать
   pri-*i-*zhat'/pri-*ye-*khat'
art искусство ⓝ is-*kust-*va
art gallery галерея ⓕ ga-*lir-*ye-ya
artist художник/художница ⓜ/ⓕ
   khu-*dozh-*nik/khu-*dozh-*nit-sa
ashtray пепельница ⓕ *pye-*pil'-nit-sa

Asia Азия ⓕ *a-*zi-ya
ask (a question) спрашивать/спросить
   *spra-*shih-vat'/spra-*sit'*
ask (for something) просить/попросить
   pra-*sit'/*pa-pra-*sit'*
aspirin аспирин ⓜ a-*spi-*rin
asthma астма ⓕ *ast-*ma
astrology астрология ⓕ ast-ra-*lo-*gi-ya
at в v
atheism атеизм ⓜ a-ti-*izm*
atheist атеист ⓜ a-ti-*ist*
atmosphere атмосфера ⓕ at-mas-*fye-*ra
aubergine баклажан ⓜ ba-kla-*zhan*
August август ⓜ *av-*gust
aunt тётя ⓕ *tyot-*ya
Australia Австралия ⓕ af-*stra-*li-ya
automated teller machine (ATM)
   банкомат ⓜ ban-ka-*mat*
autumn осень ⓕ *o-*sin'
avenue проспект ⓜ prasp-*yekt*
awful ужасный u-*zhas-*nih

B

B&W (film) чёрно-белый *chor-*nab-*ye-*lih
baby ребёнок ⓜ rib-*yo-*nak
baby food детское питание ⓝ
   *dyet-*ska-ye pi-*ta-*ni-ye
baby powder тальк ⓜ talk
babysitter приходящая няня ⓕ
   pri-khad-*ya-*sha-ya *nyan-*ya
back (body) спина ⓕ spi-*na*
back (position) задняя часть ⓕ
   *zad-*nya-ya chast'
backpack рюкзак ⓜ ryug-*zak*
bacon бекон ⓜ bi-*kon*
badge значок ⓜ zna-*chok*
bad плохой pla-*khoy*
bag мешок ⓜ mi-*shok*
baggage багаж ⓜ ba-*gash*
baggage allowance норма багажа ⓕ
   *nor-*ma ba-*ga-*zha
baggage claim выдача багажа ⓕ
   *vih-*da-cha ba-*ga-*zha
bakery булочная ⓕ *bu-*lach-na-ya
balalaika балалайка ⓕ ba-la-*ley-*ka
balance (account) баланс ⓜ ba-*lans*
balcony балкон ⓜ bal-*kon*
ball (sport) мяч ⓜ myach
ballet балет ⓜ bal-*yet*
Baltic Sea Балтийское море ⓝ
   bal-*ti-*ska-ye *mor-*ye
banana банан ⓜ ba-*nan*
band (music) группа ⓕ *gru-*pa

bandage бинт ⓜ bint
Band-Aid пластырь ⓜ pla·*stihr*
bank банк ⓜ bank
bank account банковский счёт ⓜ
  ban·kaf·ski shot
banknote банкнот ⓜ bank·*not*
bar бар ⓜ bar
barber парикмахер ⓜ pa·rik·*ma*·khir
baseball бейсбол ⓜ byeys·*bol*
basket корзина ⓕ kar·*zi*·na
bath ванна ⓕ *va*·na
bathhouse баня ⓕ *ban*·ya
bathing suit купальный костюм ⓜ
  ku·*pal'*·nih kast·*yum*
bathroom ванная ⓕ *va*·na·ya
battery (general) батарея ⓕ ba·tar·*ye*·ya
be быть biht'
beach пляж ⓜ plyash
bean фасоль ⓕ fa·*sol'*
beautiful красивый kra·*si*·vih
because потому что pa·ta·*mu* shta
bed кровать ⓕ kra·*vat'*
bedding постельное бельё ⓝ
  past·*yel'*·na·ye bil·*yo*
bedroom спальня ⓕ *spal*·nya
bee пчела ⓕ pchi·*la*
beef говядина ⓕ gav·*ya*·di·na
beer пиво ⓝ *pi*·va
beetroot свёкла ⓕ *svyo*·kla
before до do
beggar нищий/нищая ⓜ/ⓕ
  ni·shi/*ni*·sha·ya
behind за za
Belarus Белоруссия ⓕ bi·la·*ru*·si·ya
Belgium Бельгия ⓕ *byel'*·gi·ya
below под pot
berth (train) полка ⓕ *pol*·ka
berth (ship) койка ⓕ *koy*·ka
beside рядом с *rya*·dam s
best самый лучший *sa*·mih *luch*·shih
bet пари ⓝ pi *pa*·ri
between между *myezh*·du
Bible Библия ⓕ *bib*·li·ya
bicycle велосипед ⓜ vi·la·sip·*yet*
big большой bal'·*shoy*
bigger больше *bol'*·she
biggest самый большой *sa*·mih bal'·*shoy*
bike велосипед ⓜ vi·la·sip·*yet*
bike chain цепь для велосипеда ⓕ
  tsep' dlya vi·la·sip·*ye*·da
bike lock замок для велосипеда ⓜ
  za·*mok* dlya vi·la·sip·*ye*·da

bike path велодорожка ⓕ
  vi·la·da·*rosh*·ka
bike shop велосипедный магазин ⓜ
  vi·la·sip·*yed*·nih ma·ga·*zin*
bill (restaurant etc) счёт ⓜ shot
binoculars бинокль ⓜ bi·*nokl'*
bird птица ⓕ *ptit*·sa
birth certificate свидетельство о
  рождении ⓝ svid·*ye*·tilst·va o razh·*dye*·ni
birthday день рождения ⓜ
  dyen' razh·*dye*·ni
biscuit печенье ⓝ pi·*chen*·ye
bite (dog/insect) укус ⓜ u·*kus*
bitter горький *gor'*·ki
black чёрный a *chor*·nih
black market чёрный рынок ⓜ
  chor·nih *rih*·nak
Black Sea Чёрное море ⓝ
  chor·na·ye *mor*·ye
bladder мочевой пузырь ⓜ
  ma·chi·*voy* pu·*zihr'*
blanket одеяло ⓝ a·di·*ya*·la
blind слепой a sll·*poy*
blister волдырь ⓜ val·*dihr'*
blood кровь ⓕ krof'
blood group группа крови ⓕ *gru*·pa kro·vi
blood pressure кровяное давление ⓝ
  kra·vi·*no*·ye dav·*lye*·ni·ye
blood test анализ крови ⓜ a·*na*·lis kro·vi
(dark) blue синий *si*·ni
(light) blue голубой ga·lu·*boy*
board (plane/ship) садиться/сесть
  sa·*dit'*·sa/syest'
boarding house пансионат ⓜ pan·si·a·*nat*
boarding pass посадочный талон ⓜ
  pa·*sa*·dach·nih ta·*lon*
boat лодка ⓕ *lot*·ka
body тело ⓝ *tye*·la
bone кость ⓕ kost'
book книга ⓕ *kni*·ga
book заказывать/заказать
  za·*ka*·zih·vat'/za·ka·*zat'*
booked out распроданы ras·*pro*·da·nih
book shop книжный магазин ⓜ
  knizh·nih ma·ga·*zin*
boots (footwear) сапоги ⓜ sa·pa·*gi*
border граница ⓕ gra·*nit*·sa
bored скучно *skuch*·na
boring скучный *skuch*·nih
borrow брать/взять на время
  brat'/vzyat' na *vryem*·ya
botanic garden ботанический сад ⓜ
  ba·ta·*ni*·chi·ski sat

both оба/обе ⓜ/ⓕ *o-ba/ob-ye*
bottle бутылка ⓕ *bu-tihl-ka*
bottle opener (beer) открывалка ⓕ
 at-krih-val-ka
bottle opener (wine) штопор ⓜ *shto-par*
bottle shop винный магазин ⓜ
 vi-nih ma-ga-zin
bottom (body) зад ⓜ *zat*
bottom (position) дно ⓝ *dno*
boulevard бульвар ⓜ *bul'-var*
bowl миска ⓕ *mis-ka*
box коробка ⓕ *ka-rop-ka*
boxer shorts удлинённые шорты ⓜ pl
 u-dil-nyo-nih-ye shor-tih
boxing бокс ⓜ *boks*
boy мальчик ⓜ *mal'-chik*
boyfriend друг ⓜ *druk*
bra лифчик ⓜ *lif-chik*
brakes тормоза ⓜ pl *tar-ma-za*
brandy коньяк ⓜ *kan-yak*
brave a смелый *smye-lih*
bread хлеб ⓜ *khlyep*
bread rolls булочка ⓕ *bu-lach-ka*
break ломать/сломать *la-mat'/sla-mat'*
breakfast завтрак ⓜ *zaf-trak*
breast (body) грудь ⓕ *grud'*
breathe дышать *dih-shat'*
bribe взятка ⓕ *vzyat-ka*
bribe давать/дать взятку
 da-vat'/dat' vzyat-ku
bridge мост ⓜ *most*
briefcase портфель ⓜ *part-fyel'*
bring приносить/принести
 pri-na-sit'/pri-ni-sti
broccoli брокколи ⓜ *bro-ka-li*
broken (down) сломанный *slo-ma-nih*
bronchitis бронхит ⓜ *bran-khit*
brother брат ⓜ *brat*
brown коричневый *ka-rich-ni-vih*
bruise синяк ⓜ *sin-yak*
brush щётка ⓕ *shot-ka*
bucket ведро ⓝ *vi-dro*
Buddhist буддист/буддистка ⓜ/ⓕ
 bu-dist/bu-dist-ka
budget бюджет ⓜ *byud-zhet*
buffet буфет ⓜ *buf-yet*
bug жук ⓜ *zhuk*
build строить/построить *stro-it'/past-ro-it'*
builder строитель ⓜ *stra-i-til'*
building здание ⓝ *zda-ni-ye*
bumbag поясной кошелёк ⓜ
 pa-yas-noy ka-shal-yok

bureaucracy бюрократия ⓕ
 byu-ra-kra-ti-ya
burn ожог ⓜ *a-zhok*
bus автобус ⓜ *af-to-bus*
bus station автовокзал ⓜ *af-ta-vag-zal*
bus stop остановка ⓕ *a-sta-nof-ka*
business бизнес ⓜ *biz-nis*
business class бизнес-класс ⓜ *biz-nis-klas*
business person бизнесмен ⓜ
 biz-nis-myen
business trip командировка ⓕ
 ka-man-di-rof-ka
busker уличный музыкант ⓜ
 u-lich-nih mu-zih-kant
busy занят/занята ⓜ/ⓕ *za-nit/za-ni-ta*
but но *no*
butcher мясник ⓜ *mis-nik*
butter масло ⓝ *mas-la*
butterfly бабочка ⓕ *ba-bach-ka*
button пуговица ⓕ *pu-ga-vit-sa*
buy покупать/купить *pa-ku-pat'/ku-pit'*

C

cabbage капуста ⓕ *ka-pu-sta*
cable car фуникулёр ⓜ *fu-ni-kul-yor*
café кафе ⓝ *ka-fe*
cake (large) торт ⓜ *tort*
cake (small) пирожное ⓝ *pi-rozh-na-ye*
cake shop кондитерская ⓕ
 kan-di-tir-ska-ya
calculator калькулятор ⓜ *kal'-kul-ya-tar*
calendar календарь ⓜ *ka-lin-dar'*
call звонить/позвонить *zva-nit'/paz-va-nit'*
call (phone) звонок ⓜ *zva-nok*
camera фотоаппарат ⓜ *fo-to-a-pa-rat*
camera shop фотографический
 магазин ⓜ *fo-to-gra-fi-chi-ski ma-ga-zin*
camp располагаться/расположиться
 ras-pa-la-gat'-sa/ras-pa-la-zhiht'-sa
campfire костёр ⓜ *kast-yor*
camp site кемпинг ⓜ *kyem-pink*
can (be able) мочь/смочь *moch'/smoch'*
can (have permission) можно *mozh-na*
can (tin) банка ⓕ *ban-ka*
can opener открывашка ⓕ *at-krih-vash-ka*
Canada Канада ⓕ *ka-na-da*
cancel отменять/отменить
 at-min-yat'/at-mi-nit'
cancer рак ⓜ *rak*
candle свеча ⓕ *svi-cha*
candy конфеты ⓕ pl *kanf-ye-tih*
capsicum перец ⓜ *pye-rits*
car машина ⓕ *ma-shih-na*

car hire прокат автомобилей Ⓜ
pra-*kat* af-ta-ma-*bil*-yey

car owner's title свидетельство о
владении автомобилем Ⓝ
svid-*ye*-til'-stva a vlad-*ye*-ni af-ta-ma-*bil*-yem

car park автостоянка Ⓕ af-ta-sta-*yan*-ka

car registration регистрация машины Ⓕ
ri-*gist*-rat-sih-ya ma-*shih*-nih

caravan автоприцеп Ⓜ af-ta-prit-*sep*

cardiac arrest сердечный приступ Ⓜ
sird-*yech*-nih *pri*-stup

cards (playing) карты Ⓕ pl *kar*-tih

care for ухаживать за u-*kha*-zhih-*vat*' za

carpenter плотник Ⓜ *plot*-nik

carriage вагон Ⓜ va-*gon*

carriage attendant проводник Ⓜ
pra-vad-*nik*

carrot морковь Ⓕ mar-*kof*'

carry нести/понести ni-*sti*/pa-ni-*sti*

cash наличные Ⓝ pl na-*lich*-nih-ye

cash (a cheque) обменивать/обменять
ab-*mye*-ni-*vat*'/ab-min-*yat*'

cashew кешью Ⓜ *kye*-shu

cashier кассир Ⓜ ka-*sir*

casino казино Ⓝ ka-zi-*no*

Caspian Sea Каспийское море Ⓝ
kas-*pi*-ska-ya *mor*-ye

cassette кассета Ⓕ kas-*ye*-ta

castle замок Ⓜ *za*-mak

casual work временная работа Ⓕ
vrye-mi-na-ya ra-*bo*-ta

cat кошка Ⓕ *kosh*-ka

cathedral собор Ⓜ sa-*bor*

Catholic католик/католичка Ⓜ/Ⓕ
ka-*to*-lik/ka-ta-*lich*-ka

cauliflower цветная капуста Ⓕ
tsvit-*na*-ya ka-*pu*-sta

cave пещера Ⓕ pi-*she*-ra

CD компакт-диск Ⓜ kam-pakt-*disk*

celebration праздник Ⓜ *praz*-nik

cell phone мобильный телефон Ⓜ
ma-*bil*'-nih ti-li-*fon*

cemetery кладбище Ⓝ *klad*-bi-she

cent цент Ⓜ tsent

centimetre сантиметр Ⓜ san-tim-*yetr*

centre центр Ⓜ tsentr

ceramics керамика Ⓕ ki-*ra*-mi-ka

cereal хлопья Ⓕ *khlop*-ya

certificate свидетельство Ⓝ svid-*ye*-tilst-va

chain цепь Ⓕ tsep'

chair стул Ⓜ stul

chairlift (ski) подвесной подъёмник Ⓜ
pad-vis-*noy* pad-*yom*-nik

champagne шампанское Ⓝ
sham-*pan*-ska-ye

championships чемпионат Ⓜ
chim-pi-a-*nat*

chance шанс Ⓜ shans

change перемена Ⓕ pi-rim-*ye*-na

change (coins) мелочь Ⓕ *mye*-lach'

change (money) обменивать/обменять
ab-*mye*-ni-*vat*'/ab-min-*yat*'

changing room примерочная Ⓕ
prim-*ye*-rach-na-ya

chat up убалтывать/уболтать
u-*bal*-tih-*vat*'/u-bal-*tat*'

cheap дешёвый di-*sho*-vih

cheat мошенник Ⓜ ma-*she*-nik

check (banking) чек Ⓜ chek

check (bill) счёт Ⓜ shot

check-in (desk) регистрация Ⓕ
ri-gist-*rat*-sih-ya

checkpoint контрольный пункт Ⓜ
kan-*trol*'-nih punkt

Chechnya Чечня Ⓕ chich-*nya*

cheese сыр Ⓜ sihr

chef шеф-повар Ⓜ shef-*po*-var

chemist (pharmacist) фармацевт Ⓜ
far-mat-*seft*

chemist (pharmacy) аптека Ⓕ apt-*ye*-ka

cheque (banking) чек Ⓜ chek

cherry вишня Ⓕ *vish*-nya

chess (set) шахматы Ⓜ pl *shakh*-ma-tih

chessboard шахматная доска Ⓕ
shakh-mat-na-ya da-*ska*

chest (body) грудная клетка Ⓕ
grud-*na*-ya *klyet*-ka

chestnut каштан Ⓜ kash-*tan*

chewing gum жевательная резинка Ⓕ
zhih-*va*-til'-na-ya ri-*zin*-ka

chicken курица Ⓕ *ku*-rit-sa

chicken pox ветрянка Ⓕ vit-*ryan*-ka

child ребёнок Ⓜ rib-*yo*-nak

child seat детский стульчик Ⓜ
dyet-ski *stul*'-chik

childminding присмотр за детьми Ⓜ
pris-*motr* za dit'-*mi*

children дети Ⓝ pl *dye*-ti

chilli чили Ⓝ *chi*-li

China Китай Ⓜ ki-*tey*

chocolate шоколад Ⓜ sha-ka-*lat*

choose выбирать/выбрать
vih-bi-*rat*'/*vih*-brat'

Chornobyl Чернобыль Ⓜ chir-na-*bihl*'

Christian христианин/христианка Ⓜ/Ⓕ
khri-sti-a-*nin*/khri-sti-*an*-ka

Christmas (Day) Рождество ⓝ razh·*dist*·vo
Christmas Eve Сочельник ⓜ sa·*chel*'·nik
church церковь ⓕ *tser*·kaf'
cider сидр ⓜ sidr
cigar сигара ⓕ si·*ga*·ra
cigarette сигарета ⓕ si·gar·*ye*·ta
cigarette lighter зажигалка ⓕ za·zhih·*gal*·ka
cinema кино ⓝ ki·*no*
circus цирк ⓜ tsihrk
citizen гражданин/гражданка ⓜ/ⓕ grazh·da·*nin*/grazh·*dan*·ka
citizenship гражданство ⓝ grazh·*danst*·va
city город ⓜ *go*·rat
city centre центр города ⓜ tsentr *go*·ra·da
civil rights гражданские права ⓝ pl grazh·*dan*·ski·ye pra·*va*
class (category) класс ⓜ klas
classical классический kla·*si*·chi·ski
clean a чистый *chi*·stih
clean чистить/почистить *chi*·stit'/pa·*chi*·stit'
cleaning уборка ⓕ u·*bor*·ka
client клиент ⓜ kli·*yent*
climb подниматься/подняться pad·ni·*mat*'·sa/pad·*nyat*'·sa
cloakroom гардероб ⓜ gar·di·*rop*
clock часы ⓜ pl chi·*sih*
close закрывать/закрыть za·krih·*vat*'/za·*kriht*'
close (nearby) близкий *blis*·kih
closed закрытый za·*krih*·tih
clothesline верёвка для белья ⓕ vir·*yof*·ka dlya bil·*ya*
clothing одежда ⓕ ad·*yezh*·da
clothing store магазин готового платья ⓜ ma·ga·*zin* ga·to·va·va *plat*·ya
cloud облако ⓝ *ob*·la·ka
cloudy облачный *ob*·lach·nih
clutch (car) сцепление ⓝ stsep·*lye*·ni·ye
coach (bus) автобус ⓜ af·*to*·bus
coach (sport) тренер ⓜ *tre*·nir
coast берег ⓜ *bye*·rik
coat пальто ⓝ pal'·*to*
cocaine кокаин ⓜ ka·ka·*in*
cockroach таракан ⓜ ta·ra·*kan*
cocktail коктейль ⓜ kak·*teyl*
cocoa какао ⓝ ka·*ka*·o
coffee кофе ⓜ *kof*·ye
coins монеты ⓕ pl man·*ye*·tih
cold простуда ⓕ pra·*stu*·da
cold холодный kha·*lod*·nih
colleague коллега ⓜ&ⓕ kal·*ye*·ga

collect call звонок по коллекту ⓜ zva·*nok* pa kal·*yek*·tu
college техникум ⓜ *tyekh*·ni·kum
colour цвет ⓜ tsvyet
comb расчёска ⓕ ras·*chos*·ka
come приходить/прийти pri·kha·*dit*'/pri·*ti*
comfortable удобный u·*dob*·nih
commission комиссионные ⓜ pl ka·mi·si·o·nih·ye
communion (religious) Святое Причастие ⓝ svi·*to*·ye pri·*cha*·sti·ye
communism коммунизм ⓜ ka·mu·*nizm*
communist коммунист/коммунистка ⓜ/ⓕ ka·mu·*nist*/ka·mu·*nist*·ka
companion попутчик/попутчица ⓜ/ⓕ pa·*put*·chik/pa·*put*·chit·sa
company (firm) компания ⓕ kam·*pa*·ni·ya
compass компас ⓜ *kom*·pas
complain жаловаться/пожаловаться *zha*·la·vat'·sa/pa·*zha*·la·vat'·sa
complaint жалоба ⓕ *zha*·la·ba
complimentary (free) бесплатный bis·*plat*·nih
computer компьютер ⓜ kam·*pyu*·tir
computer game компьютерная игра ⓕ kam·*pyu*·tir·na·ya i·*gra*
concert концерт ⓜ kant·*sert*
concussion сотрясение мозга ⓝ sat·ris·*ye*·ni·ye *moz*·ga
conditioner (hair) бальзам ⓜ bal'·*zam*
condolence соболезнование ⓝ sa·ba·*lyez*·na·va·ni·ye
condom презерватив ⓜ pri·zir·va·*tif*
conference (big) съезд ⓜ syest
conference (small) конференция ⓕ kan·fir·*yent*·sih·ya
confirm (booking) подтверждать/подтвердить pat·virzh·*dat*'/pat·vir·*dit*'
conjunctivitis конъюнктивит ⓜ kan·yunk·ti·*vit*
connection (transport) связи ⓕ *svya*·zi
conservative консервативный kan·sir·va·*tiv*·nih
constipation запор ⓜ za·*por*
consulate консульство ⓝ *kon*·sulst·vo
contact lens solution раствор для контактных линз ⓜ rast·*vor* dlya kan·*takt*·nihkh lins
contact lenses контактные линзы ⓕ pl kan·*takt*·nih·ye *lin*·zih

contraceptives
противозачаточные средства ⓝ pl
pra·ti·va·za·*cha*·tach·nih·ye *sryetst*·va
contract контракт ⓜ kan·*trakt*
convent женский монастырь ⓜ
zhen·skih ma·na·*stihr*
cook повар ⓜ *po*·var
cook готовить/приготовить
ga·*to*·vit'/pri·*ga*·to·vit'
cookie печенье ⓝ pi·*chen*·ye
cooking кулинария ⓕ ku·li·*na*·ri·ya
cool (temperature) прохладный
pra·*khlad*·nih
corkscrew штопор ⓜ *shto*·par
corn кукуруза ⓕ ku·ku·*ru*·za
corner угол ⓜ *u*·gal
cost v стоить *sto*·it'
cotton хлопок ⓜ *khlo*·pak
cotton balls ватные шарики ⓜ pl
vat·nih·ye *sha*·ri·ki
cotton buds ватные палочки ⓕ pl
vat·nih·ye pa·*lach*·ki
cough кашель ⓜ *ka*·shel'
cough medicine жидкость от кашля ⓕ
zhiht·kast' at *kash*·lya
count считать/посчитать shi·*tat*'/pa·shi·*tat*'
country страна ⓕ stra·*na*
countryside сельская местность ⓕ
syel'·ska·ya *myes*·nast'
coupon талон ⓜ ta·*lon*
courgette кабачок ⓜ ka·ba·*chok*
court (legal) суд ⓜ sut
court (tennis) корт ⓜ kort
cover charge плата за кувер т ⓕ
pla·ta za kuv·*yert*
cow корова ⓕ ka·*ro*·va
cracker (biscuit) печенье ⓝ pi·*chen*·ye
crafts ремёсла ⓕ pl *slif*·ki
crash авария ⓕ a·*va*·ri·ya
crazy сумасшедший su·ma·*shet*·shi
cream (food) сливки ⓕ pl *slif*·ki
cream (ointment) крем ⓜ kryem
crèche ясли ⓜ pl *yas*·li
credit кредит ⓜ kri·*dit*
credit card кредитная карточка ⓕ
kri·*dit*·na·ya *kar*·tach·ka
cross (religious) крест ⓜ kryest
cross-country skiing катание на обычных
лыжах по ровной местности ⓝ
ka·*ta*·ni·ye na a·*bihch*·nihkh *lih*·zhakh pa
rov·ney *myes*·na·sti
crowded заполнено людьми
za·*pol*·ni·na lyud'·mi

cruise круиз ⓜ kru·*is*
cucumber огурец ⓜ a·gur·*yets*
cup чашка ⓕ *chash*·ka
cupboard шкаф ⓜ shkaf
currency exchange обмен валюты ⓜ
ab·*myen* val·*yu*·tih
current (electricity) ток ⓜ tok
current affairs
политические события и новости pl
pa·li·*ti*·chi·ski·ye sa·*bih*·ti·ya i *no*·va·sti
curry кэрри ⓕ *ke*·ri
custom обычай ⓜ a·*bih*·chey
customs таможня ⓕ ta·*mozh*·nya
customs declaration
таможенная декларация ⓕ
ta·*mo*·zhen·na·ya di·kla·*rat*·sih·ya
cut резать/нарезать *rye*·zat'/na·*rye*·zat'
cutlery столовый прибор ⓜ
sta·*lo*·vih pri·*bor*
CV автобиография ⓕ af·ta·bi·a·*gra*·fi·ya
cycle ездить на велосипеде
yez·dit' na vi·la·*sip*·yed·ye
cycling езда на велосипеде
yiz·*da* na vi·la·*sip*·yed·ye
cyclist велосипедист ⓜ vi·la·si·pi·*dist*
cystitis цистит ⓜ tsih·*stit*

D

dad папа ⓕ *pa*·pa
daily ежедневный yi·zhih·*dnyev*·nih
dance v танцевать tant·sih·*vat*'
dancing танцы ⓜ pl *tant*·sih
dangerous опасный a·*pas*·nih
dark тёмный *tyom*·nih
date (appointment) встреча ⓕ *fstrye*·cha
date (day) число ⓝ chis·*lo*
date (person) v встречаться с fstri·*chat*'·sa s
date of birth дата рождения ⓕ
da·ta razh·*dye*·ni·ya
daughter дочка ⓕ *doch*·ka
dawn рассвет ⓜ ras·*vyet*
day день ⓜ dyen'
day after tomorrow послезавтра
pas·li·*zaf*·tra
day before yesterday позавчера
pa·zaf·chi·*ra*
dead мёртвый *myort*·vih
deaf глухой glu·*khoy*
deal (cards) сдавать/сдать zda·*vat*'/zdat'
December декабрь ⓜ di·*kabr*'
decide решать/решить ri·*shat*'/ri·*shiht*'
deep глубокий glu·*bo*·ki
degrees (temperature) градус ⓜ *gra*·dus

E

delay задержка ① *zad-yersh-ka*
delicatessen гастроном ① *gas-tra-nom*
deliver доставлять/доставить
  da-stav-*lyat*/da-*sta*-vit'
democracy демократия ① di-ma-*kra*-ti-ya
demonstration манифестация ①
  ma-ni-fi-*stat*-sih-ya
Denmark Дания ① *da*-ni-ya
dental dam латексная салфетка ①
  la-tiks-na-ya sal-*fyet*-ka
dental floss
  вощёная нитка для чистки зубов ①
  va-*sho*-na-ya *nit*-ka dlya *chist*-ki zu-*bof*
dentist зубной врач ① zub-*noy* vrach
deodorant дезодорант ⓜ di-zo-da-*rant*
depart отправляться/отправиться
  at-prav-*lyat*'-sa/at-*pra*-vit'-sa
department store универмаг ⓜ
  u-ni-vir-*mak*
departure отъезд ⓜ *at-yest*
departure gate выход на посадку ⓜ
  vih-khat na pa-*sat*-ku
deposit задаток ⓜ *za-da*-tak
descendent потомок ⓜ pa-*to*-mak
desert пустыня ① pu-*stihn*-ya
dessert десерт ⓜ dis-*yert*
destination место назначения ⓜ
  mye-sta naz-na-*che*-ni-ya
details подробности ① pl pa-*drob*-na-sti
diabetes диабет ⓜ di-ab-*yet*
diaper подгузник ⓜ pad-*guz*-nik
diaphragm диафрагма ① di-a-*frag*-ma
diarrhoea понос ⓜ pa-*nos*
diary дневник ⓜ dnyev-*nik*
dictionary словарь ⓜ sla-*var'*
die умереть u-*mir*-yet'
diet диета ① di-*ye*-ta
different другой dru-*goy*
difficult трудный *trud*-nih
dining car вагон-ресторан ⓜ
  va-*gon*-ri-sta-ran
dinner ужин ⓜ u-*zhin*
direct прямой pri-*moy*
direct-dial (by) прямым набором
  номера pri-*mihm* na-*bo*-ram no-*mi*-ra
direction направление ⓜ na-prav-*lye*-ni-ye
director директор ⓜ dir-*yek*-tar
dirty грязный *gryaz*-nih
disaster катастрофа ① ka-tas-*tro*-fa
disabled инвалид ⓜ in-va-*lit*
disco дискотека ① dis-kat-*ye*-ka
discount скидка ① *skit*-ka
disease болезнь ① bal-*yezn'*
dish блюдо ⓜ *blyu*-da

disk (CD-ROM/floppy) диск ⓜ disk
diving подводное плавание ⓜ
  pad-*vod*-na-ye *pla*-va-ni-ye
divorced разведённый raz-vid-*yo*-nih
dizzy кружится голова kru-*zhiht*-sa ga-la-*va*
do делать/сделать *dye*-lat'/*zdye*-lat'
doctor врач ⓜ vrach
documentary документальный фильм ⓜ
  da-ku-min-*tal'*-nih film
dog собака ① sa-*ba*-ka
doll кукла ① *kuk*-la
dollar доллар ⓜ *do*-lar
dominoes домино ① da-*mi*-no
door дверь ① dvyer'
double a двойной dvey-*noy*
double bed двуспальная кровать ①
  dvu-*spal'*-na-ya kra-*vat'*
double room номер на двоих ⓜ
  no-mir na dva-*ikh*
down вниз vnis
downhill под уклон pad u-*klon*
drama драма ① *dra*-ma
dream сон ⓜ son
dress платье ⓜ *plat*-ye
drink (alcoholic) спиртной напиток ⓜ
  spirt-*noy* na-*pi*-tak
drink (general) напиток ⓜ na-*pi*-tak
drink пить/выпить pit'/*vih*-pit'
drive v водить машину va-*dit'* ma-*shih*-nu
drivers licence водительские права ① pl
  va-*di*-til'-ski-ye pra-*va*
drug dealer нарко-диллер ⓜ nar-ko-*di*-ler
drug trafficking оборот наркотиков ⓜ
  a-ba-*rot* nar-*ko*-ti-kaf
drug user наркоман ⓜ nar-ka-*man*
drugs (illegal) наркотики ① pl nar-*ko*-ti-ki
drums барабаны ⓜ pl ba-ra-*ba*-nih
drunk пьяный *pya*-nih
dry a сухой su-*khoy*
dry (clothes) сушить/высушить
  su-*shiht*/*vih*-su-shiht'
duck утка ① *ut*-ka
dummy (pacifier) соска ① *sos*-ka
DVD DVD ⓜ di-vi-*di*

E

each каждый *kazh*-dih
ear ухо ⓜ *u*-kha
early ранний *ra*-ni
earn зарабатывать/заработать
  za-ra-*ba*-tih-vat'/za-ra-*bo*-tat'
earplugs затычки для ушей ① pl
  za-*tihch*-ki dlya u-*shey*

earrings серёжки ① pl sir-*yosh*-ki
Earth земля ① *zim*-lya
east восток ⑩ va-*stok*
Easter Пасха ① *pas*-kha
easy лёгкий *lyokh*-ki
eat есть/съесть yest'/syest'
economy class пассажирский класс ⑩
   pa-sa-*zhihr*-ski klas
eczema экзема ① eg-*zye*-ma
education образование ⑩
   a-bra-za-*va*-ni-ye
egg яйцо ① yeyt-*so*
eggplant баклажан ⑩ bak-la-*zhan*
election выборы ⑩ pl vih-*ba*-rih
electrical store электронный
   универмаг ⑩ e-lik-*tro*-nih u-ni-vir-*mak*
electricity электричество ⑩
   e-lik-*tri*-chist-va
elevator лифт ⑩ lift
email и-мейл ⑩ i-*meyl*
embarrassed смущённый smu-*sho*-nih
embassy посольство ⑩ pa-*solst*-va
emergency авария ① a-*va*-ri-ya
emotional эмоциональный
   e-mot-sih-a-*nal*-nih
employee служащий/служащая ⑩/①
   slu-zha-shi/*slu*-zha-sha-ya
employer работодатель ⑩
   ra-bo-ta-*dat*-yel'
empty пустой pu-*stoy*
encephalitis энцефалит ⑩ ent-sih-fa-*lit*
end конец ⑩ kan-*yets*
engaged (person) обручённый
   ab-ru-*cho*-nih
engaged (phone) занято *zan*-ya-ta
engagement (wedding) обручение ⑩
   ab-ru-*che*-ni-ye
engine мотор ⑩ ma-*tor*
engineer инженер ⑩ in-*zhihn*-yer
engineering инженерное дело ⑩
   in-*zhihn*-yer-na-ye *dye*-la
England Англия ① *an*-gli-ya
English (language) английский an-*gli*-ski
Englishman англичанин ⑩ an-gli-*cha*-nin
Englishwoman англичанка ①
   an-gli-*chan*-ka
enjoy (oneself) наслаждаться/
   насладиться nas-lazh-*dat'*-sa/nas-la-*dit'*-sa
enough достаточно da-*sta*-tach-na
enter входить/войти fkha-*dit'*/vey-*ti*
entertainment guide путеводитель ⑩
   pu-ti-va-*di*-til'
entry вход ⑩ fkhot

envelope конверт ⑩ kanv-*yert*
environment окружающая среда ①
   a-kru-*zha*-yu-sha-ya sri-*da*
epilepsy эпилепсия ① e-pil-*yep*-si-ya
equal opportunity равные возможности
   ① pl *rav*-ni-ye vaz-*mozh*-na-sti
equality равноправие ⑩ rav-na-*pra*-vi-ye
equipment оборудование ⑩
   a-ba-*ru*-da-va-ni-ye
escalator эскалатор ⑩ e-ska-*la*-tar
estate agency риэлтер ⑩ ri-*el*-tar
Estonia Эстония ① e-*sto*-ni-ya
ethnic этнический et-*ni*-chi-ski
ethnic minority национальность ①
   nat-sih-a-*nal'*-nast'
euro евро ⑩ *yev*-ro
Europe Европа ① yev-*ro*-pa
euthanasia эйтаназия ① ey-ta-*na*-zi-ya
evening вечер ⑩ *vye*-chir
every каждый *kazh*-dih
everyone все fsye
everything всё fsyo
exactly точно *toch*-na
excellent отличный at-*lich*-nih
excess (baggage) перевес ⑩ pi-riv-*yes*
exchange менять/обменять
   min-*yat'*/ab-min-*yat'*
exchange rate обменный курс ⑩
   ab-*mye*-nih kurs
exhaust (car) выхлопная труба ①
   vih-khlap-*na*-ya *tru*-ba
exhibition выставка ① *vih*-staf-ka
exit выход ⑩ *vih*-khat
expensive дорогой da-ra-*goy*
experience опыт ⑩ *o*-piht
express (mail) экспресс ⑩ eks-*pres*
extension (visa) продление ①
   prad-*lye*-ni-ye
eye drops глазные капли ① pl
   glaz-*nih*-ye ka-pli
eyes глаза ① pl gla-*za*

F

fabric ткань ① tkan'
face лицо ⑩ lit-*so*
face cloth личное полотенце ①
   lich-no-ye pa-lat-*yent*-se
factory фабрика ① *fa*-bri-ka
factory worker рабочий/рабочая ⑩/①
   ra-*bo*-chi/ra-*bo*-cha-ya
fall (autumn) осень ① *o*-sin'
fall (down) падать/упасть *pa*-dat'/u-*past'*
family семья ① sim-*ya*

family name фамилия ① fa·*mi*·li·ya
famous знаменитый zna·mi·*ni*·tih
fan (machine) вентилятор ⓜ vin·til·*ya*·tar
fan (sport) болельщик/болельщица ⓜ/①
bal·*yel'*·shik/bal·*yel'*·shit·sa
far далеко da·li·*ko*
fare плата ① *pla*·ta
farm ферма ① *fyer*·ma
farmer фермер ⓜ *fyer*·mir
fashion мода ① *mo*·da
fast быстрый *bihst*·rih
fat толстый *tol*·stih
father отец ⓜ at·*yets*
father-in-law (wife's father)
свёкор ⓜ *svyo*·kar
father-in-law (husband's father)
тесть ⓜ tyest'
fault (someone's) вина ① vi·*na*
faulty ошибочный a·*shih*·bach·nih
fax machine факс ⓜ faks
February февраль ⓜ fiv·*ral'*
feel (touch) трогать/потрогать
tro·gat'/pa·*tro*·gat'
feelings чувства ⓝ pl *chust*·va
female женский *zhen*·ski
ferry паром ⓜ pa·*rom*
festival фестиваль ⓜ fi·sti·*val'*
fever лихорадка ① li·kha·*rat*·ka
few мало *ma*·la
fiancé жених ⓜ zhih·*nikh*
fiancée невеста ① niv·*ye*·sta
fiction художественная литература ①
khu·*do*·zhihst·vi·na·ya li·ti·ra·*tu*·ra
fight драка ① *dra*·ka
fill наполнять/наполнить
na·paln·*yat'*/na·*pol*·nit'
film (camera) плёнка ① *plyon*·ka
film (cinema) фильм ⓜ film
film speed скорость протяжки плёнки ①
sko·rast' prat·*yash*·ki *plyon*·ki
filtered с фильтром s *fil'*·tram
find находить/найти na·kha·*dit'*/ney·*ti*
fine (penalty) штраф ⓜ shtraf
fine a хороший kha·*ro*·shih
finger палец ⓜ *pa*·lits
finish конец ⓜ kan·*yets*
finish кончать/кончить kan·*chat'*/*kon*·chit'
Finland Финляндия ① fin·*lyan*·di·ya
fire (emergency) пожар ⓜ pa·*zhar*
fire (heat) огонь ⓜ a·*gon'*
firewood дрова ① *dra*·va
first a первый *pyer*·vih

first-aid kit санитарная сумка ①
sa·ni·*tar*·na·ya *sum*·ka
first class в первом классе
f *pyer*·vam *klas*·ye
first name имя ⓝ *im*·ya
fish рыба ① *rih*·ba
fishing рыболовство ⓝ rih·ba·*lofst*·va
fish shop рыбный магазин ⓜ
rihb·nih ma·ga·*zin*
flag флаг ⓜ flak
flashlight фонарик ⓜ fa·*na*·rik
flat (apartment) квартира ① kvar·*ti*·ra
flat плоский *plo*·ski
flea блоха ① bla·*kha*
fleamarket блошиный рынок ⓜ
bla·*shih*·nih *rih*·nak
flight полёт ⓜ pal·*yot*
flood наводнение ⓝ na·vad·*nye*·ni·ye
floor (room) пол ⓜ pol
floor (storey) этаж ⓜ e·*tash*
flour мука ① mu·*ka*
flower цветок ⓜ tsvi·*tok*
flu грипп ⓜ grip
fly муха ① *mu*·kha
foggy туманно tu·*ma*·na
follow следовать/последовать
slye·da·vat'/pas·*lye*·da·vat'
food еда ① yi·*da*
food supplies продовольствие ⓝ
pra·da·*volst*·vi·ye
foot нога ① na·*ga*
football (soccer) футбол ⓜ fud·*bol*
footpath тротуар ⓜ tra·tu·*ar*
foreign иностранный i·nast·*ra*·nih
forest лес ⓜ lyes
forever навсегда naf·*syeg*·da
forget забывать/забыть za·bih·*vat'*/za·*biht'*
fork вилка ① *vil*·ka
fortnight adv две недели dvye nid·*ye*·li
fortune teller гадалка ① ga·*dal*·ka
foul нарушение ⓝ na·ru·*she*·ni·ye
fragile хрупкий *khrup*·ki
France Франция ① *frant*·sih·ya
free (available) свободный sva·*bod*·nih
free (gratis) бесплатный bis·*plat*·nih
fresh свежий *svye*·zhih
Friday пятница ① *pyat*·nit·sa
fridge холодильник ⓜ kha·la·*dil'*·nik
friend друг/подруга ⓜ/① druk/pa·*dru*·ga
from от ot
frost мороз ⓜ ma·*ros*
fruit фрукты ⓜ pl *fruk*·tih
fry жарить/пожарить *zha*·rit'/pa·*zha*·rit'

frying pan сковорода ⓕ ska·va·ra·*da*
full полный *pol*·nih
full-time на полной ставке
na *pol*·ney staf·*kye*
fun adv весело vye·si·la
funeral похороны ⓜ pl *po*·kha·ra·nih
funny смешной smish·*noy*
furniture мебель ⓕ *mye*·bil'
future будущее ⓝ *bu*·du·shi·ye

G

game (match) матч ⓜ mach
game (type of sport) спорт ⓜ sport
garage гараж ⓜ ga·*rash*
garbage мусор ⓜ *mu*·sar
garbage can помойный ящик ⓜ
pa·*moy*·nih ya·*shik*
garden сад ⓜ sat
gardener садовод ⓜ sa·da·*vot*
gardening садоводство ⓝ sa·da·*votst*·va
garlic чеснок ⓜ chis·*nok*
gas (cooking) газ ⓜ gas
gas (petrol) бензин ⓜ bin·*zin*
gastroenteritis гастроэнтерит ⓜ
ga·stra·en·ti·*rit*
gate (airport) выход на посадку ⓜ
vih·khat na pa·*sat*·ku
gauze марля ⓕ *marl*·ya
gay гей ⓜ gey
Georgia Грузия ⓕ *gru*·zi·ya
German (language) немецкий ⓜ
nim·*yet*·ski
Germany Германия ⓕ gir·*ma*·ni·ya
get получить
pa·lu·*chat*/pa·lu·*chit*
get off (train, etc) сходить/сойти
skha·*dit*/sey·*ti*
gift подарок ⓜ pa·*da*·rak
gin джин ⓜ dzhihn
girl (teenage) девушка ⓕ *dye*·vush·ka
girl (pre-teen) девочка ⓕ *dye*·vach·ka
girlfriend подруга ⓕ pa·*dru*·ga
give давать/дать da·*vat*/dat'
given name имя ⓝ *im*·ya
glandular fever железистая лихорадка ⓕ
zhihl·*ye*·zi·sta·ya li·kha·*rat*·ka
glasnost гласность ⓕ *glas*·nast'
glass стакан ⓜ sta·*kan*
glasses (spectacles) очки ⓝ pl ach·*ki*
gloves перчатки ⓝ pl pir·*chat*·ki
glue клей ⓜ klyey
go (on foot) идти/пойти i·*ti*/pey·*ti*

go (by vehicle) ехать/поехать
ye·khat'/pa·*ye*·khat'
go out выходить/выйти vih·kha·*dit*/*vih*·ti
go out with встречаться с fstri·*chat*·sa s
goal гол ⓜ gol
goat козёл ⓜ kaz·*yol*
god (general) бог ⓜ bok
goggles очки ⓝ pl ach·*ki*
gold золото ⓝ *zo*·la·ta
golf ball гольф-мяч ⓜ *golf*·myach
golf course корт для гольфа ⓜ
kort dlya *gol*'fa
good хороший kha·*ro*·shih
government правительство ⓝ
pra·*vi*·til'·stva
gram грамм ⓜ gram
granddaughter внучка ⓕ *vnuch*·ka
grandfather дедушка ⓜ *dye*·dush·ka
grandmother бабушка ⓕ *ba*·bush·ka
grandson внук ⓜ vnuk
grass трава ⓕ tra·*va*
grateful благодарный bla·ga·*dar*·nih
grave могила ⓕ ma·*gi*·la
great (fantastic) отличный at·*lich*·nih
green зелёный zil·*yo*·nih
greengrocer зеленщик ⓜ zi·lin·*shik*
grey серый *sye*·rih
grocery гастроном ⓜ gast·ra·*nom*
grow расти/вырасти ra·*sti*/vih·ra·sti
guaranteed с гарантией z ga·*ran*·ti·yey
guess догадываться/догадаться
da·*ga*·dih·vat'·sa/da·ga·*dat*'·sa
guesthouse гостиница ⓕ ga·*sti*·nit·sa
guide (audio) аудио-путеводитель ⓜ
au·di·o·pu·ti·va·*di*·til'
guide (person) гид ⓜ git
guidebook путеводитель ⓜ pu·ti·va·*di*·til'
guide dog собака-поводырь ⓕ
sa·*ba*·ka·pa·va·*dihr*
guided tour организованная экскурсия
ⓕ ar·ga·ni·zo·va·na·ya ik·*skur*·si·ya
guilty виновный vi·*nov*·nih
guitar гитара ⓕ gi·*ta*·ra
Gulag (prison) ГУЛАГ ⓜ gu·*lak*
gun ружьё ⓝ ruzh·*yo*
gym спортзал ⓜ sport·*zal*
gymnastics гимнастика ⓕ gim·*na*·sti·ka
gynaecologist гинеколог ⓜ gi·ni·*ko*·lak

H

hair волосы ⓜ pl *vo*·la·sih
hairbrush щётка для волос ⓕ
shot·ka dlya *vo*·las

haircut стрижка ⓕ *strish*-ka
hairdresser парикмахер ⓜ pa-rik-*ma*-khir
halal халал ⓜ kha-*lal*
half половина ⓕ pa-la-*vi*-na
hallucination галлюцинация ⓕ
  gal-yut-sih-*nat*-sih-ya
ham ветчина ⓕ vit-chi-*na*
hammer молоток ⓜ ma-la-*tok*
hammer and sickle серп и молот ⓜ
  syerp i *mo*-lat
hammock гамак ⓜ ga-*mak*
hand рука ⓕ ru-*ka*
handbag сумочка ⓕ *su*-mach-ka
handkerchief носовой платок ⓜ
  na-sa-*voy* pla-*tok*
handlebars руль ⓜ rul'
handmade ручной работы
  ruch-*noy* ra-*bo*-tih
handsome красивый kra-*si*-vih
happy счастливый shis-*li*-vih
harbour гавань ⓕ *ga*-van'
hard (not soft) твёрдый *tvyor*-dih
hard-boiled вкрутую fkru-*tu*-yu
hardware store хозяйственный магазин
  ⓜ khaz-*yeyst*-vi-nih ma-ga-*zin*
hashish гашиш ⓜ ga-*shihsh*
hat шапка ⓕ *shap*-ka
have у ... есть у ... yest'
have a cold простужаться/простудиться
  pra-stu-*zhat*-sa/pra-stu-*dit*-sa
have fun веселиться/развеселиться
  vi-si-*lit*-sa/pa-vi-si-*lit*-sa
hay fever сенная лихорадка ⓕ
  si-*na*-ya li-kha-*rat*-ka
hazelnut лесной орех ⓜ lis-*noy* ar-*yekh*
he он on
head голова ⓕ ga-la-*va*
headache головная боль ⓕ
  ga-lav-*na*-ya bol'
headlights фары ⓕ pl *fa*-rih
health здоровье ⓝ zda-*rov*-ye
hear слышать/услышать
  slih-*shat*/us-*lih*-shat'
hearing aid слуховой аппарат ⓜ
  slu-kha-*voy* a-pa-*rat*
heart сердце ⓝ *syerd*-tsih
heart attack сердечный приступ ⓜ
  sird-*yech*-nih *pri*-stup
heart condition болезнь сердца ⓕ
  bal-*yezn'* *syerd*-tsa
heat жара ⓕ zha-*ra*
heated обогреваемый a-ba-gri-*ma*-i-vih
heater обогреватель ⓜ a-ba-gri-*va*-til'

heavy тяжёлый tya-*zho*-lih
helmet шлем ⓜ shlyem
help помощь ⓕ *po*-mash'
help помогать/помочь
  pa-ma-*gat*/pa-*moch*'
hepatitis гепатит ⓜ gi-pa-*tit*
her (possession) её yi-*yo*
herb трава ⓕ tra-*va*
herbal травяной trav-ya-*noy*
herbalist специалист по травам ⓜ
  spit-sih-a-*list* pa tra-*vam*
here здесь zdyes'
heroin героин ⓜ gi-ra-*in*
high (distance) высокий vih-*so*-ki
highchair высокий стульчик ⓜ
  vih-*so*-ki stul'-chik
high school средняя школа ⓕ
  sryed-ni-ya *shko*-la
highway шоссе ⓝ sha-*se*
hike v ходить пешком kha-*dit'* pish-*kom*
hiking поход ⓜ pa-*khot*
hill холм ⓜ kholm
Hindu индус/индуска ⓜ/ⓕ
  in-*dus*/in-*dus*-ka
hire брать/взять напрокат
  brat'/vzyat' na-pra-*kat*
his его yi-*vo*
historical исторический i-sta-*ri*-chi-ski
history история ⓕ i-*sto*-ri-ya
hitchhike путешествовать автостопом
  pu-ti-*shest*-va-vat' af-ta-*sto*-pam
HIV ВИЧ ⓜ vich
hockey хоккей ⓜ khak-*yey*
holiday праздник ⓜ *praz*-nik
holidays отпуск ⓜ *ot*-pusk
home дом ⓜ dom
homeless бездомный biz-*dom*-nih
homemaker домохозяйка ⓕ
  do-ma-khaz-*yey*-ka
homosexual гомосексуалист ⓜ
  go-mo-sik-su-a-*list*
honey мёд ⓜ myot
honeymoon медовый месяц ⓜ
  mi-*do*-vih *mye*-sits
horoscope гороскоп ⓜ ga-ra-*skop*
horse лошадь ⓕ *lo*-shat'
horse riding верховая езда ⓕ
  vir-kha-*va*-ya yiz-*da*
hospital больница ⓕ bol'-*nit*-sa
hospitality гостеприимство ⓝ
  ga-sti-pri-*imst*-va
hot жаркий *zhar*-ki

hot water горячая вода ①
  gar·*ya*-chi-ya va-*da*
hotel гостиница ① ga-*sti*-nit-sa
hour час ⓜ chas
house дом ⓜ dom
housework домашние дела ⓝ pl
  da-*mash*-ni-ye dye-*la*
how как kak
how much сколько *skol*·ka
hug обнимать/обнять ab-ni-*mat'*/*ab*-nyat'
human resources
  управление персоналом ⓝ
  u-prav-*lye*-ni-ye pir-sa-*na*-lam
human rights права человека ⓝ pl
  pra-*va* chi-lav-*ye*-ka
humid влажный *vlazh*-nih
hungry (be) голоден/голодна
  go-la-din/ga-*lad*-na
hurt v болеть bal·*yet'*
husband муж ⓜ mush
hypothermia гипотермия ①
  gi-*pat*-*yer*-mi-ya

I

I я ya
ice лёд ⓜ lyot
ice axe ледоруб ⓜ lye-da-*rup*
ice cream мороженое ⓝ ma-*ro*-zhih-na-ye
ice-cream parlour кафе-мороженое ⓝ
  ka-*fe*-ma-*ro*-zhih-na-ye
ice hockey хоккей на льду ⓜ
  khak-*yey* na ldu
ice skating катание на коньках ⓝ
  ka-*ta*-ni-ye na kan'-*kakh*
identification установление личности ①
  u-sta-nav-*lye*-ni-ye *lich*-na-sti
ID card идентификационная карта ①
  id-yen-ti-fi-*kat*-sih-o-na-ya *kar*-ta
idiot дурак ⓜ du-*rak*
if если *yes*-li
ill болен *bo*-lin
immigration иммиграция ①
  i-mi-*grat*-sih-ya
important важный *vazh*-nih
impossible невозможно ni-*vaz*-*mozh*-na
in в v
(be) in a hurry спешить spi-*shiht'*
in front of перед *pye*-rit
included включая fklyu-*cha*-ya
income tax подоходный налог ⓜ
  pa-da-*khod*-nih na-*lok*
indicator (car) указатель ⓜ u-ka-*za*-til'
indoor закрытый za-*krih*-tih

industry промышленность ①
  pra-*mihsh*-li-nast'
infection инфекция ① inf-*yekt*-sih-ya
inflammation воспаление ⓝ
  vas-pal-*ye*-ni-ye
influenza грип ⓜ grip
information информация ①
  in-far-*mat*-sih-ya
ingredient ингредиент ⓜ in-gri-di-*yent*
inject делать/сделать укол
  dye-lat'/*zdye*-lat' u-*kol*
injection инъекция ① in-*yekt*-sih-ya
injury травма ① *trav*-ma
innocent невиновный nye-vi-*nov*-nih
inside внутри vnu-*tri*
instructor инструктор ⓜ ins-*truk*-tar
insurance страхование ⓝ stra-kha-*va*-ni-ye
interesting интересный in-tir-*yes*-nih
international международный
  mizh-du-na-*rod*-nih
Internet интернет ⓜ in-ter-*net*
Internet café интернет-кафе ⓝ
  in-ter-*net*-ka-fe
interpreter переводчик ⓜ pi-ri-*vot*-chik
interview интервью ⓝ in-tir-*vyu*
invite приглашать/пригласить
  pri-gla-*shat'*/pri-gla-*sit'*
Ireland Ирландия ① ir-*lan*-di-ya
iron (clothes) утюг ⓜ ut-*yuk*
island остров ⓜ *ost*-raf
Israel Израиль ⓜ iz-ra-*il'*
it оно a-*no*
IT компьютеры ⓜ pl kam-*pyu*-ti-ri
Italy Италия ① i-*ta*-li-ya
itch зуд ⓜ zut
itemised указанный по пунктам
  u-*ka*-za-nih pa *punk*-tam
itinerary маршрут ⓜ marsh-*rut*
IUD ВМС ⓜ ve-em-*se*

J

jacket (for men) куртка ① *kurt*-ka
jacket (for women) жакет ⓜ zhak-*yet*
jail тюрьма ① tyur'-*ma*
jam джем ⓜ dzhem
January январь ⓜ yan-*var'*
Japan Япония ① ya-*po*-ni-ya
jar банка ① *ban*-ka
jaw челюсть ① *chel*-yust'
jeans джинсы ⓝ pl *dzhihn*-zih
jeep джип ⓜ dzhihp

jet lag нарушение суточного ритма организма ⓝ na-ru-*she*-ni-ye *su*-tach-na-va *rit*-ma ar-ga-*niz*-ma
jewellery ювелирные изделия ⓝ pl yu-vi-*lir*-nih-ye iz-*dye*-li-ya
Jewish еврей/еврейка ⓜ/ⓕ *yiv*-rey/yiv-*rey*-ka
job работа ⓕ ra-*bo*-ta
jogging бег трусцой byek trust-*soy*
joke анекдот ⓜ a-nik-*dot*
journalist журналист/журналистка ⓜ/ⓕ zhur-na-*list*/zhur-na-*list*-ka
journey путешествие ⓝ pu-ti-*shest*-vi-ye
judge судья ⓜ sud-*ya*
juice сок ⓜ sok
July июль ⓜ i-*yul'*
jumper (sweater) джемпер ⓜ *dzhem*-pir
jumper leads проводник для соединения напрямую ⓜ pra-vad-*nik* dlya sa-i-*din*-ye-ni-ya nap-*rya*-mu-yu
June июнь ⓜ i-*yun'*

K

Kazakhstan Казахстан ⓜ ka-zakh-*stan*
ketchup кетчуп ⓜ *kyet*-chup
key ключ ⓜ klyuch
keyboard клавиатура ⓕ kla-vi-a-*tu*-ra
kidney почка ⓕ *poch*-ka
kilo кило ⓝ ki-*lo*
kilogram килограмм ⓜ ki-la-*gram*
kilometre километр ⓜ ki-lam-*yetr*
kind (nice) добрый *dob*-rih
kindergarten детский сад ⓜ *dyet*-ski sat
king король ⓜ ka-*rol'*
kiss поцелуй ⓜ pat-sih-*luy*
kiss целовать/поцеловать tsih-la-*vat'*/pat-sih-la-*vat'*
kitchen кухня ⓕ *kukh*-nya
knee колено ⓝ kal-*ye*-na
knife нож ⓜ nosh
know знать znat'
kopeck копейка ⓕ kap-*yey*-ka
kosher кошерный *ko*-shihr-nih
Kremlin Кремль ⓜ kryeml'

L

labourer рабочий/рабочая ⓜ/ⓕ ra-*bo*-chi/ra-*bo*-cha-ya
lace кружево ⓝ *kru*-zhih-va
lake озеро ⓝ *o*-zi-ra
Lake Baikal Байкал ⓜ bey-*kal*
lamb баранина ⓕ ba-*ra*-ni-na

land земля ⓕ zim-*lya*
landlady хозяйка ⓕ khaz-*yey*-ka
landlord хозяин ⓜ khaz-*ya*-in
language язык ⓜ yi-*zihk*
laptop портативный компьютер ⓜ par-ta-*tiv*-nih kam-*pyu*-tir
large большой bal'-*shoy*
last (final) последний pas-*lyed*-ni
last (previous) прошлый *prosh*-lih
last (week) (на) прошлой (неделе) (na) *prosh*-ley (nid-*yel*-ye)
late поздний *poz*-ni
later поже *po*-zhih
Latvia Латвия ⓕ *lat*-vi-ya
laugh смеяться/рассмеяться smi-*yat'*-sa/ras-mi-*yat'*-sa
laundry (clothes) бельё ⓝ bil-*yo*
laundry (place) прачечная ⓕ *pra*-chich-na-ya
law (rule) закон ⓜ za-*kon*
law (study, profession) юриспруденция ⓕ yu-ris-prud-*yent*-sih-ya
lawyer адвокат ⓜ ad-va-*kat*
laxative слабительное ⓝ sla-*bi*-til'-na-ye
lazy ленивый li-*ni*-vih
leader руководитель ⓜ ru-ka-va-*dit*-yel'
learn учить/выучить u-*chit'*/vih-u-*chit'*
leather кожа ⓕ *ko*-zha
left (direction) левый *lye*-vih
left luggage оставленный багаж ⓜ a-*stav*-li-nih ba-*gash*
left luggage (office) камера хранения ⓕ *ka*-mi-ra khran-*ye*-ni-ya
left-wing левый *lye*-vih
leg нога ⓕ na-*ga*
legal законный za-*ko*-nih
legislation законодательство ⓝ za-ka-na-*da*-tilst-va
legumes бобовые ⓝ pl ba-*bo*-vih-ye
lemon лимон ⓜ li-*mon*
lemonade лимонад ⓜ li-ma-*nat*
lens линза ⓕ *lin*-za
lesbian лесбианка ⓕ lis-bi-*an*-ka
less меньше *myen'*-she
letter (mail) письмо ⓝ pis'-*mo*
lettuce салат ⓜ sa-*lat*
liar лгун/лгунья ⓜ lgun/lgun-ya
library библиотека ⓕ bib-li-at-*ye*-ka
lice вши ⓜ pl fshih
licence лицензия ⓕ lit-*sen*-zi-ya
license plate number номерной знак ⓜ na-mir-*noy* znak
lie (not stand) лежать li-*zhat'*

lie (untruth) лгать/солгать lgat'/sal-*gat'*
life жизнь ① *zhihzn'*
life jacket спасательный жилет ⓜ spa-*sa*-til'-nih zhihl-*yet*
lift (elevator) лифт ⓜ lift
light свет ⓜ svyet
light (colour) светлый svyet-lih
light (weight) лёгкий *lyokh*-kih
light bulb лампочка ① *lam*-pach-ka
light meter экспозиметр ⓜ ek-spo-*zim*-yetr
lighter (cigarette) зажигалка ① za-zhih-*gal*-ka
like v любить lyu-*bit'*
lime (fruit) лайм ⓜ leym
linen (bedding) бельё ① bil-*yo*
lip balm гигиеническая губная помада ① gi-gi-i-*ni*-chi-ska-ya gub-*na*-ya pa-*ma*-da
lips губы pl *gu*-bih
lipstick губная помада ① gub-*na*-ya pa-*ma*-da
liquor store винный магазин ⓜ *vi*-nih ma-ga-*zin*
listen слушать slu-*shat'*
Lithuania Литва ① lit-*va*
little (not much) немного nim-*no*-ga
little (size) маленький *ma*-lin'-ki
live (somewhere) жить zhiht'
liver печень ① *pye*-chin'
local местный *myes*-nih
lock замок ⓜ za-*mok*
locked запертый zap-*yer*-tih
lollies конфеты ① pl kanf-*ye*-tih
long длинный *dli*-nih
look смотреть/посмотреть smat-*ryet'*/pas-mat-*ryet'*
look for присматривать/присмотреть pris-mat-*ri*-vat'/pris-mar-*yet'*
loose change мелочь ① *mye*-lach'
lose терять/потерять tir-*yat'*/pa-tir-*yat'*
lost пропавший pra-*paf*-shih
lost property office бюро находок ⓝ byu-ro na-*kho*-dak
(a) lot много *mno*-ga
loud громкий *grom*-ki
love любовь ① lyu-*bof'*
love любить lyu-*bit'*
lover любовник/любовница ⓜ/① lyu-*bov*-nik/lyu-*bov*-nit-sa
low низкий *nis*-ki
lubricant смазка ① *smas*-ka
luck счастье ⓝ *shast'*ye
lucky счастливый shis-*li*-vih

luggage багаж ⓜ ba-*gash*
luggage lockers камера-автомат ① *ka*-mi-ra-af-ta-*mat*
luggage tag багажная бирка ① ba-*gazh*-na-ya *bir*-ka
lump шишка ① *shihsh*-ka
lunch обед ⓜ ab-*yet*
lung лёгкое ⓝ *lyokh*-ka-ye
luxury роскошь ① *ros*-kash'

M

machine машина ① ma-*shih*-na
mafia мафия ① *ma*-fi-ya
magazine журнал ⓜ zhur-*nal*
mail (letters/system) почта ① *poch*-ta
mailbox почтовый ящик pach-*to*-vih ya-shik
main главный *glav*-nih
main road главная дорога ① *glav*-na-ya da-*ro*-ga
make делать/сделать dye-lat'/zdye-lat'
make-up косметика ① kas-*mye*-ti-ka
mammogram маммограмма ① ma-ma-*gra*-ma
man (male) мужчина ① mush-*chi*-na
manager (general) заведующий ⓜ zav-ye-du-yu-shi
manager (hotel, restaurant) администратор ⓜ ad-mi-nist-*ra*-tar
many много *mno*-ga
map карта ① *kar*-ta
March март mart
margarine маргарин ⓜ mar-ga-*rin*
marijuana марихуана ① ma-ri-khu-*a*-na
marital status семейное положение ⓝ sim-*yey*-na-ye pa-la-*zhe*-ni-ye
market рынок ⓜ *rih*-nak
marmalade цитрусовый джем ⓜ *tsih*-tra-sa-vey dzhem
marriage брак ⓜ brak
married женатый/замужняя ⓜ/① zhih-*na*-tih/za-*muzh*-ni-ya
marry (for a man) жениться zhih-*nit'*-sa
marry (for a woman) выходить/выйти замуж vih-kha-*dit'*/*vih*-ti za-*mush*
martial arts боевые искусства ⓜ pl ba-i-*vih*-ye is-*kust*-va
Marxism марксизм ⓜ mark-*sizm*
mass (Catholic) обедня ① ab-*yed*-nya
massage массаж ⓜ ma-*sash*
masseur массажист ⓜ ma-sa-*zhist*
masseuse массажистка ① ma-sa-*zhist*-ka
match (sports) матч ⓜ match

matches (fire) спички ① pl *spich*-ki

mattress матрац ⑩ ma-*trats*

May май ⑩ mey

maybe может быть *mo*-zhiht biht

mayonnaise майонез ⑩ ma-yan-*yes*

mayor мэр ⑩ mer

me меня min-*ya*

meal еда ① yi-*da*

measles корь ① kor'

meat мясо ⑪ *mya*-sa

mechanic механик ⑩ mi-*kha*-nik

media средства массовой информации ⑪ pl *sryets*-tva *ma*-sa-vey in-far-*mat*-sih

medicine (drugs) лекарство ⑪ li-*karst*-va

medicine (study, profession) медицина ① mi-dit-*sih*-na

meditation медитация ① mi-di-*tat*-sih-ya

meet встречать/встретить fstri-*chat'*/fstrye-*tit'*

meeting собрание ⑪ sa-*bra*-ni-ye

melon арбуз ⑩ ar-*bus*

member член ⑩ chlyen

menstruation менструация ① minst-ru-*at*-sih-ya

menu меню min-*yu*

message записка ① za-*pis*-ka

metal металл ⑩ mi-*tal*

metre метр ⑩ myetr

metro (train) метро ⑪ mi-*tro*

metro station станция метро ① *stant*-sih-ya mi-*tro*

microwave (oven) микроволновка ① mi-kra-val-*nof*-ka

midday полдень ⑩ *pol*-din'

midnight полночь ⑩ *pol*-noch'

migraine мигрень ① mi-*greyn'*

military военные ⑩ pl va-*ye*-nih-ye

military service военная служба ① va-*ye*-na-ya *sluzh*-ba

milk молоко ⑪ ma-la-*ko*

milk shake молочный коктейль ⑩ ma-*loch*-nih kak-*teyl*

millimetre миллиметр ⑩ mi-lim-*yetr*

mince мясной фарш ⑩ mis-*noy* farsh

mineral water минеральная вода ① mi-ni-*ral*-na-ya va-*da*

minute (time) минута ① mi-*nu*-ta

mirror зеркало ⑪ *zyer*-ka-la

miscarriage выкидыш ⑩ *vih*-ki-dihsh

miss (person) тосковать по ta-ska-*vat'* pa

miss (train etc) опаздывать/опоздать к a-*paz*-dih-vat'/a-*paz*-dat'* k

mistake ошибка ① a-*shihp*-ka

mobile phone мобильный телефон ⑩ ma-*bil'*-nih ti-li-*fon*

modem модем ⑩ mo-*dim*

modern современный sa-vrim-*ye*-nih

moisturiser увлажняющий крем ⑩ uv-lazh-*nya*-yu-shi kryem

monastery монастырь ⑩ ma-na-*stihr*

Monday понедельник ⑩ pa-nid-*yel'*-nik

money деньги ① pl *dyen'*-gi

Mongolia Монголия ① man-*go*-li-ya

monk монах ⑩ ma-*nakh*

month месяц ⑩ *mye*-sits

monument памятник ⑩ *pam*-yit-nik

moon луна ① lu-*na*

more больше *bol'*-she

morning утро ⑪ *u*-tra

morning sickness утренняя тошнота ① *u*-tri-ni-ya tash-na-*ta*

mosque мечеть ① mi-*chet'*

mosquito комар ⑩ ka-*mar*

mosquito net противомоскитная сетка ① pra-ti-va-ma-*skit*-na-ya *syet*-ka

motel мотель ⑩ ma-*tel'*

mother мать ① mat'

mother-in-law (husband's mother) свекровь ① svi-*krof'*

mother-in-law (wife's mother) тёща ① *tyo*-sha

motorbike мотоцикл ⑩ ma-tat-*sihkl*

motorboat моторная лодка ① ma-*tor*-na-ya *lot*-ka

motorway шоссе ⑪ sha-*se*

mountain гора ① ga-*ra*

mountain bike горный велосипед ⑩ *gor*-nih vi-la-si-*pyet*

mountain range горная гряда ① *gor*-na-ya grya-*da*

mountaineering альпинизм ⑩ al'-pi-*nizm*

mouse мышь ① mihsh'

mouth рот ⑩ rot

movie фильм ⑩ film

Mr господин ⑩ ga-spa-*din*

Mrs/Ms/Miss госпожа ① ga-spa-*zha*

mud слякоть ① slya-*kat'*

mum мама ① *ma*-ma

mumps свинка ① *svin*-ka

murder убийство ⑪ u-*bist*-va

murder убивать/убить u-bi-*vat'*/u-*bit'*

muscle мускул ⑩ *mus*-kul

museum музей ⑩ muz-*yey*

mushroom гриб ⑩ grip

mushrooming собирание грибов ⑪ sa-bi-*ra*-ni-ye gri-*bof*

music музыка ⓕ *mu*·zih·ka
musician музыкант ⓜ mu·zih·*kant*
music shop музыкальный магазин ⓜ
mu·zih·*kal*·nih ma·ga·*zin*
Muslim мусульманин/мусульманка
ⓜ/ⓕ mu·sul'·*ma*·nin/mu·sul'·*man*·ka
mussel мидия ⓕ *mi*·di·ya
mustard горчица ⓕ gar·*chit*·sa
mute немой ni·*moy*
my мой moy

N

nail clippers ножницы для ногтей ⓕ pl
nozh·nit·sih dlya nakt·*yey*
name (given/first) имя ⓝ *im*·ya
name (of object) название ⓝ na·*zva*·ni·ye
name (last/family) фамилия ⓕ fa·*mi*·li·ya
napkin салфетка ⓕ salf·*yet*·ka
nappy подгузник ⓜ pad·*guz*·nik
national park заповедник ⓜ
za·pav·*yed*·nik
nationality национальность ⓕ
nat·sih·a·*nal'·nast'*
nature природа ⓕ pri·*ro*·da
nausea тошнота ⓕ tash·na·*ta*
near(by) близко (от) *blis*·ka (at)
nearest ближайший bli·*zhey*·shi
necessary нужный *nuzh*·nih
neck шея ⓕ *she*·ya
necklace ожерелье ⓝ a·zhih·*ryel*·ye
need нуждаться в nuzh·*dat'*·sa v
needle (sewing) игла ⓕ i·*gla*
needle (syringe) шприц ⓜ shprits
negative негативный ni·ga·*tiv*·nih
neither … nor … ни … ни … ni … ni …
net сеть ⓕ syet'
Netherlands Нидерланды ⓜ pl
ni·dir·*lan*·dih
never никогда ni·kag·*da*
new новый *no*·vih
New Year's Day Новый год ⓜ *no*·vih got
New Year's Eve Новогодняя ночь ⓕ
na·va·*god*·ni·ya noch'
New Zealand Новая Зеландия ⓕ
no·va·ya zi·*lan*·di·ya
news новости ⓕ pl no·va·sti
newsagency газетный киоск ⓜ
gaz·*yet*·nih ki·*osk*
newspaper газета ⓕ gaz·*ye*·ta
next (month) (в) следующем (месяце)
(f) *slye*·du·yu·shim (*mye*·sit·se)
next to рядом с *rya*·dam s
nice милый *mi*·lih

nickname прозвище ⓝ *proz*·vi·she
night ночь ⓕ noch'
nightclub ночной клуб ⓜ nach·*noy* klup
no нет nyet
noisy шумный *shum*·nih
none никаких ni·ka·*kikh*
nonsmoking некурящий ni·kur·*ya*·shi
noon полдень ⓜ *pol*·din'
north север ⓜ *sye*·vir
Norway Норвегия ⓕ narv·*ye*·gi·ya
nose нос ⓜ nos
not не nye
notebook блокнот ⓜ blak·*not*
nothing ничего ni·chi·*vo*
November ноябрь ⓜ na·*yabr'*
now сейчас si·*chas*
nuclear energy ядерная энергия ⓕ
ya·dir·na·ya e·*nir*·gi·ya
nuclear power station
ядерная электростанция ⓕ
ya·dir·na·ya e·lik·tra·*stant*·sih·ya
nuclear waste ядерные отходы ⓜ pl
ya·dir·nih·ye at·*kho*·dih
number номер ⓜ *no*·mir
numberplate номерной знак ⓜ
na·mir·*noy* znak
nun монахиня ⓕ ma·*na*·khi·ya
nurse медсестра ⓕ mit·sist·*ra*
nut орех ⓜ ar·*yekh*

O

oats овёс ⓜ av·*yos*
ocean океан ⓜ a·ki·*an*
October октябрь ⓜ akt·*yabr'*
off (spoiled) испорченный is·*por*·chi·nih
office контора ⓕ kan·*to*·ra
office worker служащий/служащая ⓜ/ⓕ
slu·zha·shi/*slu*·zha·shi·ya
often часто *cha*·sta
oil (cooking/fuel) масло ⓝ *mas*·la
old старый *sta*·rih
olive оливка ⓕ a·*lif*·ka
olive oil оливковое масло ⓝ
a·*lif*·ka·va·ye *mas*·la
Olympic Games Олимпийские игры ⓕ pl
a·lim·*pi*·ski·ye i·*grih*
on на na
on time вовремя *vov*·ryem·ya
once один раз a·*din* ras
one один/одна ⓜ/ⓕ a·*din*/ad·*na*
one-way в один конец v a·*din* kan·*yets*
onion лук ⓜ luk
only только *tol'*·ka

open открытый at-*krih*-tih
open открывать/открыть at-krih-*vat*/at-*kriht*'
opening hours часы работы ⓜ pl chi-*sih* ra-*bo*-tih
opera опера ⓕ *o*-pi-ra
opera house оперный театр ⓜ *o*-pir-nih ti-*atr*
operation (general) операция ⓕ a-pi-*rat*-sih-ya
operator оператор ⓜ a-pi-*ra*-tar
opinion мнение ⓝ *mnye*-ni-ye
opposite против *pro*-tif
optometrist оптик ⓜ *op*-tik
or или *i*-li
orange (fruit) апельсин ⓜ a-*pil*'-sin
orange (colour) оранжевый a-*ran*-zhih-vih
orange juice апельсиновый сок ⓜ a-*pil*'-si-na-vih sok
orchestra оркестр ⓜ ar-*kestr*
order заказ ⓜ za-*kas*
order заказывать/заказать za-*ka*-zih-vat'/za-*ka*-zat'
ordinary обыкновенный a-bihk-nav-*ye*-nih
orgasm оргазм ⓜ ar-*gazm*
original оригинальный a-ri-gi-*nal*'-nih
Orthodox православный pra-vas-*lav*-nih
Orthodox Church православная церковь pra-vas-*lav*-na-ya *tser*-kaf'
other другой dru-*goy*
our наш nash
outside снаружи sna-*ru*-zhih
ovarian cyst яичниковая киста ⓕ yi-*ich*-ni-ko-va-ya kis-*ta*
ovary яичник ⓜ yi-*ich*-nik
oven духовка ⓕ du-*khof*-ka
overcoat пальто ⓝ pal'-*to*
overdose передозировка ⓕ pi-ri-do-*zi*-rof-ka
overnight всю ночь fsyu noch'
overseas за границей za gra-*nit*-sey
owner владелец ⓜ vlad-*yel*-its
oxygen кислород ⓜ kis-la-*rot*
oyster устрица ⓕ *ust*-rit-sa

P

pacemaker ритмизатор сердца ⓜ rit-mi-*za*-tar *syert*-sa
pacifier (dummy) соска ⓕ *sos*-ka
package посылка ⓕ pa-*sihl*-ka
packet пачка ⓕ *pach*-ka
padlock нависной замок ⓜ na-vis-*noy* za-*mok*

page страница ⓕ *stra*-nit-sa
pain боль ⓕ bol'
painful болит ba-*lit*
painkiller болеутоляющие ⓝ pl bo-li-u-tal-*ya*-yu-shi-ye
painter художник ⓜ khu-*dozh*-nik
painting (a work) картина ⓕ kar-*ti*-na
painting (the art) живопись ⓕ *zhih*-va-pis'
pair пара ⓕ *pa*-ra
Pakistan Пакистан ⓜ pa-ki-*stan*
palace дворец ⓜ dvar-*yets*
pan сковорода ⓕ ska-va-ra-*da*
pants (trousers) брюки ⓜ pl *bryu*-ki
panty liners гигиеническая прокладка ⓕ gi-gi-i-*ni*-chi-ska-ya pra-*klat*-ka
pap smear мазок ⓜ ma-*zok*
paper бумага ⓕ bu-*ma*-ga
paperwork документы ⓜ pl da-kum-*yen*-tih
paraplegic парализованный pa-ra-li-*zo*-va-nih
parcel посылка ⓕ pa-*sihl*-ka
parents родители ⓜ pl ra-*di*-ti-li
park парк ⓜ park
park (a car) ставить/поставить (машину) *sta*-vit'/pa-*sta*-vit' (ma-*shih*-nu)
parliament дума ⓕ *du*-ma
part (component) деталь ⓕ di-*tal*'
part-time на неполной ставке na ni-*pol*-ney *staf*-kye
party (fiesta) вечеринка ⓕ vi-chi-*rin*-ka
party (politics) партия ⓕ *par*-ti-ya
pass проходить/пройти pra-kha-*dit*'/*prey*-ti
passenger пассажир ⓜ pa-sa-*zhihr*
passport паспорт ⓜ *pas*-part
passport number номер паспорта ⓜ *no*-mir *pas*-par-ta
past (time) прошлое ⓝ *prosh*-la-ye
pasta паста ⓕ *pa*-sta
pastry пирожное ⓝ pi-*rozh*-na-ye
path тропинка ⓕ tra-*pin*-ka
patriarch (in Orthodox Church) патриарх ⓜ pa-tri-*arkh*
pay платить/заплатить pla-*tit*'/za-pla-*tit*'
pay phone телефон-автомат ⓜ ti-li-*fon*-af-ta-*mat*
payment оплата ⓕ a-*pla*-ta
peace мир ⓜ mir
peach персик ⓜ *pyer*-sik
peanut арахис ⓜ a-*ra*-khis
pear груша ⓕ *gru*-sha
peasant крестьянин/крестьянка ⓜ/ⓕ krist-*ya*-nin/krist-*yan*-ka

pedal педаль ① pi·*dal'*
pedestrian пешеход ⓜ pi·shih·*khot*
pen ручка ① *ruch*·ka
pencil карандаш ⓜ ka·ran·*dash*
penis пенис ⓜ *pye*·nis
pensioner пенсионер/пенсионерка ⓜ/①
  pin·si·an·*yer*/pin·si·an·*yer*·ka
people люди ⓜ pl *lyu*·di
pepper (bell/black) перец ⓜ *pye*·rits
per в v
per cent процент ⓜ prat·*sent*
perestroika перестройка ① pi·rist·*roy*·ka
perfect прекрасный pri·*kras*·nih
performance спектакль ⓜ spik·*takl'*
perfume духи ⓜ pl du·*khi*
period pain болезненные месячные
  ⓜ pl bal·*yez*·ni·nih·ye *mye*·sich·nih·ye
permafrost вечная мерзлота ①
  vyech·na·ya mirz·la·*ta*
permission/permit разрешение ⓜ
  raz·ri·*she*·ni·ye
person человек ⓜ chi·*lav*·yek
petrol бензин ⓜ bin·*zin*
petrol station заправочная станция ①
  za·*pra*·vach·na·ye *stant*·sih·ya
pharmacy аптека ① apt·*ye*·ka
phone book телефонная книга ①
  ti·li·*fo*·na·ya *kni*·ga
phone box телефонная будка ①
  ti·li·*fo*·na·ya *but*·ka
phonecard телефонная карточка ①
  ti·li·*fo*·na·ya *kar*·tach·ka
photo снимок ⓜ *sni*·mak
photographer фотограф ⓜ fa·*to*·graf
photography фотография ① fa·ta·*gra*·fi·ya
phrasebook разговорник ⓜ raz·ga·*vor*·nik
pickaxe кирка ① *kir*·ka
picnic пикник ⓜ pik·*nik*
pigeon голубь ⓜ *go*·lub'
pie пирог ⓜ pi·*rok*
piece кусок ⓜ ku·*sok*
pig свинья ① svin·*ya*
pill таблетка ① tab·*lyet*·ka
(the) pill противозачаточная таблетка ①
  pra·ti·va·za·*cha*·tach·na·ya tab·*lyet*·ka
pillow подушка ① pa·*dush*·ka
pillowcase наволочка ① *na*·va·lach·ka
pink розовый *ro*·za·vih
place место ⓜ *mye*·sta
place of birth место рождения ⓜ
  mye·sta razh·*dye*·ni·ya
plane самолёт ⓜ sa·mal·*yot*
planet планета ① plan·*ye*·ta

plant растение ⓜ rast·*ye*·ni·ye
plastic пластмассовый plast·*ma*·sa·vih
plate тарелка ① tar·*yel*·ka
plateau плато ⓜ pla·*to*
platform платформа ① plat·*for*·ma
play (dominoes) играть в (домино)
  i·*grat'* v (da·mi·no)
play (guitar) играть на (гитаре)
  i·*grat'* na (gi·*tar*·ye)
play (theatre) пьеса ① *pye*·sa
plug (bath) пробка ① *prop*·ka
plug (electricity) вилка ① *vil*·ka
plum слива ① *sli*·va
poached варёный var·*yo*·nih
pocket карман ⓜ kar·*man*
pocket knife карманный ножик ⓜ
  kar·*ma*·nih *no*·zhihk
poetry поэзия ① pa·*e*·zi·ya
point указывать/указать
  u·*ka*·zih·vat'/u·ka·*zat'*
poisonous ядовитый ya·da·*vi*·tih
polar bear белый медведь ⓜ
  bye·lih mid·*vyet'*
Poland Польша ① *pol'*·sha
police милиция ① mi·*lit*·sih·ya
police officer милиционер ⓜ
  mi·lit·sih·an·*yer*
police station полицейский участок ⓜ
  pa·*lit*·sey·ski u·*cha*·stak
policy политика ① pa·*li*·ti·ka
politician политик ⓜ pa·*li*·tik
politics политика ① pa·*li*·ti·ka
pollen пыльца ① pihlt·*sa*
pollution загрязнение ⓜ
  za·griz·*nye*·ni·ye
pool (game) пулька ① *pul'*·ka
pool (swimming) бассейн ⓜ bas·*yeyn*
poor бедный *byed*·nih
popular популярный pa·*pul'*·yar·nih
pork свинина ① svi·*ni*·na
port (sea) порт ⓜ port
positive позитивный pa·zi·*tiv*·nih
possible возможный vaz·*mozh*·nih
postage почтовые расходы ⓜ pl
  pach·*to*·vih·ye ras·*kho*·dih
postcard открытка ① at·*kriht*·ka
postcode почтовый индекс ⓜ
  pach·*to*·vih *in*·diks
post office почта ① *poch*·ta
pot (ceramic/cooking) горшок ⓜ gar·*shok*
potato картошка ① kar·*tosh*·ka
pottery керамика ① ki·*ra*·mi·ka
pound (money/weight) фунт ⓜ funt

poverty бедность ① *byed*·nast'
powder пудра ① *pud*·ra
power энергия ① en·*yer*·gi·ya
prawn креветка ① kriv·*yet*·ka
prayer молитва ① ma·*lit*·va
prayer book молитвенник ⓜ ma·*lit*·vi·nik
prefer предпочитать/предпочесть
prit·pa·chi·*tat'*/prit·pa·*chest'*
pregnancy test kit тест на беременность
ⓜ tyest na bir·*ye*·mi·nast'
pregnant беременная bir·*ye*·mi·na·ya
premenstrual tension
предменструальная напряжённость
① prid·minst·ru·*al'*·na·ya na·pri·*zho*·nast'
prepare приготавливать/приготовить
pri·ga·*tav*·li·vat'/pri·ga·*to*·vit'
prescription рецепт ⓜ rit·*sept*
present (gift) подарок ⓜ pa·*da*·rak
present (time) настоящее ⓝ
na·sta·*ya*·shi·ye
president президент ⓜ pri·zid·*yent*
pressure давление ⓝ dav·*lye*·ni·ye
pretty хорошенький kha·*ro*·shihn'·ki
price цена ① tse·*na*
priest священник ⓜ svya·*she*·nik
prime minister премьер-министр ⓜ
prim·*yer*·mi·*nistr*
printer (computer) принтер ⓜ *prin*·tir
prison тюрьма ① tyur'·*ma*
private частный *chas*·nih
produce производить/произвести
pra·iz·va·*dit'*/pra·iz·vi·*sti*
profit прибыль ① *pri*·bihl'
program программа ① pra·*gra*·ma
promise обещать/пообещать
a·bi·*shat'*/pa·a·bi·*shat'*
protect защищать/защитить
za·shi·*shat'*/za·shi·*tit'*
protest протест ⓜ prat·*yest*
provisions провизия ① pra·*vi*·zi·ya
prune чернослив ⓜ chir·nas·*lif*
pub пивная ① piv·*na*·ya
public gardens публичный сад ⓜ
pub·*lich*·nih sat
public relations внешние связи ① pl
vnyesh·ni·ye svya·zi
public telephone публичный телефон ⓜ
pub·*lich*·nih ti·li·*fon*
public toilet общественный туалет ⓜ
ap·*shest*·vi·nih tu·al·*yet*
publishing издательское дело ⓝ
iz·*da*·til'·ska·ye *dye*·la
pull тянуть/потянуть ti·*nut'*/pi·ti·*nut'*

pump насос ⓜ na·*sos*
pumpkin тыква ① *tihk*·va
puncture прокол ⓜ pra·*kol*
pure чистый *chis*·tih
purple пурпурный pur·*pur*·nih
purse кошелёк ⓜ ka·shal·*yok*
push толкать/толкнуть tal·*kat'*/talk·*nut'*
put ставить/поставить *sta*·vit'/pa·*sta*·vit'

Q

qualifications квалификации ① pl
kva·li·fi·*kat*·si
quality качество ⓝ *ka*·chist·va
quarantine карантин ⓜ ka·ran·*tin*
quarter четверть ① *chet*·virt'
queen королева ① ka·ral·*ye*·va
question вопрос ⓜ va·*pros*
queue очередь ① o·chi·rit'
quick быстрый *bihst*·rih
quiet тихий *ti*·khi
quit бросать/бросить bra·*sat'*/*bro*·sit'

R

rabbit кролик ⓜ *kro*·lik
rabies бешенство ⓝ *bye*·shinst·va
race (sport) бег ⓜ byek
racetrack ипподром ⓜ i·pa·*drom*
racing bike гоночный велосипед ⓜ
go·nach·nih vi·la·sip·*yet*
racism расизм ⓜ ra·*sizm*
racquet ракета ① rak·*ye*·ta
radiation радиация ① ra·di·*at*·sih·ya
radiator радиатор ⓜ ra·di·*a*·tar
radio радио ⓝ *ra*·di·o
railway station вокзал ⓜ vag·*zal*
rain дождь ⓜ dozht'
raincoat плащ ⓜ plash
rally манифестация ① ma·ni·fist·*at*·sih·ya
rape изнасилование ⓝ iz·na·*si*·la·va·ni·ye
rape насиловать/изнасиловать
na·*si*·la·vat'/iz·na·*si*·la·vat'
rare (food) кровавый kra·*va*·vih
rare (uncommon) редкий *ryet*·ki
rash сыпь ① sihp'
raspberry малина ① ma·*li*·na
rat крыса ① *krih*·sa
raw сырой sih·*roy*
razor бритва ① *brit*·va
razor blade лезвие ⓝ *lyez*·vi·ye
read читать/прочитать chi·*tat'*/pra·chi·*tat'*
reading чтение ⓝ *chtye*·ni·ye
ready готов ⓜ ga·*tof*

real estate agent риэлтер ⓜ ri·*el*·tir
rear (location) a задний *zad*·ni
reason причина ⓕ pri·*chi*·na
receipt квитанция ⓕ kvi·*tant*·sih·ya
recently недавно ni·*dav*·na
recommend
рекомендовать/порекомендовать
ri·ka·min·da·*vat*'/pa·ri·ka·min·da·*vat*'
record записывать/записать
za·*pi*·sih·vat'/za·pi·*sat*'
recyclable пригодный для рецикла
pri·*god*·nih dlya rit·*sihk*·la
recycle перерабатывать/переработать
pi·ri·ra·*ba*·tih·vat'/pi·ri·ra·bo·*tat*'
red красный *kras*·nih
referee рефери ⓜ ri·fi·*ri*
reference рекомендация ⓕ
ri·ka·min·*dat*·sih·ya
refrigerator холодильник ⓜ kha·la·*dil*'·nik
refugee беженец/беженка ⓜ/ⓕ
bye·zhih·nits/*bye*·zhihn·ka
refund возвращение денег ⓜ
vaz·vra·*she*·ni ye *dye*·nik
refuse отказывать/отказать
at·*ka*·zih·vat'/at·ka·*zat*'
regional региональный ri·gi·a·*nal*'·nih
registered mail ⓕ заказной za·kaz·*noy*
regret v сожалеть sa·zhal·*yet*'
reindeer северный олень ⓜ
sye·vir·nih al·*yen*'
relationship связь ⓕ svyas'
relax расслабляться/расслабиться
ras·lab·*lyat*'·sa/ras·*la*·bit'·sa
relic реликвия ⓕ ri·*lik*·vi·ya
religion религия ⓕ ri·*li*·gi·ya
religious религиозный ri·li·gi·*oz*·nih
remote дальный *dal*'·nih
rent квартирная плата ⓕ
kvar·*tir*·na·ya *pla*·ta
rent v арендовать a·rin·da·*vat*'
repair чинить/починить chi·*nit*'/pa·chi·*nit*'
republic республика ⓕ ris·*pub*·li·ka
reservation (booking) заказ ⓜ za·*kas*
rest отдыхать/отдохнуть
a·dih·*khat*'/a·dakh·*nut*'
restaurant ресторан ⓜ ris·ta·*ran*
résumé автобиография ⓕ
af·ta·bi·a·*gra*·fi·ya
retired на пенсии na *pyen*·si
return (come back) возвращаться/
вернуться vaz·vra·*shat*·sa/vir·*nut*'·sa
return (ticket) обратный a·*brat*·nih
review рецензия ⓕ rit·*sen*·zi·ya

rhythm ритм ⓜ ritm
rib ребро ⓝ ri·*bro*
rice рис ⓜ ris
rich (wealthy) богатый ba·*ga*·tih
ride поездка ⓕ pa·*yest*·ka
ride (horse) ездить/ехать верхом
yez·dit'/*ye*·khat' vir·*khom*
right (correct) правильный *pra*·vil'·nih
right (direction) правый *pra*·vih
right-wing правый *pra*·vih
ring (jewellery) кольцо ⓝ kalt·*so*
ring (phone) звонить/позвонить
zva·*nit*'/paz·va·*nit*'
rip-off грабёж ⓜ grab·*yosh*
river река ⓕ ri·*ka*
road дорога ⓕ da·*ro*·ga
road map карта дорог ⓕ *kar*·ta da·*rok*
rob красть/обокрасть krast'/a·ba·*krast*'
robbery грабёж ⓜ grab·*yosh*
rock скала ⓕ ska·*la*
rock climbing скалолазание ⓝ
ska·la·*la*·za·ni·ye
rock group рок-группа ⓕ *rok*·gru·pa
rockmelon арбуз ⓜ ar·*bus*
rock music рок ⓜ rok
romantic романтичный ra·man·*tich*·nih
room (hotel) номер ⓜ *no*·mir
room (house) комната ⓕ *kom*·na·ta
room number номер комнаты ⓜ
no·mir *kom*·na·tih
rope верёвка ⓕ vir·*yof*·ka
rouble рубль ⓜ rubl'
round круглый *krug*·lih
route путь ⓜ put'
rubbish мусор ⓜ *mu*·sar
rubella краснуха ⓕ kras·*nu*·kha
rug ковёр ⓜ kav·*yor*
rugby регби ⓝ *reg*·bi
ruins развалины ⓕ pl raz·*va*·li·nih
rule правило ⓝ *pra*·vi·la
rum ром ⓜ rom
run бежать/побежать bi·*zhat*'/pa·bi·*zhat*'
running бег ⓜ byek
Russia Россия ⓕ ra·*si*·ya
Russian (language) русский ⓜ *rus*·ki
Russian (man/woman) a
русский/русская ⓜ/ⓕ *rus*·ki/*rus*·ka·ya

S

sad грустный *grus*·nih
safe сейф ⓜ syeyf
safe a безопасный biz·a·*pas*·nih

safe sex безопасный секс ⓜ
biz·a·*pas*·nih syeks
saint святой ⓜ svi·*toy*
salad салат ⓜ sa·*lat*
salary зарплата ⓕ zar·*pla*·ta
sale (low prices) распродажа ⓕ
ras·pra·*da*·zha
sales tax налог на продажу ⓜ
na·*lok* na pra·*da*·zhu
salmon лососина ⓕ la·sa·*si*·na
salt соль ⓕ sol'
same тот же самый tod zhe sa·mih
samovar самовар ⓜ sa·ma·*var*
sand песок ⓜ pi·*sok*
sandal сандалия ⓕ san·*da*·li·ya
sanitary napkin гигиеническая салфетка
ⓕ gi·gi·*ni*·chi·ska·ya salf·*yet*·ka
satellite спутник ⓜ *sput*·nik
Saturday суббота ⓕ su·*bo*·ta
sauce соус ⓜ *so*·us
saucepan кастрюля ⓕ kast·*ryul*·ya
sauna сауна ⓕ *sa*·u·na
sausage (cooked) сосиска ⓕ sa·*sis*·ka
sausage (salami) колбаса ⓕ kal·ba·*sa*
say говорить/сказать ga·va·*rit'*/ska·*zat'*
scalp скальп ⓜ skalp
scarf шарф ⓜ sharf
school школа ⓕ *shko*·la
science наука ⓕ na·*u*·ka
scientist учёный/учёная ⓜ/ⓕ
u·*cho*·nih/u·*cho*·na·ya
scissors ножницы ⓕ pl *nozh*·nit·sih
score (sport) забивать/забить
za·bih·*vat'*/za·*biht'*
Scotland Шотландия ⓕ shat·*lan*·di·ya
sculpture скульптура ⓕ skulp·*tu*·ra
sea море ⓝ *mor*·ye
Sea of Okhost Охотское море ⓝ
a·*khot*·ska·ye *mor*·ye
seal (animal) тюлень ⓜ tyul·*yen'*
seasickness морская болезнь ⓕ
mar·*ska*·ya bal·*yezn'*
seaside берег моря ⓜ *bye*·rik *mor*·ya
season время года ⓝ *vryem*·ya *go*·da
seat место ⓝ *myes*·ta
seatbelt ремень ⓜ rim·*yen'*
second (time) секунда ⓕ si·*kun*·da
second a второй fta·*roy*
second class на втором классе
va fta·*rom* *klas*·ye
second-hand подержанный
pad·*yer*·zha·nih
secretary секретарша ⓕ si·kri·*tar*·sha

see видеть/увидеть *vi*·dit'/u·*vi*·dit'
self-employed на себя na sib·*ya*
selfish эгоистичный e·go·is·*tich*·nih
self-service самообслуживание ⓝ
sa·ma·aps·*lu*·zhih·va·ni·ye
sell продавать/продать pra·da·*vat'*/pra·*dat'*
send посылать/послать pa·sih·*lat'*/pas·*lat'*
sensible разумный ra·*zum*·nih
sensual чувственный *chust*·vi·nih
separate отдельный ad·*yel'*·nih
September сентябрь ⓜ sint·*yabr'*
serious серьёзный sir·*yoz*·nih
service услуга ⓕ us·*lu*·ga
service charge плата за обслуживание ⓕ
pla·ta za aps·*lu*·zhih·va·ni·ye
service station заправочная станция ⓕ
za·*pra*·vach·na·ya *stant*·sih·ya
serviette салфетка ⓕ salf·*yet*·ka
several несколько *nye*·skal'·ka
sew шить/сшить shiht'/s·shiht'
sex секс ⓜ syeks
sexism сексизм ⓜ syek·*sizm*
sexy сексуальный syek·su·*al'*·nih
shade/shadow тень ⓕ tyen'
shampoo шампунь ⓜ sham·*pun'*
shape форма ⓕ *for*·ma
share (item) делить/поделить
di·*lit'*/pa·di·*lit'*
share (room) жить в одной (комнате)
zhiht' v ad·*noy* (*kom*·nat·ye)
shave бриться/побриться
brit'·sa/pa·*brit'*·sa
shaving cream крем для бритья
kryem dlya brit·*ya*
she она a·*na*
sheep овца ⓕ aft·*sa*
sheet (bed) простыня ⓕ pra·stihn·*ya*
ship корабль ⓜ ka·*rabl'*
shirt рубашка ⓕ ru·*bash*·ka
shoes туфли ⓕ pl *tuf*·li
shoe shop обувной магазин ⓜ
a·buv·*noy* ma·ga·*zin*
shoot стрелять/расстрелять
stril·*yat'*/ras·tril·*yat'*
shop магазин ⓜ ma·ga·*zin*
shop ходить по магазинам
kha·*dit'* pa ma·ga·*zi*·nam
shopping шопинг ⓜ *sho*·pink
shopping centre торговый центр ⓜ
tar·*go*·vih tsentr
short (height) короткий ka·*rot*·ki
shortage дефицит ⓜ di·fit·*siht*
shorts шорты ⓜ pl *shor*·tih

shoulder плечо ⓝ pli·*cho*
shout кричать/крикнуть kri·*chat'*/krik·*nut'*
show спектакль ⓜ spik·*takl'*
show показывать/показать
    pa·*ka*·zih·vat'/pa·ka·*zat'*
shower душ ⓜ dush
shrine святыня ⓕ svya·*tihn*·ya
shut а закрытый za·*krih*·tih
shy застенчивый za·*styen*·chi·vih
Siberia Сибирь ⓕ si·*bir'*
Siberian сибирский si·*bir*·ski
sick болен/больна ⓜ/ⓕ *bo*·lin/bal'·*na*
side сторона ⓕ sta·ra·*na*
sign знак ⓜ znak
sign (documents) подписывать/
    подписать pat·*pi*·sih·vat'/pat·pi·*sat'*
signature подпись ⓕ *pot*·pis'
silk щёлк ⓜ sholk
silver серебро ⓝ si·ri·*bro*
SIM card сим-карта ⓕ *sim*·kar·ta
similar похожий pa·*kho*·zhih
simple простой pra·*stoy*
since (May) с (мая) s (*ma*·ya)
sing петь/спеть pyet'/spyet'
singer певец/певица ⓜ/ⓕ
    piv·*yets*/pi·*vit*·sa
single (man) холост ⓜ *kho*·last
single (woman) не замужем ⓕ
    nye *za*·mu·zhihm
single room одноместный номер ⓜ
    ad·na·*mes*·nih *no*·mir
singlet майка ⓕ *mey*·ka
sister сестра ⓕ *sis*·tra
sit сидеть sid·*yet'*
size (general) размер ⓜ raz·*myer*
skate кататься на коньках
    ka·*tat'*·sa na kan'·*kakh*
skateboard скейтборд ⓜ *skeyt*·bort
ski v кататься на лыжах
    ka·*tat'*·sa na *lih*·zhakh
skiing катание на лыжах ⓝ
    ka·*ta*·ni·ye na *lih*·zhakh
skim milk снятое молоко ⓝ
    snya·*to*·ye ma·la·*ko*
skin кожа ⓕ *ko*·zha
skirt юбка ⓕ *yup*·ka
skull череп ⓜ *che*·rip
sky небо ⓝ *nye*·ba
sleep v спать spat'
sleeping bag спальный мешок ⓜ
    spal'·nih mi·*shok*
sleeping berth спальное место ⓝ
    spal'·na·ye *mye*·sta

sleeping car спальный вагон ⓜ
    spal'·nih va·*gon*
sleeping pills снотворные таблетки ⓕ pl
    snat·*vor*·nih·ye tab·*lyet*·ki
sleepy сонный *so*·nih
slice ломтик ⓜ *lom*·tik
slide (film) слайд ⓜ sleyt
slow медленный *myed*·li·nih
slowly медленно *myed*·li·na
small маленький *ma*·lin'·ki
smaller меньше *myen'*·she
smallest самый маленький
    sa·mih *ma*·lin'·ki
smell запах ⓜ *za*·pakh
smile улыбаться/улыбнуться
    u·lih·*bat'*·sa/u·lihb·*nut'*·sa
smoke курить/покурить ku·*rit'*/pa·ku·*rit'*
snack закуска ⓕ *za*·kus·ka
snack bar закусочная ⓕ za·*ku*·sach·na·ya
snake змея ⓕ zmi·*ya*
snow снег ⓜ snyek
snowboarding сноубординг ⓜ
    sno·u·*bor*·dink
soap мыло ⓝ *mih*·la
soap opera мыльная опера ⓕ
    mihl·na·ya *o*·pi·ra
soccer футбол ⓜ fud·*bol*
social welfare социальное обеспечение
    ⓝ sat·sih·*al'*·na·ye a·bis·pi·*che*·ni·ye
socialism социализм ⓜ sat·sih·a·*lizm*
socks носки ⓜ pl na·*ski*
soda содовая ⓕ *so*·da·va·ya
soft drink безалкогольный напиток ⓜ
    biz·al·ka·*gol'*·nih na·*pi*·tak
soft-boiled всмятку vsmyat·ku
soldier солдат ⓜ sal·*dat*
some несколько nye·*skal'*·ka
someone кто-то *kto*·ta
something что-то *shto*·ta
sometimes иногда i·nag·*da*
son сын ⓜ sihn
song песня ⓕ *pyes*·nya
soon скоро *sko*·ra
sore а болит ba·*lit*
soup суп ⓜ sup
south юг ⓜ yuk
souvenir сувенир ⓜ su·vi·*nir*
souvenir shop сувенирный магазин ⓜ
    su·vi·*nir*·nih ma·ga·*zin*
Soviet советский sav·*yet*·ski
Soviet Union Советский Союз ⓜ
    sav·*yet*·ski sa·*yus*

soy milk соевое молоко ⑩
  so·i·va·ye ma·la·ko
soy sauce соевый соус ⑩ so·i·vih so·us
space космос ⑩ kos·mas
Spain Испания ① i·spa·ni·ya
sparkling wine шампанское ⑩
  sham·pan·ska·ye
speak говорить ga·va·rit'
special особенный a·so·bi·nih
specialist специалист ⑩ spet·sih·a·list
speed (velocity) скорость ① sko·rast'
speed limit ограничение скорости ①
  a·gra·ni·che·ni·ye sko·ras·ti
speedometer спидометр ⑩ spi·do·mitr
spider паук ⑩ pa·uk
spinach шпинат ⑩ shpi·nat
spoiled (food) испорченный is·por·chi·nih
spoke спица ① spit·sa
spoon ложка ① losh·ka
sport спорт ⑩ sport
sports store спортивный магазин ⑩
  spar·tiv·nih ma·ga·zin
sportsman спортсмен ⑩ sparts·myen
sportswoman спортсменка ①
  sparts·myen·ka
sprain растяжение связок ⑩
  rast·ya·zhe·ni·ye svya·zak
spring (season) весна ① vis·na
square (town) площадь ① plo·shat'
stadium стадион ⑩ sta·di·on
stairway лестница ① lyes·nit·sa
stale чёрствый chorst·vih
Stalinism Сталинизм ⑩ sta·li·nizm
stamp марка ① mar·ka
stand-by ticket стенд-бай ⑩ styend·bey
star звёзда ① zvyoz·da
star sign знак ⑩ znak
start начало ⑩ na·cha·la
start начинать/начать na·chi·nat'/na·chat'
station станция ① stant·sih·ya
stationer канцелярские товары ⑩ pl
  kant·sihl·yar·ski·ye ta·va·rih
statue статуя ① sta·tu·ya
stay (hotel)
  останавливаться/остановиться
  a·sta·nav·li·vat'·sa/a·sta·na·vit'·sa
steak бифштекс ⑩ bif·shteks
steal красть/украсть krast'/u·krast'
steep крутой kru·toy
step ступень ① stup·yen'
steppe степь ① styep'
stereo стерео ⑩ stye·ri·o
stockings чулки ⑩ pl chul·ki

stolen краденый kra·di·nih
stomach желудок ⑩ zhih·lu·dak
stomachache боль в желудке ①
  bol' v zhih·lut·kye
stone камень ⑩ ka·min'
stoned (drugs) на колёсах na kal·yo·sakh
stop (bus/tram) остановка ① a·sta·nof·ka
stop (cease) переставать/перестать
  pi·ri·sta·vat'/pi·ri·stat'
stop (prevent) мешать/помешать
  mi·shat'/pa·mi·shat'
storm буря ① bur·ya
story рассказ ⑩ ras·kas
stove печь ① pyech'
straight прямой pri·moy
strange странный stra·nih
stranger незнакомец/незнакомка ⑩/①
  nyez·na·ko·mits/nyez·na·kom·ka
strawberry клубника ① klub·ni·ka
street улица ① u·lit·sa
street market уличный рынок ⑩
  u·lich·nih rih·nak
strike (work) забастовка ① za·ba·stof·ka
string верёвка ① vir·yof·ka
stroke (health) удар ⑩ u·dar
stroller детская коляска ①
  dyet·ska·ya kal·yas·ka
strong сильный sil'·nih
stubborn упрямый up·rya·mih
student студент/студентка ⑩/①
  stud·yent/stud·yent·ka
studio студия ① stu·di·ya
stupid глупый glu·pih
subtitles субтитры ⑩ pl sub·tit·rih
suburb пригород ⑩ pri·ga·rat
subway (train) метро ⑩ mi·tro
sugar сахар ⑩ sa·khar
suitcase чемодан ⑩ chi·ma·dan
summer лето ⑩ lye·ta
sun солнце ⑩ solnt·se
sunblock солнцезащитный крем ⑩
  sont·se·za·shit·nih kryem
sunburn солнечный ожог ⑩
  sol·nich·nih a·zhok
Sunday воскресенье ⑩ vas·kris·yen·ye
sunglasses очки от солнца ⑩ pl
  ach·ki at solnt·sa
sunny солнечный sol·nich·nih
sunrise заря ① zar·ya
sunset закат ⑩ za·kat
supermarket универсам ⑩ u·ni·vir·sam
superstition суеверие ① su·iv·ye·ri·ye

supporter (politics) сторонник/
сторонница @/① sta·ro·nik/sta·ro·nit·sa

supporter (sport)
болельщик/болельщица @/①
bal·yel'shik/bal·yel'shit·sa

surf v заниматься сёрфингом
za·ni·mat'·sa syor·fin·gam

surface mail обычная почта ①
a·bihch·na·ya poch·ta

surfing сёрфинг @ syor·fink

surname фамилия ① fa·mi·li·ya

surprise сюрприз @ syur·pris

sweater свитер @ svi·tir

Sweden Швеция ① shvyet·sih·ya

sweet сладкий slat·ki

swelling опухоль ① o·pu·khal'

swim v плавать pla·vat'

swimming (sport) плавание @ pla·va·ni·ye

swimming pool бассейн @ bas·yeyn

swimsuit купальный костюм @
ku·pal'·nih kast·yum

Switzerland Швейцария ① shveyt·sa·ri·ya

synagogue синагога ① si·na·go·ga

synthetic синтетический sin·ti·ti·chi·ski

syringe шприц @ shprits

T

table стол @ stol

table tennis настольный теннис @
na·stol'·nih tye·nis

tablecloth скатерть ① ska·tirt'

taiga тайга ① tey·ga

tail хвост @ khvost

tailor портной part·noy

take брать/взять brat'/vzyat'

take photos снимать/снять sni·mat'/snyat'

talk разговаривать raz·ga·va·ri·vat'

tall высокий vih·so·ki

tampon тампон @ tam·pon

tap кран @ kran

tap water водопроводная вода ①
va·da·pra·vod·na·ya va·da

tasty вкусный fkus·nih

tax налог @ na·lok

taxi такси @ tak·si

taxi rank стоянка такси ① sta·yan·ka tak·si

tea чай @ chey

teacher учитель/учительница @/①
u·chi·til'/u·chi·til'·nit·sa

team команда ① ka·man·da

teaspoon чайная ложка ①
chey·na·ya losh·ka

teeth зубы @ pl zu·bih

telephone телефон @ ti·li·fon

telephone звонить/позвонить
zva·nit'/paz·va·nit'

telephone centre телефонный центр @
ti·li·fo·nih tsentr

television телевизор @ ti·li·vi·zar

tell сказать ska·zat'

temperature (fever) лихорадка ①
li·kha·rat·ka

temperature (weather) температура ①
tim·pi·ra·tu·ra

tennis теннис @ tye·nis

tennis court теннисный корт @
tye·nis·nih kort

tent палатка ① pa·lat·ka

tent peg колышек для палатки @
ko·lih·shihk dlya pa·lat·ki

terrible ужасный u·zhas·nih

terrorism терроризм @ ti·ra·rizm

thank благодарить/поблагодарить
bla·ga·da·rit'/pab·la·ga·da·rit'

that (one) то to

theatre театр @ ti·atr

their их ikh

there там tam

they они a·ni

thick толстый tol·stih

thief вор @ vor

thin тонкий ton·ki

think думать du·mat'

third a третий trye·ti

thirsty (be) хочется пить kho·chit·sa pit'

this (month) (в) этом (месяце) ①
(v) e·tam (mye·sit·se)

this (one) это e·ta

thread нитка ① nit·ka

throat горло @ gor·la

thrush (health) молочница ①
ma·loch·nit·sa

Thursday четверг @ chit·vyerk

ticket билет @ bil·yet

ticket collector кондуктор @ kan·duk·tar

ticket machine кассовый автомат @
ka·sa·vih af·ta·mat

ticket office билетная касса ①
bil·yet·na·ya ka·sa

ticks (insects) клещи @ pl klye·shi

tide (high) прилив @ pri·lif

tide (low) отлив @ at·lif

tight узкий us·ki

time время @ vryem·ya

time difference разность времени ①
raz·nast' vrye·mi·ni

timetable расписание ⑩ ras·pi·*sa*·ni·ye
tin (can) банка ① *ban*·ka
tin opener консервный нож ⑩ kans·*yerv*·nih nosh
tiny крошечный *kro*·shich·nih
tip (gratuity) чаевые ① pl cha·i·*vih*·ye
tired устал u·*stal*
tissues салфетки ① pl salf·*yet*·ki
to в v
toast (bread) гренок ⑩ gri·*nok*
toast (to health) тост ⑩ tost
toaster тостер ⑩ *tos*·tir
tobacco табак ⑩ ta·*bak*
tobogganing санный спорт ⑩ *sa*·nih sport
today сегодня si·*vod*·nya
toe палец ⑩ *pa*·lits
tofu тофу ⑩ *to*·fu
together вместе *vmyest*·ye
toilet туалет ⑩ tu·al·*yet*
toilet paper туалетная бумага ① tu·al·*yet*·na·ya bu·*ma*·ga
tomato помидор ⑩ pa·mi·*dor*
tomato sauce кетчуп ⑩ *kyet*·chup
tomorrow завтра *zaf*·tra
tomorrow afternoon завтра после обеда *zaf*·tra *pos*·li ab·ye·da
tomorrow evening завтра вечером *zaf*·tra *vye*·chi·ram
tomorrow morning завтра утром *zaf*·tra u·tram
tonight сегодня вечером si·*vod*·nya *vye*·chi·ram
too (also) тоже *to*·zhih
too (excess) слишком *slish*·kam
tooth зуб ⑩ zup
toothache зубная боль ① zub·*na*·ya bol'
toothbrush зубная щётка ① zub·*na*·ya *shot*·ka
toothpaste зубная паста ① zub·*na*·ya *pa*·sta
torch (flashlight) фонарик ⑩ fa·*na*·rik
touch трогать/тронуть *tro*·gat'/*tro*·nut'
tour экскурсия ① eks·*kur*·si·ya
tourist турист/туристка ⑩/① tu·*rist*/tu·*rist*·ka
tourist office туристическое бюро ⑩ tu·rist·*i*·chi·ska·ye byu·*ro*
towards к k
towel полотенце ⑩ pa·lat·*yent*·se
tower башня ① *bash*·nya
track (path) дорожка ① da·*rosh*·ka
track (sport) трек ⑩ tryek

trade (commerce) торговля ① tar·*gov*·lya
trade (job) профессия ① praf·*ye*·si·ya
tradesperson ремесленник ⑩ rim·*yes*·li·nik
trade union профсоюз ⑩ praf·sa·*yus*
traffic движение ⑩ dvi·*zhe*·ni·ye
traffic light светофор ⑩ svi·ta·*for*
trail тропинка ① tra·*pin*·ka
train поезд ⑩ *po*·ist
train station вокзал ⑩ vag·*zal*
tram трамвай ⑩ tram·*vey*
transit lounge транзитный зал ⑩ *tran*·zit·nih zal
translate переводить/перевести pi·ri·va·*dit*'/pi·ri·vi·*sti*
translation перевод ⑩ pi·ri·*vot*
transport транспорт ⑩ *tran*·spart
travel путешествовать ⑩ pu·ti·*shest*·va·vat'
travel agency бюро путешествий ⑩ byu·*ro* pu·ti·*shest*·vi
travel sickness морская болезнь ① mar·*ska*·ya bal·*yezn*'
travellers cheque дорожный чек ⑩ da·*rozh*·nih chek
tree дерево ⑩ *dye*·ri·va
trip (journey) поездка ① pa·*yest*·ka
trolley тележка ① til·*yesh*·ka
trousers брюки ⑩ pl *bryu*·ki
truck грузовик ⑩ gru·za·*vik*
trust доверять/доверить da·vir·*yat*'/dav·*ye*·rit'
try (attempt) стараться/постараться sta·*rat*'·sa/pa·sta·*rat*'·sa
try (taste) пробовать/попробовать *pro*·ba·vat'/pa·*pro*·ba·vat'
T-shirt футболка ① fud·*bol*·ka
tube (tyre) камера ① *ka*·mi·ra
Tuesday вторник *ftor*·nik
tumour опухоль ① *o*·pu·khal'
tundra тундра *tun*·dra
turkey индейка ① ind·*yey*·ka
Turkish (language) турецкий tu·*rets*·ki
turn поворачивать/повернуть pa·va·*ra*·chi·vat'/pa·vir·*nut*'
TV телевизор ⑩ ti·li·*vi*·zar
tweezers щипчики ⑩ pl *ship*·chi·ki
twice дважды *dvazh*·dih
twin beds adv две односпальные кровати dvye ad·na·*spal*'·nih·ye kra·*va*·ti
twins близнецы ⑩ pl bliz·nit·*sih*
two два/две ⑩/① dva/dvye
type тип ⑩ tip

typical типичный ti-*pich*-nih
tyre шина ① *shih*-na
tsar царь ⑩ tsar'

U

Ukraine Украина ① u-kra-*i*-na
ultrasound ультразвук ⑩ ul'-*traz*-vuk
umbrella зонтик ⑩ *zon*-tik
uncomfortable неудобный nye-u-*dob*-nih
understand понимать/понять
  pa-ni-*mat'*/*pan*-yat'
underwear бельё ① bil-*yo*
unemployed безработный biz-ra-*bot*-nih
unfair несправедливый nye-spra-vid-*li*-vih
uniform форма ① *for*-ma
universe вселенная ① fsyel-*ye*-na-ya
university университет ① u-ni-vir-*sit*-yet
unleaded очищенный a-*chi*-shi-nih
until до do
unusual необычный nye-a-*bihch*-nih
up вверх vyerkh
uphill в гору v *go*-ru
Ural Mountains Урал ⑩ u-*ral*
urgent срочный *sroch*-nih
urinary infection мочевая инфекция ①
  ma-chi-*va*-ya inf-*yekt*-sih-ya
USA США ⑩ pl es-sha-*a*
useful полезный pal-*yez*-nih

V

vacancy свободный номер ⑩
  sva-*bod*-nih *no*-mir
vacation каникулы ① pl ka-*ni*-ku-lih
vaccination прививка ① pri-*vif*-ka
vagina влагалище ⑩ vla-*ga*-li-she
validate утверждать/утвердить
  ut-virzh-*dat'*/ut-vir-*dit'*
valley долина ① da-*li*-na
valuable ценный *tse*-nih
value стоимость ① *sto*-i-mast'
van фургон ⑩ fur-*gon*
veal телятина ① til-*ya*-ti-na
vegetable овощ ⑩ *o*-vash
vegetarian вегетарианец/вегетарианка
  ⑩/① vi-gi-ta-ri-*a*-nits/vi-gi-ta-ri-*an*-ka
vein вена ① *vye*-na
venereal disease венерическая болезнь ①
  vi-ni-*ri*-chi-ska-ya bal-*yezn'*
venue место концерта ⑩
  mye-sta kant-*ser*-ta
very очень *o*-chin'

video recorder видеомагнитофон ⑩
  vi-di-o-mag-ni-ta-*fon*
video tape видеокассета ①
  vi-di-o-kas-*ye*-ta
view вид ⑩ vit
village деревня ⑩ dir-*yev*-nya
vinegar уксус ⑩ *uk*-sus
vineyard виноградник ⑩ vi-na-*grad*-nik
virus вирус ⑩ *vi*-rus
visa виза ① *vi*-za
visit визит ⑩ vi-*zit*
visit посещать/посетить pa-si-*shat'*/pa-si-*tit'*
vitamins витамины ⑩ pl vi-ta-*mi*-nih
vodka водка ① *vot*-ka
voice голос ⑩ *go*-las
volleyball (sport) волейбол ⑩ va-li-*bol*
volume (sound) громкость *grom*-kast'
vote голосовать/проголосовать
  ga-la-sa-*vat'*/pra-ga-la-sa-*vat'*

W

wage зарплата ① zar-*pla*-ta
wait ждать/подождать zhdat'/pa-da-*zhdat'*
waiter официант/официантка ⑩/①
  a-fit-sih-*ant*/a-fit-sih-*ant*-ka
waiting room зал ожидания ⑩
  zal a-zhih-*da*-ni-ya
wake (someone) up будить/разбудить
  bu-*dit'*/raz-bu-*dit'*
walk гулять/погулять gul-*yat'*/pa-gul-*yat'*
want хотеть/захотеть khat-*yet'*/za-khat-*yet'*
war война ① *vey*-na
wardrobe шкаф ⑩ shkaf
warm тёплый *tyop*-lih
warn предупреждать/предупредить
  pri-du-prizh-*dat'*/pri-du-pri-*dit'*
wash (oneself) умываться/умыться
  u-mih-*vat'*-sa/u-*miht'*-sa
wash (something) стирать/выстирать
  sti-*rat'*/vih-sti-*rat'*
wash cloth (flannel) тряпочка для
  мытья ① *trya*-pach-ka dlya miht-*ya*
washing machine стиральная машина ①
  sti-*ral'*-na-ya ma-*shih*-na
watch часы ⑩ pl chi-*sih*
watch смотреть smat-*ryet'*
water вода ① va-*da*
water bottle фляшка ① *flyash*-ka
water bottle (hot) грелка ① *gryel*-ka
waterfall водопад ⑩ va-da-*pat*
watermelon арбуз ⑩ ar-*bus*
waterproof непромокаемый
  nye-pra-ma-*ka*-i-mih

wave волна ① *val·na*
way путь ⑩ *put'*
we мы *mih*
weak слабый *sla·bih*
wealthy богатый ba·*ga*·tih
wear носить na·*sit'*
weather погода ① pa·*go*·da
wedding свадьба ① *svad'*·ba
wedding cake свадебный торт ⑩
  sva·dib·nih tort
wedding present свадебный подарок ⑩
  sva·dib·nih pa·*da*·rak
Wednesday среда ① sri·*da*
week неделя ① nid·*yel*·ya
(this) week (на этой) неделе
  (na e·tey) nid·*yel*·ye
weekend выходные ⑩ pl vih·khad·*nih*·ye
weigh взвешивать/взвесить
  vzvye·shih·vat'/*vzvye*·sit'
weight вес ⑩ vyes
weights весы ⑩ pl *vye*·sih
welcome приветствовать
  priv·*yetst*·va·vat'
welfare социальное обеспечение ⑩
  sat·sih·*al'*·na·ye a·bis·*pye*·chi·ni·ye
well a здоровый zda·ro·vih
west запад ⑩ *za*·pat
western западный *za*·pad·nih
wet a мокрый *mo*·krih
what что shto
wheel колесо ⑩ ka·li·*so*
wheelchair инвалидная коляска ①
  in·va·*lid*·na·ya kal·*yas*·ka
when когда kag·*da*
where где gdye
which какой ka·*koy*
whisky виски ⑩ *vis*·ki
white белый a *bye*·lih
who кто kto
why почему pa·chi·*mu*
wide широкий shih·*ro*·ki
wife жена ① zhih·*na*
win выигрывать/выиграть
  vih·*i*·gri·vat'/*vih*·i·grat'
wind ветер ⑩ *vye*·tir
window окно ⑩ ak·*no*
windscreen ветровое стекло ⑩
  vit·ra·vo·ye sti·*klo*
wine вино ⑩ vi·*no*
winner победитель ⑩ pa·bi·*di*·til'

winter зима ① zi·*ma*
wish желать/пожелать zhih·*lat'*/pa·zhih·*lat'*
with c s
within (time) в течение f ti·*che*·ni·ye
without без byez
woman женщина ① *zhen*·shi·na
wonderful прекрасный pri·*kras*·nih
wood дерево ⑩ *dye*·ri·va
wool шерсть ① sherst'
word слово ⑩ *slo*·va
work работа ① ra·*bo*·ta
work v работать ra·*bo*·tat'
work permit разрешение на работу ⑩
  raz·ri·*she*·ni·ye na ra·*bo*·tu
world мир ⑩ mir
World Cup Кубок мира ⑩ *ku*·bak *mi*·ra
worms глисты ① pl *gli*·stih
worried обеспокоенный a·bis·pa·*ko*·i·nih
worship поклоняться pak·lan·*yat'*·sa
wrist запястье ⑩ zap·*yast*·ye
write писать/написать pi·*sat'*/na·pi·*sat'*
writer писатель/писательница ⑩/①
  pi·*sa*·til'/pi·*sa*·til'·nit·sa
wrong неправильный nye·*pra*·vil'·nih

Y

year (1 to 4 years; not age) год ⑩ got
years (5 years plus; also age) лет ⑩ pl lyet
(this) year (в этом) году (v e·tam) ga·*du*
yellow жёлтый *zhol*·tih
yes да da
yesterday вчера fchi·*ra*
(not) yet ещё (не) yi·*sho* (nye)
yoga йога ① *yo*·ga
yogurt йогурт ⑩ *yo*·gurt
you sg inf ты tih
you sg pol & pl inf&pol вы vih
young молодой ma·la·*doy*
your sg inf твой tvoy
your sg pol & pl inf&pol ваш vash
youth hostel турбаза ① tur·*ba*·za

Z

zip/zipper молния ① *mol*·ni·ya
zodiac зодиак ⑩ zo·di·*ak*
zoo зоопарк ⑩ za·*park*
zucchini кабачок ⑩ ka·ba·*chok*

Russian nouns in the **dictionary** have their gender indicated by ⓜ, ⓕ or ⓝ. If it's a plural noun you'll also see pl. When a word that could be either a noun or a verb has no gender indicated, it's a verb. For added clarity, certain words are marked as adjectives a or verbs v. Adjectives, however, are given in the masculine form only. Both nouns and adjectives are provided in the nominative case only. For information on case and gender, refer to the **phrasebuilder**. Verbs are in the imperfective form only. See the **phrasebuilder** for explanation.

For any food items, refer to the **culinary reader**.

The **russian–english dictionary** has been listed according to the Cyrillic alphabet, shown below in both roman and italic text:

Аа Бб Вв Гг Дд Ее Ёё Жж Зз Ии Йй Кк Лл Мм Нн Оо Пп
Аа Бб Вв Гг Дд Ее Ёё Жж Зз Ии Йй Кк Лл Мм Нн Оо Пп

Рр Сс Тт Уу Фф Хх Цц Чч Шш Щщ Ъъ Ыы Ьь Ээ Юю Яя
Рр Сс Тт Уу Фф Хх Цц Чч Шш Щщ Ъъ Ыы Ьь Ээ Юю Яя

А

авария ⓕ a·*va·ri·ya* accident • emergency
авиапочта ⓕ a·vi·a·*poch·ta* airmail
автобиография ⓕ
  af·ta·bi·a·*gra·fi·ya* CV • résumé
автовокзал ⓜ af·ta·vag·*zal* bus station
автоприцеп ⓜ af·ta·prit·*sep* caravan
автостоянка ⓕ af·ta·sta·*yan·ka* car park
адвокат ⓜ ad·va·*kat* lawyer
анализ крови ⓜ a·*na·*lis *kro·*vi blood test
анекдот ⓜ a·nik·*dot* joke
аптека ⓕ apt·*ye·ka* chemist • pharmacy
арендовать a·rin·da·*vat'* rent
арестовывать a·ri·*sto·vih·vat'* arrest
аудио-путеводитель ⓜ
  au·di·o·pu·ti·va·*di·til'* audio guide

Б

бабушка ⓕ *ba·bush·ka* grandmother
багажная бирка ⓕ
  ba·*gazh·na·ya bir·ka* luggage tag
бальзам ⓜ bal'·*zam* hair conditioner
банка ⓕ *ban·ka* can • jar • tin
банковский счёт ⓜ
  ban·kaf·ski shot bank account

бассейн ⓜ bas·*yeyn* swimming pool
бедность ⓕ *byed·*nast' poverty
бедный *byed·nih* poor
бежать bi·*zhat'* run
без byez without
бездомный biz·*dom·nih* homeless
безопасный biz·a·*pas·nih* safe
безработный biz·ra·*bot·nih* unemployed
белый *bye·lih* white
белый медведь ⓜ
  bye·lih mid·vyet' polar bear
бельё ⓝ bil'·*yo* bedding • laundry (clothes) •
  underwear
бензин ⓜ bin·*zin* gas • petrol
берег ⓜ *bye·rik* coast
  — моря ⓜ *mor·ya* seaside
беременная bir·ye·mi·na·ya pregnant
бесплатный bis·*plat·nih* free • gratis
бешенство ⓝ *bye·shinst·va* rabies
билет ⓜ bil·*yet* ticket
билетная касса ⓕ
  bil·*yet·na·ya ka·sa* ticket office
бинт ⓜ bint bandage
благодарить bla·ga·da·*rit'* thank
ближайший bli·*zhey·shi* nearest
близкий a *blis·kih* close

B

близко (от) *blis*·ka (at) near(by)
блокнот ⓜ *blak*·not notebook
блошиный рынок ⓜ
  bla·*shih*·nih *rih*·nak fleamarket
блюдо ⓝ *blyu*·da dish
бог ⓜ bok god (general)
богатый ba·*ga*·tih rich • wealthy
болезненные месячные ⓝ pl
  bal·*yez*·ni·ni·ye mye·*sich*·nih·ye
  period pain
болезнь ① bal·*yezn'* disease
  — сердца ① *syerd*·tsa heart condition
болен ⓜ bo·*lin* ill • sick
болеть bal·*yet'* hurt
болеутоляющие ⓝ pl
  bo·li·u·tal·*ya*·yu·shi·ye painkiller
болит ba·*lit* painful • sore
боль ① bol' pain
  — в желудке ①
  v zhih·*lut*·kye stomachache
больна ① bal'·*na* ill • sick
больница ① bol'·*nit*·sa hospital
большой bal'·*shoy* big • large
бояться v ba·*yat*·sa (be) afraid
брак ⓜ brak marriage
брат ⓜ brat brother
брать brat' take
  — на время na *vryem*·ya borrow
  — напрокат na·*pra*·kat hire
бритва ① *brit*·va razor
бриться *brit*·sa shave
бросать bra·*sat'* quit
брюки bryu·ki ⓜ pl pants • trousers
будить bu·*dit'* wake (someone) up
будущее ⓝ *bu*·du·shi·ye future
булочная ① *bu*·lach·na·ya bakery
бумага ① bu·*ma*·ga paper
буря ① *bur*·ya storm
быстрый *bihst*·rih fast • quick
быть *biht'* be
бюро находок ⓝ
  byu·*ro* na·*kho*·dak lost property office
бюро путешествий ⓝ
  byu·*ro* pu·ti·*shest*·vi travel agency

В

в v *at* • *in* • *per* • *to*
в один конец a v a·*din* kan·*yets* one-way
важный *vazh*·nih important
ванна ① *va*·na bath
ванная ⓝ *va*·na·ya bathroom
ваш vash your sg pol & pl inf&pol
вверх v*yerkh* up

велосипед ⓜ vi·la·*sip*·*yet* bicycle
велосипедист ⓜ vi·la·si·pi·*dist* cyclist
венерическая болезнь ①
  vi·ni·*ri*·chi·ska·ya bal·*yezn'* venereal disease
верёвка ① vir·*yof*·ka rope • string
  — для белья ① dlya bil·*ya* clothesline
верховая езда ①
  vir·kha·*va*·ya yiz·*da* horse riding
вес ⓜ vyes weight
веселиться vi·si·*lit*·sa have fun
весело adv *vye*·si·la fun
весна ① vis·*na* spring (season)
ветер ⓜ *vye*·tir wind
ветровое стекло ⓝ
  vit·ra·vo·ye sti·*klo* windscreen
ветрянка ① vit·*ryan*·ka chicken pox
вечер ⓜ *vye*·chir evening
вечеринка ① vi·chi·*rin*·ka party (fiesta)
вечная мерзлота ①
  vyech·na·ya mirz·*la*·ta permafrost
взрослый ⓜ *vzros*·lih adult
взрослая ① *vzros*·la·ya adult
взятка ① *vzyat*·ka bribe
вид ⓜ vit view
видеть *vi*·dit' see
вилка ① *vil*·ka fork • plug (electricity)
вина ① vi·*na* (someone's) fault
ВИЧ ⓜ vich HIV
включая fklyu·*cha*·ya included
вкусный *fkus*·nih tasty
влагалище ⓝ vla·*ga*·li·she vagina
владелец ⓜ vlad·*yel*·its owner
влажный *vlazh*·nih humid
вместе *vmyest*·ye together
ВМС ⓜ ve·em·*se* IUD
вниз vnis down
внук ⓜ vnuk grandson
внутри vnu·*tri* inside
внучка ① *vnuch*·ka granddaughter
во втором классе va fta·*rom* *klas*·ye
  second class
вовремя *vov*·ryem·ya on time
вода ① va·*da* water
водительские права ⓝ pl
  va·*di*·til'·ski·ye pra·*va* drivers licence
водить машину va·*dit'* ma·*shih*·nu drive
водопад ⓜ va·da·*pat* waterfall
военные ⓜ pl va·*ye*·nih·ye military
возвращаться vaz·vra·*shat*·sa
  return (come back)
возвращение денег ⓜ
  vaz·vra·*she*·ni·ye dye·nik refund
воздух ⓜ *voz*·dukh air
возможный vaz·*mozh*·nih possible

возраст ⓜ *voz*·rast *age*
война ⓕ vey·*na* *war*
вокзал ⓜ vag·*zal* *railway station*
вопрос ⓜ va·*pros* *question*
вор ⓜ vor *thief*
воскресенье ⓝ vas·kris·*yen*·ye *Sunday*
восток ⓜ va·*stok* *east*
вперёд fpir·*yot* *ahead*
врач ⓜ vrach *doctor*
время ⓝ *vryem*·ya *time*
— года *go*·da *season*
все pl fsye *all* • *everyone*
всё fsyo *everything*
всегда fsig·*da* *always*
встреча ⓕ *fstre*·cha *appointment* • *date*
встречать fstri·*chat'* *meet*
встречаться с fstri·*chat'*·sa s *date* v
вторник *ftor*·nik *Tuesday*
второй fta·*roy* *second*
вход ⓜ fkhot *admission price* • *entry*
входить fkha·*dit'* *enter*
вчера fchi·*ra* *yesterday*
вы vih *you* sg pol & pl inf&pol
выбирать vih·bi·*rat'* *choose*
выборы ⓜ pl *vih*·ba·rih *election*
выдача багажа ⓕ *vih*·da·cha ba·ga·*zha*
baggage claim
выигрывать vih·*i*·gri·vat' *win*
выкидыш ⓜ *vih*·ki·dihsh *miscarriage*
высокий vih·*so*·ki *high* • *tall*
высота ⓕ vih·sa·*ta* *altitude*
выставка ⓕ *vih*·staf·ka *exhibition*
выход ⓜ *vih*·khat *exit*
выход на посадку ⓜ
vih·khat na pa·*sat*·ku *airport gate*
выходить vih·kha·*dit'* *go out*
выходить замуж vih·kha·*dit'* za·mush
marry (for a woman)
выходные ⓜ pl vih·khad·*nih*·ye *weekend*

газета ⓕ gaz·*ye*·ta *newspaper*
газетный киоск ⓜ gaz·*yet*·nih ki·*osk*
newsagency • *newsstand*
гастроном ⓜ gast·ra·*nom* *delicatessen*
где gdye *where*
гигиеническая салфетка ⓕ
gi·gi i·*ni*·chi·ska·ya salf·*yet*·ka
sanitary napkin
главная дорога ⓕ
glav·na·ya da·*ro*·ga *main road*
главный *glav*·nih *main*
глаз ⓜ glas *eye*

глисты ⓜ pl *gli*·stih *worms*
глубокий glu·*bo*·ki *deep*
глухой glu·*khoy* *deaf*
говорить ga·va·*rit'* *say* • *speak*
год ⓜ got *year (1 to 4 years' duration)*
голова ⓕ ga·la·*va* *head*
головная боль ⓕ ga·lav·*na*·ya bol'
headache
голоден *go*·la·din *be hungry*
голос ⓜ *go*·las *voice*
голосовать ga·la·sa·*vat'* *vote*
голубой ga·lu·*boy* *light blue*
гора ⓕ ga·*ra* *mountain*
горло ⓝ *gor*·la *throat*
горный велосипед ⓜ
gor·nih vi·la·sip·*yet* *mountain bike*
город ⓜ *go*·rat *city*
горшок ⓜ gar·*shok* *pot (ceramics/cooking)*
горячая вода ⓕ
gar·*ya*·chi·ya va·*da* *hot water*
гостеприимство ⓝ
ga·sti·pri·*imst*·va *hospitality*
гостиница ⓕ
ga·*sti*·nit·sa *guesthouse* • *hotel*
готов ⓜ ga·*tof* *ready*
готовить ga·*to*·vit' *cook*
грабёж ⓜ grab·*yosh* *rip-off* • *robbery*
гражданин ⓜ grazh·da·*nin* *citizen*
гражданка ⓕ grazh·*dan*·ka *citizen*
гражданство ⓝ grazh·*danst*·va *citizenship*
граница ⓕ gra·*nit*·sa *border*
гренок ⓜ gri·*nok* *toast (bread)*
грипп ⓜ grip *influenza*
гроза ⓕ gra·*za* *thunderstorm*
громкий *grom*·kih *loud*
грудная клетка ⓕ grud·*na*·ya klyet·ka
chest (body)
грудь ⓕ grud' *breast (body)*
Грузия ⓕ *gru*·zi·ya *Georgia*
грузовик ⓜ gru·za·*vik* *truck*
группа крови ⓕ *gru*·pa *kro*·vi *blood group*
грустный *grus*·nih *sad*
грязный *gryaz*·nih *dirty*
губы ⓜ pl *gu*·bih *lips*
гулять gul·*yat'* *walk*

давать da·*vat'* *bribe* • *give*
далеко da·li·*ko* *far*
дата рождения ⓕ *da*·ta razh·*dye*·ni·ya
date of birth
дважды *dvazh*·dih *twice*
две недели adv dvye nid·*ye*·li *fortnight*

E

две односпальные кровати adv dvye ad·na·*spal*'·nih·ye kra·*va*·ti twin beds
дверь ① *dvyer*' door
двойной dvey·*noy* double
дворец ⓜ dvar·*yets* palace
двуспальная кровать ①
dvu·*spal*'·na·ya kra·*vat*' double bed
девочка ① *dye*·vach·ka pre-teen girl
девушка ① *dye*·vush·ka teenage girl
дедушка ① *dye*·dush·ka grandfather
делать *dye*·lat' do · make · share (item)
— **укол** lat' u·*kol* inject
день ⓜ dyen' day
— **рождения** ① razh·*dye*·ni·ya birthday
деньги ① pl *dyen*'·gi money
деревня ① dir·*yev*·nya village
дерево ⓝ *dye*·ri·va tree · wood
деталь ① di·*tal*' component · part
дети ① pl *dye*·ti children
детская коляска ① dyet·ska·ya
kal·*yas*·ka pram · pushchair · stroller
детское питание ⓝ
dyet·ska·ye pi·*ta*·ni·ye baby food
дефицит ⓜ di·fit·*siht* shortage
дешёвый di·*sho*·vih cheap
длинный *dli*·nih long
дневник ⓜ dnyev·*nik* diary
дно ⓝ dno bottom (position)
днём dnyom afternoon
до do before · until
добрый *dob*·rih kind · nice
доверять da·vir·*yat*' trust
догадываться da·*ga*·dih·vat'·sa guess
дождь ⓜ dozht' rain
должен *dol*·zhihn owe
долина ① da·*li*·na valley
дом ⓜ dom home · house
домашние дела ⓝ pl
da·*mash*·ni·ye dye·*la* housework
домохозяйка ①
do·ma·khaz·*yey*·ka homemaker
дорога ① da·*ro*·ga road
дорогой da·ra·*goy* expensive
дорожка ① da·*rosh*·ka path · track
дорожный чек ⓜ da·*rozh*·nih chek
travellers cheque
доставлять da·stav·*lyat*' deliver
достаточно da·*sta*·tach·na enough
дочка ① *doch*·ka daughter
драка ① *dra*·ka fight
древний *dryev*·ni ancient
дрова ① dra·*va* firewood
друг ⓜ druk boyfriend · friend

другой dru·*goy* different · other
дума ① *du*·ma parliament
думать *du*·mat' think
духовка ① du·*khof*·ka oven
душ ⓜ dush shower

Е

еврей/еврейка ⓜ/① yiv·*rey*/yiv·*rey*·ka
Jewish
его yi·*vo* his
еда ① yi·*da* food · meal
её yi·*yo* her (possessive)
ежедневный yi·zhih·*dnyev*·nih daily
езда на велосипеде
yiz·*da* na vi·la·sip·*yed*·ye cycling
ездить верхом yez·dit' vir·*khom* ride (horse)
если yes·li if
есть yest' eat
ехать ye·*khat*' go (by vehicle)
ещё (не) yi·*sho* (nye) (not) yet
ещё один/одна ⓜ/①
yi·*sho* a·*din*/ad·*na* another
ещё раз yi·*sho* ras again

Ж

жалоба ① zha·la·ba complaint
жаловаться zha·la·vat'·sa complain
жаркий zhar·ki hot
ждать zhdat' wait (for)
железистая лихорадка ①
zhihl·*ye*·zi·sta·ya li·kha·*rat*·ka
glandular fever
желудок ⓜ zhih·*lu*·dak stomach
жена ① zhih·*na* wife
женатый zhih·*na*·tih married
жениться zhih·*nit*'·sa marry (for a man)
жених ⓜ zhih·*nikh* fiancé
женский zhen·skih female
— **монастырь** ⓜ ma·na·*stihr* convent
женщина ① *zhen*·shi·na woman
жёлтый zhol·tih yellow
живопись ① *zhih*·va·pis' painting (art)
животное ⓝ zhih·*vot*·na·ye animal
жизнь ① zhihzn' life
жить zhiht' live (somewhere)
— **в одной (комнате)**
v ad·*noy* (*kom*·nat·ye) share (room)

З

за za behind
— **границей** gra·*nit*·sey abroad
забастовка ① za·ba·*stof*·ka strike (work)

заведующий ⓜ zav·ye·du·yu·shi
manager (general)
завтра zaf·tra *tomorrow*
— **вечером**
vye·chi·ram tomorrow evening
— **после обеда**
pos·li ab·ye·da tomorrow afternoon
— **утром** u·tram *tomorrow morning*
завтрак ⓜ zaf·trak *breakfast*
зад ⓜ zat *bottom (body)*
задаток ⓜ za·da·tak *deposit*
задержка ⓕ zad·yersh·ka *delay*
задний a zad·ni *rear (location)*
задняя часть ⓕ
zad·nya·ya chast' back (position)
зажигалка ⓕ za·zhih·gal·ka *lighter*
заказ ⓜ za·kas *booking · order*
заказной za·kaz·noy *by registered mail*
заказывать za·ka·zih·vat' *book · order*
закат ⓜ za·kat *sunset*
закон ⓜ za·kon *law*
законный za·ko·nih *legal*
законодательство ⓝ
za·ko·na·da·tilst·va legislation
закрывать v za·krih·vat' *close*
закрытый za·krih·tih *closed · indoor · shut*
закуска ⓕ za·kus·ka *snack*
закусочная ⓕ za·ku·sach·na·ya *snack bar*
зал ожидания ⓜ
zal a·zhih·da·ni·ya waiting room
замерзать za·mir·zat' *freeze*
замок ⓜ za·mok *lock*
замужняя ⓕ za·muzh·ni·ya *married*
занят/занята ⓜ/ⓕ za·nit/za·ni·ta *busy*
занято zan·ya·ta *engaged (phone)*
запад ⓜ za·pat *west*
западный za·pad·nih *Western*
запах ⓜ za·pakh *smell*
запертый zap·yer·tih *locked*
запирать za·pi·rat' *lock*
записка ⓕ za·pis·ka *message*
заповедник ⓜ
za·pav·yed·nik national park
заправочная станция ⓕ za·pra·vach·na·ye
stant·sih·ya service station
запястье ⓝ zap·yast·ye *wrist*
зарабатывать za·ra·ba·tih·vat' *earn*
зарплата ⓕ zar·pla·ta *salary · wage*
заря ⓕ zar·ya *sunrise*
защищать za·shi·shat' *protect*
звонить zva·nit' *call · ring · phone*
звонок ⓜ zva·nok *call (phone)*

звонок по коллекту ⓜ
zva·nok pa kal·yek·tu collect call
здание ⓝ zda·ni·ye *building*
здесь zdyes' *here*
здоровый zda·ro·vih *well*
здоровье ⓝ zda·rov·ye *health*
зеленщик ⓜ zi·lin·shik *greengrocer*
зелёный zil·yo·nih *green*
земля ⓕ zim·lya *Earth · land*
зеркало ⓝ zyer·ka·la *mirror*
зима ⓕ zi·ma *winter*
знак ⓜ znak *star sign*
знаменитый zna·mi·ni·tih *famous*
знать znat' *know*
зубная боль ⓕ zub·na·ya bol' *toothache*
зубной врач ⓜ zub·noy vrach *dentist*
зубы ⓜ pl zu·bih *teeth*

И

и i *and*
игла ⓕ i·gla *needle (sewing)*
играть в (домино)
i·grat' v (da·mi·no) play (dominoes)
играть на (гитаре)
i·grat' na (gi·tar·ye) play (guitar)
идти i·ti *go (on foot)*
изнасилование ⓝ iz·na·si·la·va·ni·ye *rape*
или i·li *or*
имя ⓝ im·ya *given name*
инвалид ⓜ in·va·lit *disabled*
иногда i·nag·da *sometimes*
иностранный i·nast·ra·nih *foreign*
искусство ⓝ is·kust·va *art*
испорченный is·por·chi·nih *off · spoiled*
их ikh *their*

К

к k *towards*
каждый kazh·dih *each · every*
как kak *how*
какой ka·koy *which*
камера ⓕ ka·mi·ra *tube (tyre)*
камера-автомат ⓕ
ka·mi·ra·af·ta·mat luggage lockers
камера хранения ⓕ
ka·mi·ra khran·ye·ni·ya left-luggage office
каникулы ⓕ pl ka·ni·ku·lih *vacation*
карандаш ⓜ ka·ran·dash *pencil*
карман ⓜ kar·man *pocket*
карманный ножик ⓜ
kar·ma·nih no·zhik pocket knife
карта ⓕ kar·ta *map*
— **дорог** da·rok *road map*

катание на коньках ⑩
ka·*ta*·ni·ye na kan'·*kakh* ice skating
катание на лыжах ⑩
ka·*ta*·ni·ye na *lih*·zhakh ski · skiing
кататься на коньках
ka·*tat*'·sa na kan'·*kakh* skate
качество ⑩ *ka*·chist·va quality
кашель ⑩ *ka*·shel' cough
квартира ① kvar·*ti*·ra apartment · flat
квартирная плата ①
kvar·*tir*·na·ya *pla*·ta rent (payment)
квитанция ① kvi·*tant*·sih·ya receipt
кислород ⑩ kis·la·*rot* oxygen
Китай ⑩ ki·*tey* China
кладбище ⑩ *klad*·bi·she cemetery
ключ ⑩ klyuch key
книга ① *kni*·ga book
когда kag·*da* when
кожа ① *ko*·zha leather · skin
койка ① *koy*·ka berth (ship)
колготки pl kal·*got*·ki pantyhose
колено ⑩ kal·*ye*·na knee
колесо ⑩ ka·li·*so* wheel
кольцо ⑩ kalt·*so* ring (jewellery)
команда ① ka·*man*·da team
комната ① *kom*·na·ta room (house)
конец ⑩ kan·*yets* end · finish
контора ① kan·*to*·ra office
контрольный пункт ⑩
kan·*trol*'·nih punkt checkpoint
конфеты ① pl kanf·*ye*·tih
candy · lollies · sweets
кончать kan·*chat*' finish
корабль ⑩ ka·*rabl*' ship
коричневый ka·*rich*·ni·vih brown
коробка ① ka·*rop*·ka box
— **передач** ① pi·ri·*dach* gearbox
короткий ka·*rot*·ki short (height)
корь ① kor' measles
кость ① kost' bone
кошелёк ⑩ ka·shal·*yok* purse
краденый *kra*·di·nih stolen
кран ⑩ kran tap
красивый kra·*si*·vih beautiful · handsome
краснуха ① kras·*nu*·kha rubella
красный *kras*·nih red
красть krast' rob · steal
крем ⑩ kryem cream (ointment)
кричать kri·*chat*' shout (yell)
кровать ① kra·*vat*' bed
кровь ① krof' blood
кровяное давление ⑩
kra·vi·*no*·ye dav·*lye*·ni·ye blood pressure

круглый *krug*·lih round
крутой kru·*toy* steep
кто kto who
кто-то *kto*·ta someone
Кубок мира ⑩ *ku*·bak *mi*·ra World Cup
кулинария ① ku·li·*na*·ri·ya cooking
купальный костюм ⑩
ku·*pal*'·nih kast·*yum* swimsuit
купе ⑩ ku·*pe* train compartment
курить ku·*rit*' smoke
куртка ① *kurt*·ka jacket (for men)
кусок ⑩ ku·*sok* piece
кухня ① *kukh*·nya kitchen

латексная салфетка ① *la*·tiks·na·ya
sal·*fyet*·ka dental dam
левый *lye*·vih left (direction) · left-wing
лёгкий *lyokh*·kih easy · light (weight)
лёгкое ⑩ *lyokh*·ka·ye lung
лёд ⑩ lyot ice
ледоруб ⑩ lye·da·*rup* ice axe
лезвие ⑩ *lyez*·vi·ye razor blade
лекарство ⑩ li·*karst*·va medication
ленивый li·*ni*·vih lazy
лес ⑩ lyes forest
лестница ① *lyes*·nit·sa stairway
лет ⑩ pl lyet years (5 years or longer)
лето ⑩ *lye*·ta summer
лист ⑩ list leaf
лифчик ⑩ *lif*·chik bra
лихорадка ① li·kha·*rat*·ka fever
лицо ⑩ lit·*so* face
лодка ① *lot*·ka boat
лодыжка ① la·*dihsh*·ka ankle
ложка ① *losh*·ka spoon
ломать la·*mat*' break
ломаться la·*mat*'·sa break down (car)
ломтик ⑩ *lom*·tik slice
луна ① lu·*na* moon
любить lyu·*bit*' like · love
любовник ⑩ lyu·*bov*·nik lover
любовница ① lyu·*bov*·nit·sa lover
любовь ① lyu·*bof*' love
любой lyu·*boy* any
люди ⑩ pl *lyu*·di people

магазин ⑩ ma·ga·*zin* shop
— **готового платья** ① ga·*to*·va·va
plat'·ya clothing store
магазинчик ⑩ ma·ga·*zin*·chik
convenience store

мазок ⓜ ma·*zok* pap smear
маленький ma·*lin*'ki little • small
мало *ma*·la few
мальчик ⓜ *mal*'·chik boy
марка ⓕ *mar*·ka stamp
маршрут ⓜ marsh·*rut* itinerary
масло ⓝ *mas*·la butter • oil (cooking/fuel)
мастерская ⓕ ma·*stir*·ska·ya workshop
мать ⓕ mat' mother
машина ⓕ ma·*shih*·na car • machine
мебель ⓕ *mye*·bil' furniture
медовый месяц ⓜ me·*do*·vih *mye*·sits
   honeymoon
медсестра ⓕ mit·sist·*ra* nurse
между *myezh*·du between
международный mizh·du·na·*rod*·nih
   international
мелочь ⓕ *mye*·lach' change (coins)
меньше *myen*'·she less • smaller
меня min·*ya* me
менять min·*yat'* exchange
местный *myes*·nih local
место ⓝ *mye*·sta place • seat
   — назначения ⓝ
      naz·na·*che*·ni·ya destination
   — рождения ⓝ razh·*dye*·ni·ya birthplace
месяц ⓜ *mye*·sits month
мешать mi·*shat'* stop (prevent)
мешок ⓜ mi·*shok* bag
мёртвый *myort*·vih dead
милиционер ⓜ
   mi·li·tsih·an·*yer* police officer
милиция ⓕ mi·*lit*·sih·ya police
милый *mi*·lih nice
мир ⓜ mir peace • world
миска ⓕ *mis*·ka bowl
мнение ⓝ *mnye*·ni·ye opinion
много *mno*·ga (a) lot • many
мобильный телефон ⓜ ma·*bil'*·nih
   ti·li·*fon* cell phone • mobile phone
может быть *mo*·zhiht biht maybe
можно *mozh*·na can (have permission)
мой moy my
мокрый a *mo*·krih wet
молния ⓕ *mol*·ni·ya zip • zipper
молодой ma·la·*doy* young
молочница ⓕ ma·*loch*·nit·sa thrush (health)
монеты ⓕ pl man·*ye*·tih coins
море ⓝ *mor*·ye sea
мороз ⓜ ma·*ros* frost
морская болезнь ⓕ mar·*ska*·ya
   bal·*yezn'* seasickness • travel sickness
мост ⓜ most bridge

моторная лодка ⓕ
   ma·*tor*·na·ya *lot*·ka motorboat
мочевая инфекция ⓕ ma·chi·*va*·ya
   inf·*yekt*·sih·ya urinary infection
мочевой пузырь ⓜ
   ma·chi·*voy* pu·*zihr'* bladder
мочь moch' can (be able)
мошенник ⓜ ma·*she*·nik cheat
муж ⓜ mush husband
мужчина ⓜ mush·*chi*·na man
мусор ⓜ *mu*·sar garbage • rubbish • trash
мы mih we
мыло ⓝ *mih*·la soap
мясник ⓜ mis·*nik* butcher
мяч ⓜ myach ball (sport)

на na on
   — борту bar·*tu* aboard
   — неполной ставке
      ni·*pol*·ney *staf*·kye part-time
   — полной ставке
      pol·ney *staf*·kye full-time
   — себя sib·*ya* self-employed
наводнение ⓝ na·vad·*nye*·ni·ye flood
над nat above
наличные ⓕ pl na·*lich*·nih·ye cash
налог ⓜ na·*lok* tax
   — на вылет ⓜ na *vih*·lit airport tax
   — на продажу ⓜ na pra·*da*·zhu sales tax
напиток ⓜ na·*pi*·tak drink
наполнять na·paln·*yat'* fill
направление ⓝ
   na·prav·*lye*·ni·ye direction
насиловать na·*si*·la·vat' rape
наслаждаться
   nas·lazh·*dat'*·sa enjoy (oneself)
настоящее ⓝ na·sta·*ya*·shi·ye present (time)
находить na·kha·*dit'* find
начало ⓝ na·*cha*·la start
начинать na·chi·*nat'* start
наш nash our
не nye not
   — замужем ⓕ *za*·mu·zhihm single
невеста ⓕ niv·*ye*·sta fiancée
невиновный nye·vi·*nov*·nih innocent
неделя ⓕ nid·*yel*·ya week
невозможно ni·vaz·*mozh*·na impossible
недавно ni·*dav*·na recently
незнакомец ⓜ nyez·na·*ko*·mits stranger
незнакомка ⓕ nyez·na·*kom*·ka stranger
некурящий ni·kur·*ya*·shi nonsmoking

немецкий ⓜ
nim·*yet*·ski German (language)
немного nim·*no*·ga little (not much)
необычный nye·a·*bihch*·nih unusual
неправильный nye·*pra*·vil'·nih wrong
непромокаемый
nye·pra·ma·*ka*·i·mih waterproof
несколько *nye*·skal'·ka several · some
нести ni·*sti* carry
нет nyet no
низкий *nis*·ki low
никаких ni·ka·*kikh* none
никогда ni·kag·*da* never
ничего ni·chi·*vo* nothing
но no but
Новогодняя ночь ①
na·va·*god*·ni·ya noch' New Year's Eve
новости ⓜ pl *no*·va·sti news
новый *no*·vih new
Новый год ⓜ *no*·vih got New Year's Day
нога ① na·*ga* foot · leg
нож ⓜ nosh knife
номер ⓜ *no*·mir hotel room · number
— комнаты ⓜ *kom*·na·tih room number
— на двоих ⓜ na dva·*ikh* double room
номерной знак ⓜ
na·mir·*noy* znak license plate number
норма багажа ①
nor·ma ba·ga·*zha* baggage allowance
носить na·*sit'* wear
носки ⓜ pl na·*ski* socks
ночь ① noch' night
нуждаться в nuzh·*dat*'·sa v need
нужный *nuzh*·nih necessary

О

оба/обе ⓜ/① *o*·ba/*ob*·ye both
обед ⓜ a·*yet* lunch
обедня ① ab·*yed*·nya mass (Catholic)
обеспокоенный a·bis·pa·*ko*·i·nih worried
обещать a·bi·*shat'* promise
обмен ⓜ ab·*myen* exchange
— валюты ⓜ val·*yu*·tih
currency exchange
обменивать ab·*mye*·ni·vat'
cash a cheque · change money
обменный курс ⓜ ab·*mye*·nih kurs
exchange rate
обнимать ab·ni·*mat'* hug
обогремаевый a·ba·gri·*ma*·i·vih heated
оборудование ⓝ a·ba·*ru*·da·va·ni·ye
equipment
образование ⓝ a·bra·za·*va*·ni·ye
education
обратный a·*brat*·nih return (ticket)
обручение ⓝ ab·ru·*che*·ni·ye engagement
обручённый ab·ru·*cho*·nih
engaged (person)
общественный туалет ⓜ
ap·*shest*·vi·nih tu·al·*yet* public toilet
обычай ⓜ a·*bih*·chey custom
обычная почта ①
a·*bihch*·na·ya *poch*·ta surface mail
огонь ⓜ a·*gon'* fire (heat)
ограничение скорости ①
a·gra·ni·*che*·ni·ye *sko*·ras·ti speed limit
одежда ① ad·*yezh*·da clothing
одеяло ⓝ a·di·*ya*·la blanket
один раз a·*din* ras once
один/одна ⓜ/① a·*din*/ad·*na* alone · one
одноместный номер ⓜ
ad·na·*mes*·nih *no*·mir single room
озеро ⓝ *o*·zi·ra lake
океан ⓜ a·ki·*an* ocean
окно ⓝ ak·*no* window
около *o*·ka·la about
окружающая среда ①
a·kru·*zha*·yu·sha·ya sri·*da* environment
он on he
она a·*na* she
они a·*ni* they
оно a·*no* it
опаздывать к a·*paz*·dih·vat' k miss (train)
опасный a·*pas*·nih dangerous · unsafe
оплата ① a·*pla*·ta payment
опухоль ① *o*·pu·khal swelling · tumour
опыт ⓜ *o*·piht experience
осень ① *o*·sin' autumn · fall
особенный a·*so*·bi·nih special
оставаться a·sta·*vat*'·sa stay (in one place)
оставленный багаж ⓜ
a·*stav*·li·nih ba·*gash* left luggage
останавливаться a·sta·*nav*·li·vat'·sa
stay (at a hotel) · stop (be still)
остановка ① a·sta·*nof*·ka stop (bus/tram)
остров ⓜ *ost*·raf island
от at from
ответ ⓜ at·*vyet* answer
отдельный a ad·*yel*'·nih separate
отдыхать a·dih·*khat'* rest
отец ⓜ at·*yets* father
открывать v at·krih·*vat'* open
открытый a at·*krih*·tih open
отлив ⓜ at·*lif* tide (low)
отличный at·*lich*·nih excellent · fantastic

отменять at·min·*yat'* cancel
отопление ⑩ a·tap·*lye*·ni·ye heating
отправляться at·prav·*lyat'·sa* depart
отпуск ⑩ *ot*·pusk holidays
отъезд ⑩ at·*yest* departure
официант ⑩ a·fit·sih·*ant* waiter
официантка ① a·fit·sih·*ant*·ka waitress
очень *o*·chin' very
очередь ① *o*·chi·rit' queue
очищенный a·*chi*·shi·nih unleaded
очки ① pl ach·*ki* glasses • goggles
— от солнца at *solnt*·sa sunglasses
ошибка ① a·*shihp*·ka mistake
ошибочный a·*shih*·bach·nih faulty

П

падать pa·*dat'* fall (down)
подруга ① pa·*dru*·ga friend
палатка ① pa·*lat*·ka tent
палец ⑩ *pa*·lits finger • toe
пальто ⑩ pal'·*to* coat • overcoat
пансионат ⑩ pan·si·a·*nat* boarding house
пара ① *pa*·ra pair (couple)
парикмахер ⑩
  pa·rik·*ma*·khir barber • hairdresser
паром pa·*rom* ferry
партия ① *par*·ti·ya party (politics)
пассажирский класс ⑩
  pa·sa·*zhihr*·ski klas economy class
Пасха ① *pas*·kha Easter
пачка ① *pach*·ka packet (general)
перевес ⑩ pi·riv·*yes* excess (baggage)
переводить pi·ri·va·*dit'* translate
переводчик ⑩ pi·ri·*vot*·chik interpreter
перед *pye*·rit in front of
перерабатывать pi·ri·ra·*ba*·tih·vat' recycle
переставать pi·ri·sta·*vat'* stop (cease)
перочинный нож ⑩
  pi·ra·*chin*·nih nosh penknife
перчатки ① pl pir·*chat*·ki gloves
песня ① *pyes*·nya song
петь ruet' sing
печень ① *pye*·chin' liver
печь ① pyech' stove
пешеход ⑩ pi·shih·*khot* pedestrian
пивная ① piv·*na*·ya pub • tavern
пиво ⑩ *pi*·va beer
писатель ⑩ pi·*sa*·til' writer
писательница ① pi·sa·*til'*·nit·sa writer
писать pi·*sat'* write
письмо ⑩ pis'·*mo* letter (mail)
пить pit' drink
плавать pla·*vat'* swim

плата ① *pla*·ta fare
— за куверт ① za kuv·*yert* cover charge
— за обслуживание ①
  za aps·*lu*·zhih·va·ni·ye service charge
платить pla·*tit'* pay
платье ⑩ *plat*·ye dress
плащ ⑩ plash raincoat
плёнка ① *plyon*·ka film (for camera)
плечо ⑥ pli·*cho* shoulder
плохой pla·*khoy* bad
площадь ① *plo*·shat' town square
пляж ⑩ plyash beach
поворачивать pa·va·*ra*·chi·vat' turn
погода ① pa·*go*·da weather
под pot below
под уклон pad u·*klon* downhill
подарок ⑩ pa·*da*·rak gift • present
подгузник ⑩ pad·*guz*·nik diaper • nappy
подниматься pad·ni·*mat'*·sa climb v
подписывать pat·*pi*·sih·vat' sign (forms)
подпись ① *pot*·pis' signature
подробности ① pl pa·*drob*·na·sti details
подруга ① pa·*dru*·ga girlfriend
подтверждать
  pat·virzh·*dat'* confirm (booking)
подушка ① pa·*dush*·ka pillow
поезд ⑩ *po*·ist train
поездка ① pa·*yest*·ka ride • trip
пожар ⑩ pa·*zhar* fire (emergency)
позже *po*·zhih later
позавчера
  pa·zaf·chi·*ra* day before yesterday
поздний *poz*·ni late
показывать pa·*ka*·zih·vat' show
поклоняться pak·lan·*yat'*·sa worship
покупать pa·ku·*pat'* buy
полдень ⑩ *pol*·din' midday • noon
полезный pal·*yez*·nih useful
полёт ⑩ pal·*yot* flight
полицейский участок ⑩
  pa·*lit*·sey·ski u·*cha*·stak police station
полка ① *pol*·ka berth (train) • shelf
полночь ① *pol*·noch' midnight
полный *pol*·nih full
половина ① pa·la·*vi*·na half
полотенце ⑩ pa·la·*tyent*·se towel
получать pa·lu·*chat'* get
помещение ⑥
  pa·mi·*she*·ni·ye accommodation
помогать pa·ma·*gat'* help
помощь ① *po*·mash' help
понедельник ⑩ pa·nid·*yel'*·nik Monday
понимать pa·ni·*mat'* understand

понос ⓜ pa·nos *diarrhoea*
портфель ⓜ part·*fyel'* *briefcase*
посадочный талон ⓜ
  pa·*sa*·dach·nih ta·*lon* *boarding pass*
посещать pa·si·*shat'* *visit*
после *pos*·lye *after*
послезавтра
  pas·li·*zaf*·tra *day after tomorrow*
посол ⓜ pa·*sol* *ambassador*
посольство ⓝ pa·*solst*·va *embassy*
постельное бельё ⓝ
  past·*yel'*·na·ye bil·*yo* *bedding*
посылать pa·sih·*lat'* *send*
посылка ⓕ pa·*sihl*·ka *package · parcel*
поток ⓜ pa·*tok* *stream*
потому что pa·ta·*mu* shta *because*
поход ⓜ pa·*khot* *hiking*
похожий pa·*kho*·zhih *similar*
похороны pl *po*·kha·ra·nih *funeral*
поцелуй ⓜ pat·sih·*luy* *kiss*
почему pa·chi·*mu* *why*
почка ⓕ *poch*·ka *kidney*
почта ⓕ *poch*·ta *mail · post office*
почти pach·*ti* *almost*
почтовые расходы ⓜ pl
  pach·*to*·vih·ye ras·*kho*·dih *postage*
почтовый индекс ⓜ
  pach·*to*·vih *in*·diks *post code*
почтовый ящик ⓜ
  pach·*to*·vih *ya*·shik *mailbox*
правило ⓝ *pra*·vi·la *rule*
правильный *pra*·vil'·nih *right (correct)*
правительство ⓝ
  pra·*vi*·til'·stva *government*
православная церковь
  pra·vas·*lav*·na·ya *tser*·kaf' *Orthodox Church*
православный pra·vas·*lav*·nih *Orthodox*
правый *pra*·vih *right (direction) · right-wing*
праздник ⓜ *praz*·nik *celebration · holiday*
прачечная ⓕ *pra*·chich·na·ya *laundry*
предпочитать prit·pa·chi·*tat'* *prefer*
предупреждать pri·du·prizh·*dat'* *warn*
презерватив ⓜ pri·zir·va·*tif* *condom*
прекрасный pri·*kras*·nih *perfect · wonderful*
прибытие ⓝ pri·*bih*·ti·ye *arrivals*
приветствовать priv·*yetst*·va·vat' *welcome*
прививка ⓕ pri·*vif*·ka *vaccination*
приглашать pri·gla·*shat'* *invite*
пригород ⓜ *pri*·ga·rat *suburb*
приготавливать pri·ga·*tav*·li·vat' *prepare*
приезжать pri·i·*zhat'* *arrive*
прилив ⓜ pri·*lif* *high tide*

примерочная ⓕ
  prim·*ye*·rach·na·ya *changing room*
приносить pri·na·*sit'* *bring*
природа ⓕ pri·*ro*·da *nature*
присматривать pris·*mat*·ri·vat' *look for*
присмотр за детьми
  pris·*motr* za dit'·*mi* *childminding*
приходить pri·kha·*dit'* *come*
приходящая няня ⓕ
  pri·khad·*ya*·sha·yan yan·ya *babysitter*
причина ⓕ pri·*chi*·na *reason*
пробовать *pro*·ba·vat' *try (taste)*
проверять pra·vir·*yat'* *check*
проводник ⓜ
  pra·vad·*nik* *carriage attendant*
продавать pra·da·*vat'* *sell*
продление ⓕ prad·*lye*·ni·ye *visa extension*
продовольствие ⓝ
  pra·da·*volst*·vi·ye *food supplies*
прозвище ⓝ *proz*·vi·she *nickname*
прокат автомобилей ⓜ
  pra·*kat* af·ta·ma·*bil*·yey *car hire*
промышленность ⓕ
  pra·*mihsh*·li·nast' *industry*
пропавший pra·*paf*·shih *lost*
просить pra·*sit'* *ask (for something)*
проспект ⓜ prasp·*yekt* *avenue*
простой pra·*stoy* *simple*
простуда ⓕ pra·*stu*·da *cold*
простужаться pra·stu·*zhat'*·sa *have a cold*
простыня ⓕ pra·stih·*nya* *sheet (bed)*
противозачаточная таблетка ⓕ
  pra·ti·va·za·*cha*·tach·na·ya tab·*lyet*·ka
  the pill
противозачаточные средства ⓝ pl
  pra·ti·va·za·*cha*·tach·nih·ye sryetst·va
  contraceptives
профессия ⓕ praf·*ye*·si·ya *trade (job)*
профсоюз ⓜ praf·*sa*·yus *trade union*
проход ⓜ pra·*khot* *aisle (on transport)*
проходить pra·kha·*dit'* *pass*
прошлое ⓝ *prosh*·la·ye *past*
прошлый *prosh*·lih *last (previous)*
прямой pri·*moy* *direct · straight*
прямым набором номера pri·*mihm*
  na·*bo*·ram *no*·mi·ra *direct-dial (by)*
публичный сад ⓜ
  pub·*lich*·nih sat *public gardens*
пустой pu·*stoy* *empty*
пустыня ⓕ pu·*stihn*·ya *desert*
путеводитель ⓜ pu·ti·va·*di*·til'
  entertainment guide · guidebook
путешествие ⓝ pu·ti·*shest*·vi·ye *journey*

путешествовать pu·ti·*shest*·va·vat' *travel*
— автостопом af·ta·*sto*·pam *hitchhike*
путь ⓜ put' *route · way*
пьяный *pya*·nih *drunk*
пятница ⓕ *pyat*·nit·sa *Friday*

Р

работа ⓕ ra·*bo*·ta *job · work*
работать ra·*bo*·tat' *work*
работодатель ⓜ ra·bo·ta·*dat*·yel' *employer*
рабочая ⓕ ra·*bo*·cha·ya *manual worker*
рабочий ⓜ ra·*bo*·chi *manual worker*
разведённый raz·vid·*yo*·nih *divorced*
разговаривать raz·ga·*va*·ri·vat' *talk*
разговорник ⓜ raz·ga·*vor*·nik *phrasebook*
размер ⓜ raz·*myer* *size (general)*
разность времени ⓕ
    raz·nast' *vrye*·mi·ni *time difference*
разрешение ⓝ
    raz·ri·*she*·ni·ye *permission · permit*
— на работу ⓝ na ra·*bo*·tu *work permit*
рак ⓜ rak *cancer*
ранний *ra*·ni *early*
расписание ⓝ ras·pi·*sa*·ni·ye *timetable*
располагаться ras·pa·la·*gat*'·sa *camp*
распродажа ⓕ ras·pra·*da*·zha *sale*
распроданы ras·*pro*·da·nih *booked out*
рассвет ⓜ ras·*vyet* *dawn*
рассказ ⓜ ras·*kas* *story*
расслабляться ras·lab·*lyat*'·sa *relax*
растение ⓝ rast·*ye*·ni·ye *plant*
расти ra·*sti* *grow*
растяжение связок ⓝ
    rast·ya·*zhe*·ni·ye *svya*·zak *sprain*
расчёска ⓕ ras·*chos*·ka *comb*
ребёнок ⓜ rib·*yo*·nak *baby · child*
ребро ⓝ ri·*bro* *rib*
ревнивый riv·*ni*·vih *jealous*
резать rye·*zat*' *cut*
река ⓕ ri·*ka* *river*
ремень ⓜ rim·*yen*' *seatbelt*
ремёсла ⓕ pl rim·*yos*·la *crafts*
ремесленник ⓜ rim·*yes*·li·nik *tradesperson*
рецензия ⓕ rit·*sen*·zi·ya *review*
рецепт ⓜ rit·*sept* *prescription*
решать ri·*shat*' *decide*
ритмизатор сердца ⓜ
    rit·mi·*za*·tar *syert*·sa *pacemaker*
родители ⓜ pl ra·*di*·ti·li *parents*
Рождество ⓝ razh·dist·*vo* *Christmas (Day)*
розовый *ro*·za·vih *pink*
роскошь ⓕ *ros*·kash' *luxury*
рот ⓜ rot *mouth*

рубашка ⓕ ru·*bash*·ka *shirt*
ружьё ⓝ ruzh·*yo* *gun*
рука ⓕ ru·*ka* *arm · hand*
руководитель ⓜ ru·ka·va·*dit*·yel' *leader*
ручка ⓕ *ruch*·ka *pen*
рыболовство ⓝ rih·ba·*lofst*·va *fishing*
рынок ⓜ *rih*·nak *market*
ряд ⓜ ryat *row (theatre)*
рядом с *rya*·dam s *beside · next to*

С

с s *since · with*
сад ⓜ sat *garden*
садиться sa·*dit*'·sa *board (plane/ship)*
садовод ⓜ sa·da·*vot* *gardener*
салфетка ⓕ salf·*yet*·ka *napkin · serviette*
салфетки ⓕ pl salf·*yet*·ki *tissues*
самолёт ⓜ sa·mal·*yot* *plane*
санитарная сумка ⓕ
    sa·ni·*tar*·na·ya *sum*·ka *first-aid kit*
санный спорт ⓜ
    sa·nih sport *tobogganing*
сапоги ⓜ pl sa·pa·*gi* *boots*
свадьба ⓕ *svad*'·ba *wedding*
свежемороженный
    svi·zhi·ma·*ro*·zhih·nih *frozen*
свежий *svye*·zhih *fresh*
свёкор ⓜ
    svyo·kar *father-in-law (wife's father)*
свекровь ⓕ
    svi·*krof*' *mother-in-law (husband's mother)*
свет ⓜ svyet *light*
светлый *svyet*·lih *light (colour)*
светофор ⓜ svi·ta·*for* *traffic light*
свидетельство ⓝ svid·*ye*·tilst·va *certificate*
— о владении автомобилем ⓝ a
    vlad·*ye*·ni af·ta·ma·*bil*·yem *car owner's title*
— о рождении ⓝ a razh·*dye*·ni
    birth certificate
свинка ⓕ *svin*·ka *mumps*
свободный
    sva·*bod*·nih *available · not bound*
связи ⓕ *svya*·zi *connection (transport)*
связь ⓕ svyas' *relationship*
святой svi·*toy* *saint*
священник ⓜ svya·*she*·nik *priest*
север ⓜ *sye*·vir *north*
сегодня si·*vod*·nya *today*
— вечером *vye*·chi·ram *tonight*
сейчас si·*chas* *now*
сельское хозяйство ⓝ
    syel'·ska·ye khaz·*yeyst*·va *agriculture*

семейное положение ⓝ sim-*yey*-na-ye pa-la-*zhe*-ni-ye *marital status*

семья ⓕ sim-*ya family*

сердечный приступ ⓜ sird-*yech*-nih *pri*-stup *cardiac arrest • heart attack*

сердитый sir-*di*-tih *angry*

сердце ⓝ *syerd*-tsih *heart*

серп и молот ⓜ syerp i *mo*-lat *hammer and sickle*

серый *sye*-rih *grey*

сеть ⓕ syet' *net*

сидеть sid-*yet'* *sit*

сильный *sil'*-nih *strong*

синий *si*-ni *dark blue*

сказать ska-*zat'* *tell*

скидка ⓕ *skit*-ka *discount*

сколько *skol*-ka *how much*

скорая помощь ⓕ *sko*-ra-ya *po*-mash *ambulance*

скоро *sko*-ra *soon*

скорость ⓕ *sko*-rast' *speed (velocity)*

— протяжки плёнки ⓕ prat-*yash*-ki *plyon*-ki *film speed*

слабительное ⓝ sla-*bi*-til'-na-ye *laxative*

слабый *sla*-bih *loose • weak*

сладкий *slat*-ki *sweet*

следовать *slye*-da-vat' *follow*

слепой sli-*poy* *blind*

слишком *slish*-kam *too (excess)*

словарь ⓜ sla-*var'* *dictionary*

слово ⓝ *slo*-va *word*

сломанный *slo*-ma-nih *broken (down)*

служащая/служащий ⓕ/ⓜ slu-zha-shi/ slu-zha-sha-ya *(office) employee*

слушать *slu*-shat' *listen*

слышать *slih*-shat' *hear*

смазка ⓕ *smas*-ka *lubricant*

смешной smish-*noy funny*

смеяться smi-*yat'*-sa *laugh*

смотреть smat-*ryet'* *look (after) • watch*

смущённый smu-*sho*-nih *embarrassed*

снег ⓜ snyek *snow*

снимать sni-*mat'* *take a photo*

снимок ⓜ *sni*-mak *photo*

собор ⓜ sa-*bor cathedral*

собрание ⓝ sa-*bra*-ni-ye *meeting*

совет ⓜ sav-*yet advice*

Советский Союз ⓜ sav-*yet*-ski sa-*yus Soviet Union*

современный sa-vrim-*ye*-nih *modern*

соглашаться sa-gla-*shat'*-sa *agree*

солнце ⓝ *solnt*-se *sun*

сон ⓜ son *dream*

соска ⓕ *sos*-ka *dummy • pacifier*

сотрясение мозга ⓝ sat-ris-*ye*-ni-ye *moz*-ga *concussion*

Сочельник ⓜ sa-*chel*-nik *Christmas Eve*

спальное место ⓝ *spal'*-na-ye *mye*-sta *sleeping berth*

спальный вагон ⓜ *spal'*-nih va-*gon sleeping car*

спальный мешок ⓜ *spal'*-nih mi-*shok sleeping bag*

спасательный жилет ⓜ spa-sa-til'-nih zhihl-*yet life jacket*

спать spat' *sleep*

СПИД ⓜ spit *AIDS*

спина ⓕ spi-*na back (body)*

спиртной напиток ⓜ spirt-*noy* na-*pi*-tak *drink (alcoholic)*

спички ⓕ pl *spich*-ki *matches*

спорить spo-*rit'* *argue*

спортзал ⓜ spart-*zal gym (place)*

спрашивать *spra*-shih-vat' *ask (a question)*

среда ⓕ sri-*da Wednesday*

средняя школа ⓕ *sryed*-ni-ya shko-la *high school*

срочный *sroch*-nih *urgent*

ставить *sta*-vit' *put*

— машину ma-*shih*-nu *park a car*

стараться sta-*rat'*-sa *try (attempt)*

старый *sta*-rih *old*

стена ⓕ sti-*na wall*

стирать sti-*rat'* *wash (something)*

стоимость ⓕ *sto*-i-mast' *value*

стоить v sto-*it'* *cost*

стол ⓜ stol *table*

столовая ⓕ sta-*lo*-va-ya *canteen*

страна ⓕ stra-*na country*

страница ⓕ stra-*nit*-sa *page*

страхование ⓝ stra-kha-*va*-ni-ye *insurance*

стрелять stril-*yat' shoot*

строить *stro*-it' *build*

суббота ⓕ su-*bo*-ta *Saturday*

суд ⓜ sut *court (legal)*

судья ⓕ sud-*ya judge*

суеверие ⓝ su-iv-*ye*-ri-ye *superstition*

сумочка ⓕ *su*-mach-ka *handbag*

сушить su-*shiht' dry (general)*

сходить skha-*dit' get off (a train, etc)*

сцепление ⓝ stsep-*lye*-ni-ye *clutch (car)*

счастливый shis-*li*-vih *happy • lucky*

счастье ⓝ *shast*-ye *luck*

счёт ⓜ shot *bank account • bill • check*

считать shi-*tat'* *count*

США ⓜ pl es-sha-*a USA*

сын ⓜ sihn *son*

Т

там tam *there*
таможенная декларация ①
ta·*mo*·zhih·na·ya di·kla·*rat*·sih·ya
customs declaration
таможня ① ta·*mozh*·nya *customs*
танцевать tant·*sih*·vat' *dance*
танцы ⑩ pl *tant*·sih *dancing*
тарелка ① tar·*yel*·ka *plate*
твёрдый *tvyor*·dih *hard (not soft)*
твой tvoy *your* sg inf
телефон-автомат ⑩
ti·li·*fon*·af·ta·*mat* *pay phone*
телефонная будка ①
ti·li·*fo*·na·ya *but*·ka *phone box*
тело ⑩ *tye*·la *body*
тёмный *tyom*·nih *dark*
тень ① tyen' *shade* • *shadow*
тёплый *tyop*·lih *warm*
терять tir·*yat'* *lose*
тест на беременность ⑩ tyest na
bir·*ye*·mi·nast' *pregnancy test kit*
тесть ⑩
tyest' *father-in-law (husband's father)*
тётя ① *tyot*·ya *aunt*
техникум ⑩ *tyekh*·ni·kum *college*
тёща ①
tyo·sha *mother-in-law (wife's mother)*
тихий *ti*·khi *quiet*
ткань ① tkan' *fabric*
то to *that (one)*
тоже *to*·zhih *also* • *too*
ток ⑩ tok *current (electricity)*
толстый *tol*·stih *fat* • *thick*
только *tol'*·ka *only*
тому назад ta·*mu* na·*zat* *ago*
тонкий *ton*·ki *thin*
торговля ① tar·*gov*·lya *trade (commerce)*
торговый центр ⑩
tar·*go*·vih tsentr *shopping centre*
тормоза ⑩ pl tar·ma·*za* *brakes*
тосковать по ta·ska·*vat'* pa *miss (person)*
тост ⑩ tost *toast (to health)*
тот же самый tod zhe sa·mih *same*
точно *toch*·na *exactly*
тошнота ① tash·na·*ta* *nausea*
трава ① tra·*va* *grass* • *herb*
травма ① *trav*·ma *injury*
травяной trav·ya·*noy* *herbal*
трогать *tro*·gat' *feel* • *touch*
тропинка ① tra·*pin*·ka *path* • *trail*
тротуар ⑩ tra·tu·*ar* *footpath*
трудный *trud*·nih *difficult*

тряпочка для мытья ①
trya·pach·ka dlya miht·*ya* *wash cloth*
туалетная бумага ①
tu·al·*yet*·na·ya bu·*ma*·ga *toilet paper*
турбаза ① tur·*ba*·za *tourbase* • *youth hostel*
турецкий tu·*rets*·ki *Turkish*
туфли ⑩ pl *tuf*·li *shoes*
ты tih *you* sg inf
тюрьма ① tyur'·*ma* *jail* • *prison*
тяжёлый tya·*zho*·lih *heavy*

У

у ... есть u ... yest' *have*
убийство ⑩ u·*bist*·va *murder*
уборка ① u·*bor*·ka *cleaning*
увлажняющий крем ⑩
uv·lazh·*nya*·yu·shi kryem *moisturiser*
угол ⑩ u·*gal* *corner*
удар ⑩ u·*dar* *stroke (health)*
удобный u·*dob*·nih *comfortable*
ужасный u·*zhas*·nih *awful* • *terrible*
уже u·*zhe* *already*
ужин ⑩ u·*zhihn* *dinner*
указывать u·*ka*·zih·vat' *point*
укус ⑩ u·*kus* bite *(dog/insect)*
улица ① u·*lit*·sa *street*
уличный рынок ⑩
u·lich·nih *rih*·nak *street market*
улыбаться u·lih·*bat*·sa *smile*
ультразвук ⑩ ul'·*traz*·vuk *ultrasound*
умереть u·*mir*·yet' *die*
умываться u·mih·*vat*'·sa *wash (oneself)*
универмаг ⑩
u·ni·vir·*mak* *department store*
универсам ⑩ u·ni·vir·*sam* *supermarket*
услуга ① us·*lu*·ga *service*
устал u·*stal* *tired*
установление личности ⑩
u·sta·nav·*lye*·ni·ye lich·*na*·sti *identification*
утверждать ut·virzh·*dat'* *validate*
утро ⑩ *u*·tra *morning*
ухаживать за u·*kha*·zhih·vat' za *care for*
ухо ⑩ *u*·kha *ear*
учитель ⑩ u·*chi*·til' *teacher*
учительница ① u·*chi*·til'·nit·sa *teacher*
учить u·*chit* *learn*

Ф

фабрика ① *fa*·bri·ka *factory*
фамилия ① fa·*mi*·li·ya *surname*
фары ① pl *fa*·rih *headlights*
фонарик ⑩ fa·*na*·rik *flashlight* • *torch*

фунт ⓜ funt *pound (money/weight)*
фургон ⓜ fur·*gon* van
футболка ⓕ fud·*bol*·ka *T-shirt*

X

хвост ⓜ khvost *tail*
хлопок ⓜ *khlo*·pak *cotton*
ходить пешком kha·*dit'* pish·kom *hike*
ходить по магазинам kha·*dit'* pa
  ma·ga·*zi*·nam *go shopping • shop*
хозяин ⓜ khaz·*ya*·in *landlord*
хозяйка ⓕ khaz·*yey*·ka *landlady*
холм ⓜ kholm *hill*
холодильник ⓜ kha·la·*dil'*·nik *refrigerator*
холодный kha·*lod*·nih *cold*
холост ⓜ *kho*·last *single (man)*
хорошенький kha·ro·*shihn'*·ki *pretty*
хороший kha·ro·*shih* *fine • good*
хотеть khat·*yet'* *want*
хочется пить *kho*·chit·sa pit' *thirsty*
хрупкий *khrup*·ki *fragile*
художник ⓜ khu·*dozh*·nik *artist*
художница ⓕ khu·*dozh*·nit·sa *artist*

Ц

цвет ⓜ tsvyet *colour*
цветок ⓜ tsvi·*tok* *flower*
целовать tsih·la·*vat'* *kiss*
цена ⓕ tse·*na* *price*
ценный *tse*·nih *valuable*
центр города ⓜ tsentr *go*·ra·da *city centre*
церковь ⓕ *tser*·kaf' *church*

Ч

чаевые ⓕ pl cha·i·*vih*·ye *tip (gratuity)*
час ⓜ chas *hour*
частный *chas*·nih *private*
часто cha·*sta* *often*
часы ⓜ pl chi·*sih* *clock • watch*
часы работы ⓜ pl
  chi·*sih* ra·bo·tih *opening hours*
чашка ⓕ *chash*·ka *cup*
чек ⓜ chek *check • cheque*
человек ⓜ chi·*lav*·yek *person*
челюсть ⓕ *chel*·yust' *jaw*
чемодан ⓜ chi·ma·*dan* *suitcase*
через *che*·ris *across*
череп ⓜ *che*·rip *skull*
чёрно-белый *chor*·nab·*ye*·lih *B&W (film)*
Чёрное море ⓝ
  chor·na·ye *mor*·ye *Black Sea*

чёрный *chor*·nih *black*
  — рынок ⓜ *rih*·nak *black market*
четверг ⓜ chit·*vyerk* *Thursday*
четверть ⓕ *chet*·virt' *quarter*
чинить chi·*nit'* *repair*
число ⓝ chis·*lo* *date (day)*
чистить a chi·*stit'* *clean*
чистый chi·stih *clean • pure*
читать chi·*tat'* *read*
чтение ⓝ *chtye*·ni·ye *reading*
что shto *what*
что-то *shto*·ta *something*
чувства ⓝ pl *chust*·va *feelings*

Ш

шапка ⓕ *shap*·ka *hat*
шахматы ⓜ pl *shakh*·ma·tih *(chess) set*
Швейцария ⓕ shveyt·*sa*·ri·ya *Switzerland*
Швеция ⓕ *shvyet*·sih·ya *Sweden*
шерсть ⓕ sherst' *wool*
шея ⓕ *she*·ya *neck*
шина ⓕ *shih*·na *tire • tyre*
широкий shih·*ro*·ki *wide*
шить shiht' *sew*
шкаф ⓜ shkaf *cupboard • wardrobe*
школа ⓕ *shko*·la *school*
шоссе ⓝ sha·*se* *highway • motorway*
шприц ⓜ shprits *needle • syringe*
штраф ⓜ shtraf *fine (penalty)*
шумный *shum*·nih *noisy*

Э

этаж ⓜ e·*tash* *floor (storey)*
это e·ta *this (one)*

Ю

юбка ⓕ *yup*·ka *skirt*
юг ⓜ yuk *south*
юриспруденция ⓕ yu·ris·prud·*yent*·sih·ya
  law (study, profession)

Я

я ya *I*
ядовитый ya·da·*vi*·tih *poisonous*
язык ⓜ yi·*zihk* *language*
яичник ⓜ yi·*ich*·nik *ovary*
яичниковая киста ⓕ yi·*ich*·ni·ko·va·ya
  kis·*ta* *ovarian cyst*
янтарь ⓜ yin·*tar'* *amber*
ясли ⓜ pl *yas*·li *crèche*

INDEX

What kind of traveller are you?

A. You're eating chicken for dinner *again* because it's the only word you know.

B. When no one understands what you say, you step closer and shout louder.

C. When the barman doesn't understand your order, you point frantically at the beer.

D. You're surrounded by locals, swapping jokes, email addresses and experiences – other travellers want to borrow your phrasebook.

If you answered A, B, or C, you NEED Lonely Planet's phrasebooks.

- **Talk to everyone everywhere**
  Over 120 languages, more than any other publisher

- **The right words at the right time**
  Quick-reference colour sections, two-way dictionary, easy pronunciation, every possible subject

- **Lonely Planet Fast Talk** – essential language for short trips and weekends away

- **Lonely Planet Phrasebooks** – for every phrase you need in every language you want

'Best for curious and independent travellers' – *Wall Street Journal*

Lonely Planet Offices

ustralia
Maribyrnong St, Footscray,
oria 3011
3 8379 8000
8379 8111
us@lonelyplanet.com.au

USA
150 Linden St, Oakland,
CA 94607
☎ 510 893 8555
fax 510 893 8572
✉ info@lonelyplanet.com

bery Ave,
R 4RW
9000
001
anet.co.uk

www.lonelyplanet.com